att 517
J2-20

GW01003676

EARTH LIGHTS

A radical and compelling new study of the UFO enigma that spans seismology, megalithic sites, the psycho-kinetic abilities of the human mind and ancient shamanistic powers.

By the same author
THE LEY HUNTER'S COMPANION
  (with Ian Thomson)

EARTH LIGHTS

Towards an Explanation of the UFO Enigma

by
Paul Devereux

With additional material by
Paul McCartney

TURNSTONE PRESS LIMITED
Wellingborough, Northamptonshire

First published 1982

For Jay,
who also saw

© PAUL DEVEREUX 1982

*This book is sold subject to the condition that it shall not, by way of trade
or otherwise, be lent, re-sold, hired out, or otherwise circulated without the
publisher's prior consent in any form of binding or cover other than that in
which it is published and without a similar condition including this
condition being imposed on the subsequent purchaser.*

British Library Cataloguing in Publication Data

Devereux, Paul
    Earth lights: towards an understanding of the
    UFO enigma
    1. Unidentified flying objects
    I. Title
    001.9'42   TL789

    ISBN 0-85500-123-2

Printed and bound in Great Britain.

Contents

List of Illustrations

Acknowledgements

I must thank Lawrence Dale, Tony Pace, Lionel Beer and Norman Oliver, then officers of BUFORA, for their valuable help in various important areas of my research.

To author Tony Roberts I owe hours of useful discussion and argument, as well as my gratitude to him and his wife Jan for getting a particular text to me very swiftly. Bob Rickard, the remarkable editor of *Fortean Times*, has likewise provided valuable ideas and information during the years this book was in the making and, perhaps more importantly, encouragement when my confidence sometimes faltered. John Steele, one of my colleagues on the *Dragon Project*, provided me with rare reference material and a great deal of insight and spiritual support. I also owe much to other workers on the project, including Don Robins. The *Dragon Project* and I owe a special debt to Threshold Foundation.

I am indebted to Frank Earp, Barry Gooding, John Rowston, David Morris, Vivien Corser and Jan Heering of Amsterdam for going out of their way to supply me with remarkable items of information pertinent to the theme of this inquiry. To Bob Cowley of RILKO I owe epiphany.

Large sections of this book could not have been written without the knowledgeable and vital collaboration of Paul McCartney, with whom it has been a great pleasure to work. (I should mention, too, that Sue McCartney's Civil Service experience directed us to the use of the most suitable population information for our purposes.)

One of the most enjoyable aspects of writing this book has been the memories it has summoned up of my work in Leicestershire with Andy York, whose intelligent, tireless research helped to provide the springboard for the ideas presented in the following pages.

I must record here how much I have appreciated the endless patience and understanding of Alick Bartholomew and Michael Cox of Turnstone Press.

Finally, I am grateful for the co-research provided by my wife Jay at various times, and I owe her and my son Solomon a special debt for the way they allow my too-frequent absences from the family hearth to deal with the endless and complex research little-understood phenomena demand. I'll make it up to them one day.

I am most grateful to the following for permission to use photographs: to the Fortean Picture Library for the photographs on pp. 27 and 30; to Frank Lane for the photograph on p. 98, and to those others for whom credit is given next to their photographs. For diagrams: to Souvenir Press for the one on p. 93; to Neville Spearman Ltd. for the diagram on p. 181 and to Nelson Hall Inc. for the diagram on p. 93.

Preface

The purpose of this book is to try and establish a set of possibilities and correlations that can stand as an alternative to the usual explanations of what we have come to term UFOs — Unidentified Flying Objects. This alternative approach started life as a largely unpublished essay called *The Thor Factor* in 1975, during a period of research into the phenomena, geology and ancient sites of an English county (see Chapter 7). In this current version the paradigm is still by no means a complete theory; it is still what a paradigm is supposed to be — a pattern, a prototype. But I feel it is sufficiently well formed for it to provide a genuine 'conceptual handle' for fresh approaches to the UFO mystery.

It is beyond my resources of time, finance and expertise to provide a completely watertight 'scientifically acceptable' answer to the UFO problem, but I think enough pointers are given in the following pages for the commencement of research that could, one day, reach that point of completion. Indeed, I think uncoordinated pockets of such research already exist.

While the conceptual framework constructed in this book may not cover every reported aspect of the UFO phenomenon, I am confident that it covers more aspects than any other single proposal so far put forward. As such, I hope at least some researchers will feel they cannot honestly ignore it, however crude and inadequate it may be at the moment. Nevertheless, I resign myself to the probability that the approach I outline in the following chapters will be controversial, not only outside ufological circles but also within. Sacred cows graze everywhere.

I urge the experienced researcher not to 'skip' chapters as they all contain material relevant to the new paradigm: the case put forward in this book unfolds in stages.

What I have written is the work not only of someone who has studied the UFO problem for many years but also of one who has witnessed a number of remarkable UFO events. If at times I seem very positive about certain aspects of the phenomenon, it is only because I am relating to facts as I have witnessed them.

One of the peculiarities of the approach to UFOs employed here is the association of ancient sites with the whole problem. This is really a secondary pattern which shows, as I attempt to persuade the reader, that ancient peoples may have had an understanding of the nature of UFOs, of their origin and application to human consciousness. If this idea is correct, then a study of *all* the characteristics of the megalithic structures built by these early peoples may enable us to learn what they knew and in so doing to obtain a greater insight into the nature of UFO phenomena for ourselves. This I feel could be a valuable new angle on an enigma that has frustrated us for too long. From the solving of ancient mysteries may come forth the foundation for a future science.

Paul Devereux
Powys, Cymru
May 1981

PART ONE
Signs in the Heavens

1.
Experiences, Directions
—And a Challenge

And Albion knew that it
Was the Lord, the Universal Humanity; & Albion saw his Form
A Man . . . .

William Blake, *Jerusalem*

The starting point for any study of UFOs has to be the UFO experience itself. If it is not accepted that there is a real phenomenon to be understood, then all books on UFOs are a waste of time. For that reason I begin by describing two of my own UFO experiences because I *know* from them that there really is an unknown type of event taking place on our planet and I want to present them in such a manner that it will be difficult for anyone to ignore that fact.

My first clear-cut UFO experience took place in May 1967 at Ravensbourne College of Art, situated about a mile south of Bromley in Kent, where I was in my final term of a Fine Art Diploma course. As I recall, it was around eight o'clock in the evening, shortly before sunset. I had moved to a north-facing window in order to mix some colours in daylight as it was becoming dark within the top floor studio where I and a handful of other students were working. The window was three or four floors up and afforded a view across some fields to Bromley. Nothing more was on my mind than the looming final diploma exhibition we had to mount in a month or so. Although it was the flowery year of pyschedelia, I had ingested nothing stronger than coffee from the college canteen.

Something made me glance up from my palette. In the sky in the direction of Bromley was an orange light. A pulsing, praeternaturally brilliant orange light in the form of an upright rectangle. My mind tumbled: it was impossible to make sense of what I was seeing. My mouth agape, I witnessed the glowing orange rectangle move through the sky towards the college. I stepped back a pace or two from the window and without diverting my eyes from the phenomenon managed to call to the other students. Wondering casually at my excitement, they lethargically moved to various windows, where they froze—conceptual shock rooting each one of them to the spot. At one moment I remember glancing around at the others in the hope of some reassuring smile, but everyone, without exception, was looking out of the studio windows with their mouths hanging open.

The phenomenon had come to a halt in the sky, a few hundred feet above the fields and a short distance to the north-west of the college. I was looking up at it through the top left hand corner of the window I was standing at. It was easy to discern the remarkably regular form of the orange light: it had the proportions of a door, with crisp edges and corners. The pulsing orange glow subsided slightly as we observed the stationary aerial shape. I was unable to determine whether the shape was fully three-dimensional or somehow flat.

Quite suddenly, something even more disturbing happened: the form of the glowing phenomenon began to decay; the crisp rectangular shape collapsing into amorphous, organic configurations that kept churning in the sky. It appeared like a sort of animated, glowing aerial Rorschach test in which many forms could be fancied. Even before this phase of the event took place, other students from the ground floor workshops had come out onto the car park below my vantage point and were staring up at the remarkable sight.

At this time it had not occurred to me that we were witnessing what was known as a 'UFO': this was no machine. This was like some happening out of the Old Testament. I began to feel profoundly disturbed. This was something that had no place outside of a dream; yet here we were, different groups of people, looking up at the same patch of sky, all of us shocked with the unfamiliarity of what we were seeing. I felt indescribably lonely even though surrounded by other witnesses. I wanted this thing to go away, for it to be a cloud, to be something explicable. Then we could all laugh and joke about it and go about our business. To most people, this event probably seems exciting and not the sort of thing to cause such mental disturbance. I can only speak for myself. When faced with an event of the order I am describing here, the word 'awe' takes on a dimension of meaning more than its definition of 'a mixture of fear and wonder' can hope to communicate. The *idea* of seeing a UFO is quite different to *actually witnessing* one.

The phenomenon, stationary in the sky, was moving within itself like a time-lapse film of a billowing, boiling cloud, albeit a small and glowing one. What I am now going to describe does not come easy, even after all these years and many re-tellings of the incident. Just as one can imagine shapes in the ruddy embers of a fire, so too could forms be 'seen' in the glowing orange turmoil of configurations before us. At one point the shape of a human form suggested itself—at least, it did to me. (Faces and figures are perhaps the easiest patterns to determine in a Rorschach-type situation.) At the moment this shape was fleetingly suggested the quality of the phenomenon changed again into something crisp and definite, only this time instead of a rectangle it was glowing, featureless form of a human figure with its arms outstretched that presented itself. At least, *I* saw it as that; others saw it slightly differently. One student, Gillian, was gasping repeatedly 'What *is* it?', putting into words the 'loop tape' situation created by racing minds unable to come up with the necessary combination of explanations to cope with the event being witnessed by the senses. For the purposes of this book I contacted Gillian after a period of almost a dozen years and asked her to put down her memories of the Ravensbourne event. She wrote:

> I certainly do remember this event, but must admit that I cannot remember it in clarity. Nevertheless I shall try to give the best recollection that I can.
>   While working in the studio at Ravensbourne Art College one evening in May 1967, my attention was drawn to the window by another student. It was already fairly dark outside and in the sky was a light in the shape of a cross. It seemed to be a few hundred

yards away, far larger than the size of a house or maybe several
times larger, and suspended in the sky. I felt sure the light came from
a solid object of some sort and it remained in the sky for some
minutes. It was certainly not caused by cloud formations but I can
give no explanation for it. I believe there were about six of us in that
room who witnessed the event, the other students having already
left the building earlier. Another student on a different level of the
building also saw the phenomenon, and joined us later to tell us
about it.

Clearly Gillian interpreted what she witnessed along similar
lines to myself, a cross having similarities of shape with a figure
with outstretched arms. The cross shape is significant as we shall
shortly see. Nevertheless, what I remember seeing, and what I
and others thought we were seeing at the time, was a figure.
Also, there is no doubt that it was not very dark outside,
because I was mixing paints in the daylight coming through the
window. It was growing dark *within* the studio, however. (No
one liked putting on the strip lighting as it adversely affected
colour tone.)

Perhaps because of my Catholic upbringing, I interpreted the
figure as long-haired and robed, creating a Christ-like or
perhaps angelic glowing 'silhouette'. Another student, Jay, who
was later to become my wife, also saw the form as a figure, but in
a slightly different way. This is her account:

Along with several other students I was working late in the top floor
studio . . . The windows looked out in the direction of Bromley
town, possibly due north. It was a very pleasant evening shortly
before sunset, sometime between seven and eight o'clock, possibly
nearer to eight.

Our attention was drawn to the window by Paul Devereux who
was very excited. On approaching the window I saw in the sky
directly opposite a red, glowing door-shaped rectangle. It appeared
to be somewhere over the fields between the college and Bromley,
possibly a little over half a mile away. It appeared very large and
fairly close.

Several other people on this floor were watching and began
asking each other what it was. After a while the rectangle began to
break down and change shape but still keeping the same intensity of
light and colour (a glowing orangey-red). It took on the shape of a
figure in silhouette contained within the area which had originally
been the door-shaped rectangle. It reminded me strongly of
Leonardo's 'universal man'.

Whilst being unable to take my eyes from it, I also wished it would go away. It seemed to be going on far too long and did not fit into any acceptable area of reality. Gradually, the figure began to fade and when I left the window there was just a faint pinkish haze left in that area of the sky.

I would not like to hazard a guess at the duration of the figure/cross form, but it could not have been very long in real terms. I may be adding to my memories, but I had the impression that the phenomenon was almost imperceptibly losing brilliance all the time I was witnessing it, right from the first moment when it appeared to be over Bromley. At all events, the figure decayed as the rectangle had done earlier, but this time there was no animated jumbling of forms. The phenomenon gradually became just a rosy cloud, and then a duller and duller patch in the sky. At no point did I, or anyone else as far as I know, notice anything leave the area of the aerial event, but there was a distinct sense that whatever had been animating it was no longer present. While the active part of the event may have lasted in all a few minutes, the final rosy cloud could still be made out a quarter of an hour later, until it resembled a vague smudge of rouge in the sky.

The aftermath of the experience was strange. Instead of shouting about what we had seen, we were in a sort of shocked state. What was there to say? We had seen something that had no cosy conceptual cubby-hole to slot it into, yet we had been observing it just as we would any mundane object.

The sky at the time of the incident was vaguely blue, with a few wispy clouds. There was certainly no low, heavy cloud. The event seemed calculated to be inexplicable. Having been a teenage amateur astronomer I knew the phenomenon had not been astronomical. In any case, this thing had come from the *north*—not a direction for planetary, solar or lunar events. The aerial shape had been a self-luminous orange, had moved and then become stationary. It was quite large and was not round in shape. At no point had it arched to the ground or the horizon, nor had it simply disappeared. This ruled out satellites and that new favourite of the debunkers, 'space debris'. The one explanation that remained was some form of plasma effect in the atmosphere. But do any known plasma effects have corners and straight edges? Do they move to a maintained stationary position and then 'perform'? Do they leave long-lasting glows in the sky?

That there was no 'off the peg' explanation soon became

obvious. Nor did the notion of extra-terrestrial astronauts have anything to do with what we witnessed. The meaningless catch-all explanation of 'mass hallucination' stood no chance either: the phenomenon was witnessed by at least three, independent, non-communicating groups of people—the classic test against hallucinatory situations. The favourite gimmick of one school of ufology, that of a commonly experienced psychic event, does not hold water, because there was a definite objective element to the phenomenon. The independent groups of witnesses and the long-lasting rosy cloud attest to that. I do not deny, though, that there were definite psychic factors associated with the phenomenon.

There were clearly slight personal disparities about the nature of the figure/cross amongst the witnesses, as there are amongst witnesses of more mundane events; but equally clearly something objective was causing the narrow range of witness response.

The day after the aerial phenomenon had manifested was a curious one. I cannot speak for the others, but I seemed to have an inability to even think about the previous evening's experience. I simply got on with my work. A student who had seen the phenomenon from the car park came up to the painting studio to see if anyone would discuss the event with him. When he approached me I was helplessly non-commital. He became quite angry and stormed off. Another student who had not been present the previous evening but had heard of the incident told us we had witnessed a UFO and set about getting all the witnesses to sign a basic account of the affair which he then sent off to a UFO organization.

I have kept in touch with another student, Paul, who witnessed the early phase of the event. Judging by his description of the colour and location of the aerial light it seems he must have seen the thing shortly before I did. He was leaving the college at the time:

Below is an account of an incident that ocurred twelve to thirteen years ago whilst walking down the main staircase at Ravensbourne College in Kent . . . On passing the window of the fourth floor landing I was aware of an unusually intense area of bright sky in the direction of Bromley town centre. This caught my attention but I did not stop.

On passing the third-floor landing I noticed that the area of bright sky had acquired a more intense centre of strong whitish light about the size of the moon. Again, I did not stop to inspect the situation more closely.

On arriving at ground level at the main entrance I do not recall seeing the area of strongly lit sky or its intense centre over Bromley centre.

Paul has admitted to me that his recollection of the whole thing is now somewhat hazy. I recall that he had left the studio a short time before I moved to the window, but I am myself unable to remember the exact timing of events.

It transpired that either at the time of the college sighting, or shortly after it, another group of students filming a tale of King Arthur at ancient Keston Ponds (overlooked by a hill-top pre-historic earthwork known as Caesar's Camp) was also visited by a strange light. This one was, apparently, a brilliant white sphere containing within its form an even more intense white crescent shape. The sphere bobbed down close to one of the ponds—both of which have poltergeist accounts associated with them—then moved rapidly up into the air again and was lost to sight.

I have not gone to any great lengths to chase up other witnesses to either incidents, but there must be another dozen people at least who witnessed one or the other of these curious events. But enough has been presented here to confirm that a most unusual set of events *did* occur on that May evening in 1967. The Ravensbourne phenomenon cannot remotely be explained by mundane methods. It was not a rectangular cloud, a rectangular misperception or a rectangular hallucination. The *truly* scientific, objective response must be that some factor we are not currently aware of was at work. A silly distortion of the evidence, claiming the sighting to be 'Venus' or what-have-you, is simply unscientific and unacceptable; and yet I recall giving an account of my experience to someone extremely well-informed on UFO matters: at the end of my description he was able to say 'Yes, Paul, but it *is* easy to misinterpret space satellites, you know'! His own subjectivity had prevented him from absorbing what I had been saying.

There is, of course, the possibility that I am fabricating the whole thing, even though I present eye-witness accounts by other people. Well, I refuse to let sceptics off the hook here: I am always prepared to undertake any test that can confirm the objective nature of my account, be it polygraph or voice graph tests, deep hypnosis, 'truth serum' or whatever—provided, naturally, that such tests are conducted in a responsible and professional manner, as part of a full, serious programme of research and at the sceptic's own expense. Certain other conditions would have to be met too: I would, for example, expect that when the positive nature of the enquiries was forthcoming the investigating sceptic would change his or her attitude in public. And the research would have to be such that it would be recognized by other sceptical parties: I cannot spend my life being tested by every Tom, Dick or Harry who has an aimless whim to do so.

To those serious sceptics who have psychological problems in accepting the actuality of UFO phenomena, here then is a challenge. I am aware of the shortcomings of all these methods of determining the truth,[1] but perhaps a series of them, linked with a full enquiry into the other witnesses (and perhaps some of them would also be prepared to be tested), may be able to establish to some degree of unavoidable objectivity the fact— and fact it is—that the unidentified phenomenon described here did really take place. And if the Ravensbourne event took place, as it did, then enquiries into the nature of UFOs are both valid and necessary.

I have gone into some depth with the analysis of this UFO experience for the reasons I have already stated: it is necessary to establish the rock of certainty upon which this enquiry is based. Of necessity, further accounts in this work will have to be far briefer.

Altogether, 1967 was an amazing year, the culmination of a few years in the 1960s in which Western youth contacted mental, and possibly spiritual, realities *en masse*. This was accompanied by a surge in UFO sightings. The magnitude of this UFO wave is graphically shown in a table derived from a partial set of UFO sightings from 1921 to 1970 (UFOCAT-70) reproduced in the early 1970s by *Flying Saucer Review*. Here is the relevant section:

Year	Number of sightings
1960	125
1961	80
1962	122
1963	86
1964	60
1965	193
1966	373
1967	1561

Interestingly, many of the UFO sightings in 1967 were reported by members of the population who were not part of the 'psyche-delic generation'—airline pilots, policemen, suburban housewives, radio reporters, and so on.

In July of 1967 I was to have one more UFO experience. After setting up a painting exhibition in Norwich, two friends and I were coming back to London in a left-hand drive Volkeswagen. I was in the back seat. It was a warm, sunny late afternoon. About half way through the journey, presumably somewhere in Suffolk or Essex, I glanced to my right and saw a *totally* black, round shape pacing the car at about a field's distance from the road. The other passenger, seated in front of me, also saw the shape. Awestruck, neither of us could utter a word to the driver, who was blissfully unaware of what was going on. The shape could have been a globe, a disc on edge or some kind of supra-dimensional hole for all we could make out: its utter blackness was quite inexplicable on such a sunny day. As we looked, the phenomenon disappeared. It was the only time I have ever wit-nessed disappearance of that kind in real life. We have all seen it on films and television of course, but to see it happen in actuality leaves a sort of cold aftershock. No jump in the film of life—the thing simply was not there any more. Moments later it, or a similar form, appeared about half a mile further on across the fields, fractions of a second before moving off and disappearing into the glare of the sun.

Our tongues suddenly loosened, we both shouted 'UFO!', causing our slightly excitable driver to put us into a braking skid. He berated us both for not telling him about the event while it was happening; but like virtually all non-witnesses he under-estimated the profound shock that accompanies the sighting of a UFO. Our culture simply has not prepared us for the experience.

When you see a UFO it is suddenly not comic strip, not *Star Wars*, not a hoax, not misperception. It is a forbidden corner of reality.

Again, I am open to suitable tests to ascertain the truthfulness of this account?

The entire year of 1967 ws filled with similar remarkable events. An airline pilot coming into Shannon airport complained about a strange green fireball that was following him in. Devon patrolmen chased a brilliantly-lit cross-shaped UFO (one of many such sightings made by police and others in the autumn of 1967) at tree-top height at speeds up to ninety miles per hour. A Northamptonshire housewife saw a glowing cross-shape in the sky, with what seemed to be a figure silhouetted on it. Lights, crosses, fireballs: Britain—and elsewhere—was alive with reports of inexplicable aerial events. Even the media had a shock: I remember with amusement a radio reporter, on what was then BBC Home Service, being somewhat cynically sent to accompany a group of ufologists on a nightime hill-top sky-watch. To the consternation of the programme presenter the reported 'phoned into the studio to report that he had actually witnessed a multi-coloured UFO through binoculars.

UFOs were headline news throughout much of the latter part of 1967 in Britain. The sense of a new pulse of life was everywhere being felt, the possibilities of new beginnings took on clearer dimensions. It was fertile soil indeed for a little more human spirit and awareness to emerge. Although it now seems that this period was one of isolated, naive optimism, I think the seeds of an extension of human awareness were planted then that are now maturing and cautiously, gradually, reaching out into the light of current understanding.

After having had my UFO experience I began to read UFO literature. At that time this mainly consisted of sensationalist American material that seemed obsessed with UFOs as extra-terrestrial machines, often coloured with a highly paranoid tint. Although I could see that beneath all the dross an area of real human experience was being referred to, the approach of the literature failed to make useful connections with the experiences I had had and which I was mentally trying to digest.

One day in 1967 a new book appeared. It was called *The Flying Saucer Vision* by John Michell. The juxtaposition of the two terms in the title was like a lightning bolt of inspiration: here at last was someone talking about strange aerial phenomenon from a quite different and more meaningful viewpoint.

The book contained an odd collection of flying saucer themes and a discussion of a former race on Earth. For its time, it was a sensitive and far-reaching approach to the UFO enigma. Along the way, Michell introduced the concept of lines of electromagnetic energy running through the landscape and presented a new audience with the 1920s 'ley' line (alignment of ancient sites) ideas of Alfred Watkins (see Chapter 6). Intuitively, Michell had picked up on a new stream of awareness coming into archaeology—a seemingly unlikely corner of human activity for revelatory new concepts.

In the early 1960s C. A. Newham had been doing work at Stonehenge, showing that the constructors of the site thousands of years ago seem to have had a clear awareness of solar and lunar movement. In articles in *Nature* in 1963 and 1964, and in *Stonehenge Decoded* in 1965, Professor Gerald Hawkins of the Smithsonian Institute detailed his own work at Stonehenge, showing it to be a 'stone age computer' preserving certain solar and lunar alignments within its structure. It was capable of eclipse prediction.

In 1967 itself, Professor Alexander Thom's *Megalithic Sites In Britain* was published which, using a dense mathematical approach, provided evidence of prehistoric astronomical practices that had staggering implications.

All this was a revival and detailed extension of pioneer work done by researchers earlier this century into the nature of prehistoric sites. The revival was a signal that prehistoric societies and their understanding were going to have to be reappraised.

This exciting prospect gave impetus to a curious, and probably mistaken idea that was developed in the early 1960s by an ex-R.A.F. pilot called Tony Wedd. He was an ufologist who had also read the books on leys published in the 1920s and the 1930s by Alfred Watkins. In 1955 Aimé Michel published the results of his analysis of a French UFO wave or 'flap'. He had found that landings and near landings of UFOs occurred in alignments he called 'orthotonies'. It was Wedd's brainwave to suggest the possibility that ley alignments and orthotonies were related and that the UFOs might be extracting some form of telluric, terrestrial magnetic force from the leys for propulsion. Wedd further postulated that the ancient markers on ley alignments—stone circles, monoliths, burial mounds, hill-top earthworks and the like—might be used by UFO pilots as landmarks during their aerial perambulations. One senses here something of the ex-R.A.F. pilot in Wedd's theorizing! Nevertheless, a fresh if parochial interest in Watkins' theory was awakened in some ufologists, and the ley concept was rescued from obscurity. Another new angle on the UFO mystery had also be signposted.

The publication of Michell's *The Flying Saucer Vision* occurred at exactly the right time: here was a work making rudimentary links between ancient sites, UFOs and leys when serious research was opening up new vistas of possible prehistoric skills, when the ley theory was being revived and when the skies were alive with UFO activity to such an extent that more mundane news was being elbowed from the headlines. A potent mental brew had been concocted and was to cause the development of an important new arena of thought that has come to be known as 'Earth Mysteries' (Chapter 6).

So the historical accidents of 1967 pushed me, and others, into a simultaneous study of prehistory and UFOs. This curious connection was—and still is—something of a hunch, but a rather persistent one. Whatever the validity of such a connection, the remainder of this book is the summation of aspects of research commenced amidst this *mileu*.

There *is* a UFO phenomenon and it needs study to make it understandable. The UFO sceptic who dismisses it or who claims it cannot be scientifically studied is like a fisherman with a small gauge net who will not believe in big fish till he catches one! It is not for the UFO phenomenon to constrict itself to scientific rigours: it is for the scientists to apply their ingenuity to devise ways of studying something dwelling on the outer perimeters of their knowledge. If it is not accepted that those perimeters have to be extended, then science is merely a belief system dogmatically defended.

It really is time the UFO engima was given credibility. It may contain much of value to our current situation. To stand in the way of developing human understanding is nothing for the sceptics to feel proud of.

It is time for them to begin making nets of a different gauge.

2.
The UFO Pageant

Those who believe in these myths have our sympathy
. . . an obvious falsity, a physically impossible event.

An eighteenth-century physicist dismissing a report of a
fall of meteoric fragments witnessed by 300 people
before it was known stones do exist in the sky.

It is not the purpose of this book to present endless lists of UFO
sightings. This has been done by authors more informed than I
am on UFO case histories. Nevertheless, we must spend one
fairly extensive chapter breaking down the basic patterns of
claimed UFO manifestations in order to have a reference point
and to clearly identify the type of phenomenon we are seeking to
explain. In the course of doing this I will refer to a few events that
I hope will be unfamiliar even to UFO enthusiasts, and a new
category of UFO sighting will be identified.

Anyone remotely interested in the subject must surely know
by now that modern interest in unexplained aerial events has its
origins in the June 1947 sighting of aerial ellipsoid forms near
Mount Rainier in Washington State, U.S.A., that were described as looking like saucers. This triggered the 'flying saucer'
terminology in the media (and which, incidentally, helped to
trivialize the phenomenon from the outset) and the ensuing
worldwide interest in such events.

It must be equally well known that this modern awareness of
inexplicable flying forms is only the latest chapter in the history
of UFO observations. Some researchers claim to be able to
detect UFO sightings in Biblical texts and maintain that there are
clear records of UFOs in medieval and later documents, where
they are interpreted as signs from God, swords, spears and,

more recently, as spectral airships and ghost aircraft. In the Second World War glowing orbs of light that accompanied both Allied and German aircraft became known as 'foo fighters'.

Since the late 1940s there have been many thousands of UFO sightings from every corner of the world. With a common language for the aerial phenomena and with better communications the whole subject has grown into a rich, complex web of speculation, argument and, in certain cases, escapism.

Over the years UFO events have been broken down into certain well-defined categories, though each one is in itself a complicated study. Perhaps what is now generally considered to be the definitive set of categories has been provided by J. Allen Hynek—although even this is being subjected to further modification by other researchers.

Hynek is a highly qualified astronomer and was consultant to Project Blue Book inaugurated by the U.S. Air Force. This project was supposedly aimed at sifting and evaluating reports of UFO sightings. When it was terminated in 1969 the official view was that there was nothing further to investigate; that nearly all the alleged UFO sightings that had been studied by the project could be 'explained away' as misperception or hoax. Only a minority of the reports remained unidentified.

After being released from his Blue Book commitments, Hynek surprised the world by stating his belief that the UFO phenomenon, whatever its nature, was at core an actuality and that Project Blue Book had not always fully or properly investigated UFO sighting cases. In short, that it had not been scientific.

Different researchers use different methods of classifying UFO sightings but the categories put forward by Hynek have come closest to being accepted as standard. In brief they are:

1. DISTANT UFOS. Phenomena seen at a distance, which Hynek breaks down into *Nocturnal Lights, Daylight Discs* and *Radar-Visual* (where radar echoes seem to have been confirmed by visual observation at the same time). He admits that Nocturnal Lights and Daylight Discs may not be mutually exclusive.

2. CLOSE ENCOUNTERS OF THE FIRST KIND (CE1). The 'simple' close encounter with a UFO where it does not interact with its environment.

3. CLOSE ENCOUNTERS OF THE SECOND KIND (CE2). Close observation of a UFO in which the phenomenon interacts with its environment in some way, such as leaving marks on the ground.

4. CLOSE ENCOUNTERS OF THE THIRD KIND (CE3). The now famous classification in which close observation of a UFO includes the perception of 'occupants' or 'entities' in or around the phenomenon. This is not necessarily the same as 'contactee' reports, where an individual claims to be in telepathic or physical contact with 'space beings'.

Reports can also be classified according to a 'strangeness' index which gives a measure as to the amount of explanation required.

In this chapter I will, by and large, adhere to these categories, except that I divide the first one into two: 'Lights', whether seen in daylight or at night and whether aerial or earthbound; and 'Daylight Sightings', where an UFO is seen in daylight, whether in the air or on the ground, but gives the impression of being a solid object visible by reflected light. Also, I prefer to designate the CE3 category simply as 'Entities' because the UFO link is not always apparent.

Finally, I add a fresh category I call 'Proto-Entities', which I will clarify later.

So that we can get some measure of the beast that confronts us I now give some examples of each of the main categories. They are not necessarily intended to be 'classic' cases but have been chosen simply to illustrate the main forms the UFO phenomenon can adopt.

Lights
Lights in the sky (usually abbreviated to LITS) and ground-based UFO lights constitute the greatest number of UFO sightings: one researcher, John Keel, estimates that they form about 75 per cent of reports. They are often the most easily 'explained away', but there are clearly some incidents that cannot be ascribed to any simple, known cause.

CASE 1: In the early decades of this century a light was seen on several occasions in the vicinity of Loch Gruinard, Wester Ross, Scotland, by local inhabitants. It came from the heights above the loch and usually made for a large rock in the water known as

Frame from a film taken at 9 a.m. from the Thame-Aylesbury road of an 'orange ball' travelling above the treetops 'in a straight plane at about 300 m.p.h. . . . it disappeared in a split second'. (*Photo: Peter H. Day*)

Fraoch Eilean Mor. There the light always disappeared suddenly. A peculiarity of the light was that it resembled a ball of light without giving off any rays. One fellow, a Mr John Gunn, once witnessed the light at close quarters. He said it created 'a strange noise' in his ears.[1]

CASE 2: One evening, while staying at Dilkusha, the residence at that time of the Maharaja at Gangtok in the Himalayas, Lama Anagarika Govinda saw swift-moving lights gliding through a range of distant hills. Thinking them to be car headlights on a new mountain road, the Lama mentioned his observation to his host the next morning. The Maharaja assured him there was no such road in the hills and that the lights had no human origin: 'They move about over the most difficult ground with an ease and speed no human being could attain, apparently floating in the air,' he said. 'Nobody has yet been able to explain their nature, and I myself have no theory about them, though the people of my country believe them to be a kind of spirit.' The Maharaja then described to Lama Govinda how he had once witnessed the lights moving through the palace grounds towards the site where the temple now stands. *This location had always been a sanctified place,* he claimed.

Govinda gave this account in his book *The Way of the White Clouds,* where he makes a further interesting observation regarding mysterious lights. A centre for such lights, he writes, is the mountain of Wu T'ai Shan in China. On the southern peak of this mountain there is a tower which gives pilgrims an unimpeded view of the landscape. The purpose of this tower, however, is to give pilgrims the opportunity to witness a strange manifestation that many have claimed to be a form of the Bodhisattva himself. Govinda quotes from John Blofeld's *The Wheel Of Life,* which describes the phenomenon as the author himself witnessed it:

> Shortly after midnight, a monk, carrying a lantern, stepped into our room and cried: 'The Bodhisattva has appeared!' The ascent to the door of the tower occupied less than a minute. As each one entered the little room and came face to face with the window beyond, he gave a shout of surprise, as though all our hours of talk had not sufficiently prepared us for what we now saw. There in the great open spaces beyond the window, apparently not more than one or two hundred yards away, innumerable balls of fire floated majestically past. We could not judge their size, for nobody knew how far

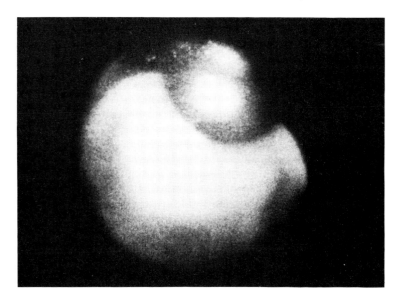

UFO photographed at Uzes, southern France, on 19 November 1974. (*Photo: Christophe Fernandez*)

away they were. Where they came from, what they were, and where they went after fading from sight in the West nobody could tell. Fluffy balls of orange-coloured fire, moving through space, unhurried and majestic—truly a fitting manifestation of divinity!

CASE 3: People dwelling by Loch Rannoch in Scotland have sometimes reported a strange ball of light which skims over a particular stretch of the loch's surface. In Perthshire, it seems such phenomena are called *gealbhan.*[2]

CASE 4: In the summer of 1960 near Walkerton, Ontario, several witnesses, including policemen, a newspaper reporter and a man who was to later become a professional astronomer, 'cornered' a swiftly-moving aerial light in a field. There it hovered around a lone tree and was seen to pass in front of and behind its branches. The circular light was estimated to be something under three feet is diameter. As the witnesses approached it, the light sped away noiselessly at a high rate of acceleration and was lost to view.[3]

CASE 5: On 24 January 1970, Mr Leon Herbosch witnessed a ground-based anomalous light in the town of Rhode-Saint-Genese, in Belgium. Taking a walk near a relative's home on a bright moonlit evening, Mr Herbosch saw a luminous object on a patch of waste ground. On approaching the phenomenon, the light was seen to be an elliptical 'blob' several metres long by about a metre and a half high. As Mr Herbosch came closer to it, the blob turned a light green phosphorescent colour. At this point the witness stopped his approach. Shortly afterwards the blob became brighter, seemed to vibrate and 'inflated' into a golden bell-shape. This grew to about five metres in height, at which point the light issuing from it—described as 'neon white'—had become almost blinding. Although vibrating, the phenomenon maintained a clear bell-shape. Mr Herbosch was able to observe that the interior of the light seemed to be made up of tiny luminous particles swarming around. The witness noticed no sound, heat or smell emanating from the illuminated shape, which lit up the ground for at least a hundred metres around. After a while, the phenomenon 'collapsed' back to its blob form and moved off over the surface of the ground until hidden from sight. The next day, no marks could be found that the object might have left.[4]

CASE 6: On 23 February 1975 some witnesses near the town of Leicester in the English Midlands also had a close view of a light-form hovering close to the ground. It was, they said, circular but did not appear to be solid; it was composed of twinkling light, the dominant colour being orange mixed with strong white and dull red. The whole mixture appeared to revolve around itself, although the object was stationary.[5]

CASE 7: Mr Henry Dalzell, an employee of the Atomic Energy Authority at Harwell, along with his son, witnessed a cross-shaped set of lights through a telescope at their home in Wantage, on 14 December 1970. The object looked like five round balls of light arranged in the shape of a cross. It stayed in the sky for a few minutes before one of the lights shot away from the main formation. The rest of the spheres simply disappeared 'as if a light had gone out'. This was the second UFO to be seen in a week in the area. Earlier, a man had seen a light descend to the nearby Berkshire Downs.[6]

CASE 8: At Gedling, Nottinghamshire, an experienced amateur astronomer saw an orange ball of light he initially took to be an exploding fireball. It then split into five or six separate lights that slowed down and changed into thin crescents. These fell in a falling leaf motion, rocking from side to side, before merging again and disappearing.[7]

CASE 9: About midnight one winter's night in 1976, Len Franklin was escorting a babysitter from his home to hers in Wantage, Oxfordshire. As the two of them left the house, Len caught sight of a peculiar object in the cloudless sky. Intrigued as Len was, the babysitter did not want to know about it—she seemed a little alarmed. Len nevertheless remained looking at the light, which was very bright white and oval in shape. Surrounding this core of white light was a plasma-like 'cloud of tiny, speckly bits'. This 'cloud' was moving in and out, looking rather like an amoeba. The whole aerial phenomenon seemed to be moving eastwards at no more than three or four miles an hour. Len, along with the reluctant babysitter, followed the direction of the light. He could see stars through the cloudy surround of the central white light. Suddenly the centre of the thing glowed a bright orange, dimmed a little, then intensified again. The 'cloud' changed instantly into a delta-shape, then the whole assemblage of light shot off at a tremendous speed and disappeared from sight[8]

These nine cases represent a fair sample of the type of UFO appearance which is seen only in terms of light. We can perhaps see that *only one type of phenomenon is being described*: one that can change its shape, that seems to have little mass and that, on the rare occasions when it is observed closely, seems to have a twinkling or churning inner activity. These lights are seen on land and water as well as in the air. There is a hint in the Scottish and Himalayan material quoted that these lights can return repeatedly to a particular area.

In some reports the lights seem to behave intelligently, usually expressed by their moving away from or towards the witness. But is this really intelligence on the part of the light phenomenon? If one knew nothing about magnetism, a ball-bearing rolling across a smooth surface towards a magnet might seem like a display of intelligence on the part of the ball-bearing, as might two bar magnets spinning away from each other when the same poles are placed in juxtaposition. Perhaps there are electromagnetic—or subtler—fields around human beings that

UFO photographed over Trindade Island, off South America. (*anon*)

can cause these tenuous, shape-shifting lights to react in certain ways.

So while this form of UFO manifestation seems varied and complex at first glance, it looks highly probable that it reduces to recognizable patterns of behaviour and structure when studied a little more closely.

Daylight Sightings

Here we consider UFOs that appear as solid objects seen by daylight rather than by self-illumination. A survey of the UFO literature tends to suggest that this type of sighting is nowhere near as commonplace as the 'Lights' category.

CASE 10: Anne Pickover was in the backyard of her home in Barnoldswick, Lancashire, at about 8 a.m. one day in 1977 when she noticed sunlight glinting off a silvery cigar-shaped object. No sound was coming from it, and the only noticeable thing about the aeroform was that it had a dark band around its centre. Almost overhead when Anne first saw it, the object remained in sight for about five minutes as it slowly traversed the sky.[9]

CASE 11: In September 1954 a worker on the scenic railway on the pleasure beach at Great Yarmouth, Norfolk, saw an object come out of some clouds and stop in mid-air. The witness stated: 'It just hovered, spinning, it seemed, round its own axis, changing its shape from a cigar to a disc. It was blue-grey in colour. For five minutes it was in that position then suddenly it was gone. I looked to the north and to my surprise it was hovering over the sea, then it was gone again. It must have moved a distance of approximately two miles in the time it takes to blink an eye. When I told people about it they said it was a balloon. It must have been a very fast and large balloon to travel against the wind.'[10]

CASE 12: In early October 1970 three members of the Koscielniak family observed a curious aerial object for about half an hour early one bright, clear morning over the Denham Valley near Uxbridge. A large, flattened ellipse-shaped object came suddenly at great speed from the south-west. It flashed across the sky until it reached the zenith, where it stopped for a few seconds. It then moved off again in a straight line to the east, where it stopped and hovered again, about one hundred feet up in the air. It had hard outlines and shone with a metallic sheen. The sunshine was reflected off it, yet it also seemed to be emitting a kind of irridescence which 'lay in streaks around it and seemed to pulsate and glow'. The aeroform also had lights and a kind of antenna attached to it. The witnesses stressed that the disc itself did not glow and was silvery-blue in colour. An interesting part of this account is that the UFO was finally observed to *fade from vision*. Other UFOs, some apparently quite similar in appearance to this one, were reported over the same area of Middlesex before and after this sighting, over a period of a few years.[11]

CASE 13: Mr and Mrs Clarkson and a friend in the western English county of Shropshire encountered a UFO one Sunday in June 1976. It was twilight and the headlights had been switched on but the witnesses said visibility was still good. They slowed down to 35 m.p.h. to negotiate a bridge over a disused railway line, but before they reached it a large circular object came up from behind a hedge and passed low over the car, moving upwards. The object was dark, silent and about thirty feet in diameter. It had numerous orange lights or jets along the perimeter of the underside; these were not very bright and gave only a faint orange glow on the surface of the aeroform. The sighting lasted about ten seconds and there was no apparent effect on the functioning of the car.[12]

CASE 14: While sunbathing on the afternoon of Sunday 12 November (year not given, but probably 1978), ship's captain Frank Jolly observed a dome-shaped object fly over his house in Brighton, Melbourne, Australia. He estimated its height to be about 3000 feet and its speed between 100 and 200 knots. It appeared to be about sixty feet in diameter and to have brown stripes on its underside. The flying dome was dark grey and Captain Jolly thought it was of thin metallic substance because he noticed a 'slight buckling'. The object made no sound and it was a cloudless day.[13]

This sample of cases presents sightings typical of the sort that are reported of apparently solid objects observed in daylight conditions. Dr Hynek observes[14] that UFOs of this variety often display the characteristic of hugging the contours of the land. They often stop over small bodies of water. Sometimes, he also notes, these types of object are reported to have dark bands across their surfaces (Cases 10 and 14).

Not all 'solid' UFOs are seen first in the air—Case 13 for example. When seen on the ground such UFOs are assumed to have 'landed'. This is a dangerous assumption in my view.

Although *apparently* hard, solid objects, aeroforms of this category do display characteristics that, again, make such an assumption a risky one. Although solid enough to give a metallic appearance and reflect sunlight on many reported occasions, the same forms can then disappear in an instant. If this effect is caused by rapid acceleration, then it is likely that these UFOs are of low mass, lower than might be expected of any truly metallic object. If it is caused by some sort of 'dimensional shift', then the substance of these things might well be of a quite different order to solid matter. The slow and silent behaviour of other examples of daylight sightings (e.g. Cases 10 and 13) also suggests the movement of something other than a dense, heavy object. The observation in Case 14 that the metal appeared to be thin because it was buckling might be very significant here. If UFOs of this type are in fact composed of a tenuous substance giving the appearance of a metallic sheen, then such a report becomes less curious. The Denham Valley case (Case 12) is most interesting in this respect as it was seen to *fade* from view and displayed odd chromatic effects around its 'metallic' body. Even these 'hard' UFOs can shapeshift, as Case 11 testifies.

My Suffolk/Essex sighting (p. 19) would also come into this category. I can still recall the shock of seeing something apparently solid and utterly dense suddenly vanish. All may not be what it appears to be in the realm of the UFO.

CE1
This is the second of the 'large observational divisions of UFO sightings' suggested by Hynek—Close Encounters of the First Kind. This category involves the witnessing of a very close UFO but where no material interaction occurs between the object and its physical environment.

The witnessing of an UFO at all, in general terms, is a rare event and so it is to be expected that close encounters are themselves relatively rare occurrences within the totality of UFO experiences.

CASE 15: Clive Turner was walking home from his girlfriend's house in Dudley, West Midlands, in the early hours of Sunday 2 October 1977 when a 'humming roar' stopped him in his tracks. There was little cloud and a full moon was visible. Directly above him the witness saw a stationary object. It was a circular form of immense size—about 150 feet across—hovering at about 200 to 300 feet in the air. Its flat underside was a 'dirty silver colour' in the centre with multi-coloured lights rotating around the perimeter in a clockwise direction. The colours exhibited covered most of the range of the spectrum and blended into one another. The lights were themselves moving around the object. The witness noticed no apertures or protrusions on the object. It remained stationary for a little under half a minute then shot away at tremendous speed towards the Malvern Hills (from where there have been a number of UFO reports over the years[15]). Mr Turner, aged twenty-one at the time of the incident, said: 'If I'd blinked I would have missed it', so quick was the UFO's departure.[16]

CASE 16: Late in the evening of 20 August 1955, at Kenora, Ontario, the president of a small Canadian air service company and his nightwatchman saw an object 'like two saucers with their open tops touching, one above the other'. The executive had gone down to a lakeside to check the moorings of his seaplanes. The object was a silvery white colour and glowed bright 'but did not have a glare'. It streaked towards the two men from the west, avoided some low cloud and tilted on ts side when about 600 feet away from the witness. It then straightened out parallel with the horizon and came to a dead stop, about forty feet above the water and some seventy-five feet from the witnesses. No sound came from the object and the observers could see no discernible features on the saucer-shaped UFO. They estimated the object to be no more than five feet across and only eight to ten inches thick. It appeared to sparkle 'as if some electric force or very hot air was flowing from all the surfaces'. After its first stop, the saucer slid sideways for about fifty feet at a walking speed. After a couple of minutes it suddenly accelerated away from the witnesses so quickly that it 'disappeared like a shrinking star in three seconds from a standing start'.[17]

CASE 17: A retired electrician, Max Krauss, had a remarkable close encounter on 9 April 1970. He was walking along a country road towards his home in Langenschemmern, West Germany. It was four o'clock in the afternoon and the weather was overcast. He heard two bangs, like those made when the sound-barrier is broken, but more muffled. He carried on walking along the road when, for some reason he cannot explain, he turned round. The witness was astonished to see 'what looked like a torn-off skeleton of a plant coming whirling along the right-hand side of the road'. Despite a boisterous cross-wind the object maintained a steady course, close to the ground. It slowly overtook Mr Krauss and he could see that what had at first appeared to him as a plant's skeleton was in fact a transparent ball some forty centimetres across with spokes inside it. 'From a dark spherical nucleus with hazy edges' came eight spokes which tapered off towards their extremities, their tips almost as clear as glass, but non-reflecting. Krauss takes up the account:

As the thing passed me, I increased my pace and stepped out after it. At the moment of the encounter I was not frightened, merely astonished and curious. But I was incapable of doing anything whatsoever, such as picking up a stone, or going over to the thing and giving it a kick with my foot. I was stopped from doing so, and could only look on and observe. The thing may have rolled along in this way beside me for about 150 metres or so. Then it halted, did a right-angle turn towards the little stream of water, and stopped there. The rotation stopped too.

What I now observed is beyond my power to comprehend. From the dark centre of the ball there emerged, downwards, something resembling a hosepipe, which bent itself back and upwards like a 'U' and then writhed about sideways several times. In the bend that was nearest to the ball there appeared a gleam like brightly glowing hot iron. The glowing colour grew darker towards the more distant convolutions, and was only visible on the outward facing sides of each convolution of the hosepipe.

The hosepipe started wriggling about like a worm, extended itself, and went down to the ground. I am convinced that it reached into the water. The 'worm' remained there for a short while, and then was drawn back in again. At the same time, the central part of the ball changed colour throughout half of its radius, becoming milky, like water just before it boils. The outer shell of the ball now displayed a bluish tinge, somewhat like the ionized air to be seen around electrical high tension generators. Then the strange object slowly started its rotating, gliding movement again, passed across the road, quite close to me, to a point a pace or so into the field. And there it vanished, so absolutely silently, and at such lightning speed, straight upwards into the sky, that I was unable to follow it with my eyes.

One thing however that did strike me was that, shortly before the occurrence, all the birds had flown off in the opposite direction. Never before have I seen a crow move its wings so fast. Next day I made a search of the surroundings, but without finding anything remarkable. I also took a photograph of the section of road in question. At the time of the experiences I suffered no harmful effects in any respect. My wife dismisses my story as a piece of fantasy. If the affair ever becomes known here locally, I suppose it will be all up with my reputation.

I assure you that I have told the truth in every respect.

Mr Krauss gave additional details to investigator Hubert Malthaner: in the dark central portion of the ball a tetrahedral prism was seen briefly by the witness as the object passed by him. The spokes looked telescopically extensible and were grey-green. Over the 150 metres the witness and the UFO were side by side the distance between them was no greater than the width of the road.[18]

What is apparent even from this brief sample of CE1 cases is that UFOs seem able to assume any shape or size—some of the forms are as bizarre as they are dumbfounding. In this respect they are similar to the 'Lights' phenomena, and again we can note instances in this category as we did in the 'Daylight Sightings' section where apparently dense solid objects can accelerate instantaneously in a way that suggests that they can have hardly any mass despite their appearance. Hynek notes this acceleration characteristic of UFOs at close encounter and adds the further—in my view very important—observation that there is 'little tendency for the UFO to "cruise about the country" except locally'.[19]

CE2

This is Hynek's category of UFO sightings where a UFO is viewed at reasonably close range with accompanying physical effects on the witness, the immediate environment, or both.

CASE 18: Patricia Carter, then aged twenty-three, was the witness in this case. She was driving a van from Bristol to Minehead in the early morning of 26 September 1977. At about

7.35 a.m. she noticed something hovering over a hedge on the far side of a field to the north of the road. She stopped the van and went to investigate. She noted cattle in the field were huddled together in one corner. Patricia moved closer towards the object which appeared to be a slightly egg-shaped, smooth, silver-grey UFO about fifteen to twenty feet across. As she approached the thing she suddenly entered a zone around it where, she said, her skin prickled and her hair stood on end. The feeling was similar to that produced by a high static charge she had once experienced during a school physics experiment. After a few moments of this she thought better of approaching the thing any further and returned to her van and drove off. Shortly afterwards she saw an object moving rapidly across the sky and disappear. She was unable, of course, to confirm whether or not this was the same object she had seen in the field.[20]

CASE 19: A retired industrial psychologist, who had had considerable flying experience in all types of aircraft, witnessed a UFO at about 8.35 p.m. on 15 February 1978, near his home at Ivybridge, Devon. He was watching television when it blacked out. Shortly afterwards the street lights followed suit. The house lights remained on. Looking out of his window in a westerly direction he saw an object about 2000 feet in the air bathed in a blue light. It was at a distance, he estimated, of about one mile. It had a dome-shaped top and a band around the middle which seemed to have something like windows emitting a pinkish light. He could hear a low rhythmical noise coming from the object which he estimated was about 250 feet in diameter. It was rocking gently from side to side and was in view for a full two minutes. It finally moved away at a speed the witness 'did not think possible'. The man also described feeling attracted towards the object as though by some magnetic force that gave a sensation akin to vertigo.[21]

CASE 20: Mrs Burnette Fox, along with several neighbours, witnessed a number of silvery objects over Jonesboro, Tennessee, around noon on 12 October 1966. These objects discharged 'some substance in sheets' that broke up into strands. It was sticky and burned Mrs Fox's finger when she touched some of it. All the witnesses were affected by nausea and suffered itching sensations. Everyone who entered their back yards felt this itching effect until the following Saturday when it rained. Mrs Fox's dog refused to go into the yard until after it had rained and likewise cattle refused to enter a field where the substance had fallen until the rain came.[22]

CASE 21: The witness to the following incident is a teacher (and formerly an air hostess). On 3 April 1968, shortly after 8 p.m., she was motoring near Cochrane, Wisconsin, when an object emerged swiftly and smoothly from a dip in a hill. It hovered over a car that had just overtaken the witness' vehicle. The lights of the car in front of her went out. The woman pulled over onto the gravel at the roadside because she did not want run into the vehicle in front and because her own lights, too, were beginning to dim. She brought the car to a halt but the engine was still running. Passing on from the first car, the UFO came towards that of the witness, who had her ten-year-old son with her. The UFO was a red colour and roughly boomerang shaped but 'more rolled than flat'. It looked solid, although it became fuzzy towards the edges. It hovered low over the witness' car and she leaned forward over the steering wheel to gaze up through the windscreen at it. The car engine, the lights and the radio had now stopped functioning. At this point the witness noted a striking, eerie silence. She could not get the car to start all the time the UFO hovered above her. She also noticed a curious sensation of weightlessness and even the air itself was 'light and weightless'. The object finally moved off behind the car in the direction of a farmhouse. The car could now be started and the witness accelerated out of the area, observing as she did so that the object was moving slowly across some railway tracks.[23]

CASE 22: A well-publicized close encounter in Britain was an incident that occurred on 9 November 1979, near Livingston, West Lothian, Scotland. On the morning in question the percipient, 61-year-old Robert Taylor, a local forester of sound reputation, was inspecting a young forest to the north of Livingston. He was accompanied by his dog. He left his van and proceeded down a forest track. Turning a corner he was confronted by a large dome-shaped object hovering just clear of the ground. It was about twenty feet in diameter, was soundless, and did not appear to be rotating. It was a dark grey colour with a texture similar to that of emery-paper. The exceptionally interesting quality of the UFO that Mr Taylor noticed was that *it became transparent in one place, then in another*. The witness stood stock-still in amazement for about half a minute, then two smaller spheroids appeared 'presumably' from beneath the large object and rushed towards him. These objects were of a similar appearance to the main UFO but rolled along. They had 'spikes' sticking out of their globular bodies making Mr Taylor think of the appearance of a sea mine. There was a 'plopping' sound as these spikes touched the ground. The description of these things, in 'fact, bears a striking resemblance to Mr Krauss' 'plant skeleton' UFO (Case 17). These objects attached their spikes to Mr Taylor's trousers and he felt them tug at him. He was pulled to the ground, aware of an acrid smell. He began to lose consciousness and the last thing he recalls is the sensation of being dragged along the ground towards the large UFO. When he came round, he was lying face down, the UFOs had gone and his dog was with him. Mr Taylor was unable to speak or walk. He crawled back to his van but was unable to use the two-way radio because of his speech-loss. In his confusion he backed his vehicle into some mud and was unable to free it. He walked back to his home. His speech returned during the journey. On seeing him his wife thought he had been attacked by thugs and wanted to call the police, but he persuaded her to ring his superior in the Forestry Department. He accompanied Mr Taylor back to the scene of the incident where distinct curious ground marks, holes and grooves, were visible. Mr Taylor's trousers were also torn. The ground marks were confirmed and measured by police and they were photographed.[24]

Here we have again the usual motley range of UFO forms and the same characteristics of sudden acceleration that we have come across before. In the Livingston case we have yet another observation that questions the solidity of apparently physical UFOs. (It is interesting to note that it is usually the case that the better observation a witness gets of a 'real' UFO, the more likely factors are noticed that tend to clash with the generalized appearance of a solid, heavy machine.) In this particular case, of course, as in a small number of other sightings, physical markings were left on the ground that seem to confirm beyond any doubt that a substantial object had been present. Yet this could be deceptive. Ball lightning, for example, has been know to leave holes, furrows and scorch marks on the ground as a result of energy effects of some kind. These are just the sort of markings left by UFOs. If UFO traces just occasionally seem more organized, then it could be that we are dealing with a more coherent phenomenon than ball lightning.

A common effect noted in CE2s is the presence of a field similar to static electricity surrounding UFOs, as seen in the examples presented here. This can give a prickly sensation to a witness' skin, make the hair rise, or, possibly, cause the interference frequently noted with car engines and electrical equipment. This does not *always* happen in close encounters, though it is a widely reported feature. This has caused some of the more sceptical ufologists to throw up their hands in despair, complaining that if the UFO phenomenon is genuine, why is it that similar effects are not *always* reported. This attitude is naive. If I may return to the magnetism analogy: to someone knowing nothing about the force, the unlike poles of two magnets attracting each other would seem a straightforward demonstration of magnetism. Yet another demonstration in which the like poles repelled one another would seem to be a totally contrary proposition. *A coherent system can have widely diverse, even contradictory, effects.* The more caustic breed of new researchers should dwell on their ignorance of the UFO phenomenon a little more.

Substances left by UFO appearances—such as the 'angel hair' reported in Case 20—are occasionally observed. However physically insubstantial the UFO phenomenon might be, the energy processes that go into its creation do sometimes seem to generate more stable material that can remain for some time after the phenomenon itself has ceased. This is precisely what I felt during my Ravensbourne experience: the rosy cloud that was left in the sky *was* of a genuine, physical nature, I am sure of that; it was being dispersed by air currents. Later in this book we will come across a number of accounts where 'smokey' or 'gaseous' vapour effects are produced as a by-product of UFO manifestations. I think 'angel hair' is another tenuous material that is incidentally produced in the UFO process.

Hynek notes that the vast majority of CE2 UFOs *are seen on the ground,* and mostly at night.

Entities
We now move into what *appears* to be a completely different dimension of the UFO phenomenon. In this category we deal with reports of apparently animated beings usually, though not

always, in association with UFO-type manifestations. This looks to be a 'quantum leap' in the UFO enigma but, as I will suggest later, these reports might not be so fundamentally different as they at first seem.

This category is, as might be expected, smaller than many of the other types of sighting. We are dealing with an exceedingly rare phenomenon indeed, and it is worth bearing this in mind when studying a list of such events that have been collected from sources over long periods of time and from many parts of the world. This tends to give the false impression that such happenings are fairly frequent.

CASE 23: There were five witnesses to the following encounter, which occurred between 8 p.m. and 10 p.m. on an early January evening in 1968 at the Lagoa Negra Fazenda in the southern Brazilian state of Rio Grande do Sul. When the UFO was first noted it was hovering about two metres above the ground at a distance of almost 400 metres from the house. The fazenda owner, his wife, son and daughter, as well as the fazenda manager, witnessed the UFO and its 'occupants' for about twenty minutes. The object was about three metres high, ten metres wide and was emitting a cold reddish light which penetrated the house and lit up the whole area. The UFO had a metallic gleam, it was not rotating, had a round, hat-shaped cupola and a protuberance on the underside which none of the witnesses could make out at all clearly. Two 'ufonauts' appeared by the UFO (no details given as to how exactly the figures emerged from the object) and were about two metres tall. They walked without bending their legs, they had shoulder-length hair and were white-skinned. They had unusually long arms and large, bare feet. They walked towards the house, then returned to the vicinity of the UFO. This procedure was repeated. By this time three smaller entities had emerged from the object and remained beneath it. They too had long hair and white skins. While all this was going on, the fazenda owner and manager had left the house and had taken up a position between it and the UFO by some trees, where they remained hidden. The tall entities made a third move towards the house. In the course of this they passed through a gate which the witness felt they opened and closed. As they came closer to the house the wife and daughter of the fazenda owner could see their features distinctly. 'They look like saints!' the daughter exclaimed. This unnerved the mother who shouted out to her husband to come back to the house. As though on hearing her voice, the approaching beings stopped and, haltingly, retraced their steps back to the UFO. All five entities 'got back on board' (again no details given) and the UFO developed a rotational movement, rose vertically and sped away.[25]

CASE 24: This encounter involves an entity and a curious light effect but no clearly-defined UFO as such. The area involved is the vicinity of Norbotten, Sweden. On 19 August 1970, Mr and Mrs Mohlinder and a friend were motoring between Narken and Lulea. It was dark and rainy and they had the car headlights on. Suddenly, in the beams of these, they all saw a tiny figure no more than a metre tall standing on a pathway in the forest alongside the road. The entity immediately put up its hands as if to shield itself from the headlights. As the car came closer to the figure, the interior of the vehicle and the road round about 'went totally white' with a blinding light. The driver naturally slowed down. At the same time a crack like a gunshot was heard. After the flash and bang the little figure was still on the forest path but the witnesses drove on, not caring to stop. From the look they had had of it, the figure was apparently dressed in a grey garment and was wearing something that looked like a helmet.

A few months later, in the same general area of Sweden, another witness saw a very similar figure.[26]

CASE 25: While driving back to their home at Santa Maria del Tempo, Piedmont, Italy, from a religious festival in a nearby village during the early hours of 16 April 1974, Carla and Mauro Bellingeri spotted an unusual light in the sky. The light was high up and possessed 'an unusual motion' that captured their attention. The witnesses were startled when the light lost height in a rapid dive to stop, without wavering, directly above their house, which they were now approaching. After stopping the car in front of their house, the couple got out to observe the light. It hung motionless in the air about twelve to thirteen metres above the ground. It made no sound. The top portion of the object was a sort of dome (the Bellingeri's called it a 'cockpit'), bright inside and completely transparent. It was roughly hemispherical in shape. The 'cockpit' was surrounded at its base by 'a disc-shaped ring'. This seemed to be separate to the dome. It carried lights like coloured electric bulbs, red, yellow and green, which rotated slowly clockwise in a horizontal plane. Mauro felt they looked something like the strobe lights on a police vehicle. The UFO also reflected the light coming from floodlamps in the yard of a nearby building. It was Carla's personal view that the UFO had been attracted by these lights. The witnesses could see three apparently humanoid shapes arranged in a horizontal row inside the dome. A 'lightly shaded zone' surrounded the silhouettes which made slight movements. The shape nearest to the witnesses seemed to have a big round helmet on its 'head', but it was entirely opaque and had a protuberance like a valve near its base. Suddenly this figure rotated its head to look at the husband and wife, but then returned to its original position. Then all three shapes moved to the right as if they were on a moving base. At this point three or four jets blazed out beneath the object and a pulsating 'whizzing' noise was heard. The lights increased their speed of rotation, and the UFO moved off, maintaining its altitude and rotating as it did so. The object was seen by an amateur astronomer located some distance away, and was heard by Mauro's sister-in-law who lives in the same house as the Bellingeris.[27]

CASE 26: On the evening of 14 November 1976, a celebrated British entity case took place. At 8.05 p.m. Mrs Joyce Bowles and a friend, Mr Ted Pratt, were driving to Chilcomb Farm, close to Winchester, to pick up Mrs Bowles' seventeen-year-old son. They were travelling in Mrs Bowles' car and she was driving. While they were on the A272 they noted an orange light in the sky which disappeared from view. Mrs Bowles saw it reappear and then immediately dip down towards a low-lying minor road leading to Chilcomb that they were about to turn into from the A272. This Chilcomb road is a narrow country lane which has a broad grass verge wider than itself. Immediately on turning into this lane the car began to shudder and Mrs Bowles could not keep control of it. It careered off the road at an angle and came to rest on the verge. The engine had been roaring while this was going on and the lights had considerably increased their brightness.

When the car came to a stop the engine cut out but Mr Pratt recalls that it sprang back into life of its own accord. The witnesses were now aware of a cigar-shaped object on the verge about five yards from the car. It was about fifteen feet long and a foot or so off the ground. The object seemed to be issuing some

sort of vapour along its underside. The top left portion of the
object was a 'window' with three heads peering out. The
witnesses were disturbed and Mr Pratt reached over and
switched the engine off. A figure 'emerged' from the cigar-shape
and approached the witnesses' car. (I have closely questioned
Mrs Bowles as to how the entity actually left the UFO. She was
unable to say. In fact, the whole incident seems to be remembered by her in a series of episodic, almost dream-like fragments.) The figure was that of a male, about six feet tall, slimly
built with long blond hair swept back from its forehead. It was
wearing a garment that looked like a silvery boiler-suit: *this
seemed to flap although there was no wind*. As the figure came
closer to the car, Mrs Bowles heard a whistling sound. Close to,
the witnesses observed that the entity had a dark beard and that
its skin was pale and clear. The figure placed one hand on the
roof of the car and looked inside through the driver's window.
Its nose was pointed but not particularly long; its eyes were
without pupils and were completely pink—'like an albino
rabbit' as Mrs Bowles put it. She recalled that the entity's eyes
were so penetrating that she still retained after-images of them
when she turned away to grab onto Mr Pratt. He had the impression that the entity had transmitted some sort of calming effect
to him. After a short while, the figure moved as if to walk round
the back of the car, but it never reappeared. The witnesses were
suddenly aware that the UFO had disappeared. After a little
difficulty Mrs Bowles started the car and moved off, stopping
after a short distance to light a cigarette before continuing to
Chilcomb Farm. There were other sightings of orange lights and
silver-suited figures by other witnesses all over the Winchester
area that weekend.[28, 29, 30, 31]

These cases indicate some of the varieties of experiences
recorded in close encounter cases with entities. Essentially, the
'ufonauts' come in three sizes—small, often around three to four
feet in height and having a hairy or zoomorphic appearance,
normal human size and, thirdly, what might be called a 'small
giant' size where figures between seven and ten feet are reported.
The larger entities usually have recognizably human features,
though sometimes robotic-looking figures are reported and also
'big hairy monsters'.

    I am always struck how frequently in such accounts the

entities, when they appear outside of the UFO, are never clearly observed entering and leaving the 'craft'. One minute they are not there, the next they are, and *vice versa*. Moreover, the entities often display quirky appearances—as indicated in the examples given above—in that they move in an awkward, even somnambulic manner; their limbs are strangely dispropor-tionated, or they are missing details like eye pupils. The menagerie of UFO 'occupants' seems so often to be composed of careless drawings of figures: heads, hands and feet are too large or too small, or sometimes missing altogether. UFO entities seem to me like 'rushed jobs' by some overworked creator, who makes the same mistakes as would a poorly trained art enthusiast.

Hynek has admitted to a feeling of unease when dealing with these sort of cases; and yet, I have a feeling that the entities may be the key into an important understanding concerning the whole UFO phenomenon.

Proto-Entities

I was deeply impressed while watching the Ravensbourne event how the glowing figure *formed out of the UFO material itself*. It is my contention that UFO entities are formed in the same way as the UFO shape itself, and that they partake of the same sub-stance. In my view they represent merely a different develop-ment of the same phenomenon—a rare further stage of it.

It has become clear to me that there exists a body of testimony that suggests this integral property of UFO entities. That it has not been readily perceived by ufologists may be because the sources of such accounts sometimes lie outside the normal pro-venance of UFO research, and—in no small measure in my opinion—because there has been a deep-seated *assumption* that UFO entities are travellers within a separate aeroform structure. I consider that assumption to be mistaken. But let us tackle this hitherto unrecognized area of testimony in stages.

CASE 27: One evening around the middle of this century, an Edinburgh doctor, while staying at an inn at Broadford in the Isle of Skye, sauntered out for an after-supper stroll. When he reached the shore he noticed a bright light far out in the bay. He first thought this to be a fisherman's flare until he realized that it was approaching his position at a smooth and regular speed. As it came close the doctor saw that it was a globe of light. As the phenomenon reached the tide's edge, it suddenly went out. In its place the witness now saw—for fleeting moments—a cloaked woman clutching an infant. She hurried across the sands in front of the doctor then, in an instant, her image too was extinguished.[32]

CASE 28: A party of overnight campers were located by Lake Manchester near Brisbane in Queensland, Australia. One of the party took a midnight stroll across a rope bridge to the wall of a nearby dam. There he encountered an 'electric blue sphere'. The eight-inch diameter ball of light seemed to be attracted to the witness who made his way back across the rope bridge. As this had to be negotiated slowly, the sphere caught up with him and positioned itself almost within arms reach of his right shoulder. At such close quarters the witness was shocked to see that not only did he have a glowing ball of light to contend with but also inside the sphere there was the image of a tiny, human-like entity. The being was bald, sitting cross-legged with its elbows resting on its knees and was staring intently at the witness. Bemused and alarmed, the witness scrambled back to camp and tumbled into one of the vehicles parked there.[33]

CASE 29: As a result of the previous event, the campers requested a psychic to attend the spot. This he did on a number of occasions in their presence. As nothing of interest transpired, the psychic investigator returned by himself one night. He left his car about midnight. A short while later he encountered a small blue sphere of light. The ball of light had an electric rather than a gaseous quality, the man stated. He had armed himself with a bayonet for protection and pointed this at the sphere, but realizing that if the phenomenon was electrical he would be in the discharge path, withdrew the implement. The psychic investigator obtained a close and valuable observation of the UFO. Inside the sphere of light were cloud-like tonings. Suddenly, *the darker areas of this shading coalesced into the shape of a tiny man*, again cross-legged and seated with his arms folded. The figure seemed curiously disproportioned. *As the witness watched, the figure became clearer 'very much like a photo will in developer'.* The investigator was unable to get closer than about fifteen feet from the phenomenon. During the sighting, the globe contracted and expanded periodically and fluctuated in brightness. The globe finally disappeared 'like the bursting of a bubble'.

Spheres of light have been seen so frequently around Lake Manchester, apparently, that the aboriginals—who call the lights 'min min globes'—have built a corroboree there, thinking the phenomena to be spirits of the dead.[34]

CASE 30: Jarmo Nykanen was staying at his lakeside summer cottage near Suonenjoki, Finland, on 30 June 1973. He was awoken in the early hours of the morning by a buzzing sound. The cottage was being irradiated by a strong blue light. Going outside Jarmo saw a blue light 'twice as big as a row-boat' approaching. This then stopped and hovered above the water of the lake. The light seemed to radiate from a kind of 'jelly', glowing in an unusual manner. Jarmo thought he could see a strange being inside the light. The next thing he remembered was lying on the cottage porch at about 6 a.m.[35]

CASE 31: Joseph Smith, founder of the Mormon religion, had his first other-worldly encounter one night at Palmyra, New York State. The year must probably have been 1819 or 1820. While praying in a grove near his home the boy saw a brilliant light that travelled down to the ground, growing ever more brilliant. As it settled close to him, Smith saw two beings within the light. These apparently communicated to him that he would be the recipient of a true revelation.[36]

CASE 32: A few weeks before Christmas in 1910, two men from County Kerry, Ireland, encountered strange lights near Listowel. It was about midnight, and very dark. They noticed a light about a mile ahead of them. At first they thought it was simply a light in a house, but on drawing closer they could see that it was moving up and down, to and fro; diminishing to a spark, then expanding into a yellow luminous flame. Before coming to Listowel they were able to distinguish two lights. Suddenly both of these expanded into yellow sheets of light about six feet high by four feet across. In the midst of each light they saw 'a radiant being having human form'. Only the general shape of the figures could be seen. The lights came together so that the beings could be seen side by side within the brilliant illumination. A house intervened between the travellers (who were still moving on) and the lights, and they saw no more of them. 'In our hurry to get home', said one of the witnesses, 'we were not wise enough to stop and make further examination.'[37]

CASE 33: In 1643 in Boston, Massachusetts, a group of men saw two lights arise from the water in the form of a man. Then more people witnessed the event. The lights shot out flame and sparkled. The form moved from its location to a distance and back again on several occasions.[38]

CASE 34: After a chapel meeting in Bryncrug, Wales, in 1905, a professional gentleman returning homeward suddenly saw a gigantic figure rising over a hedgerow, with right arm extended over the road. Then a ball of fire appeared above from which a long white ray descended. This struck the figure which then vanished. The phenomena were witnessed also by a prominent local farmer from another standpoint. This event took place at a time and in an area where other extraordinary light phenomena were occurring—what we would today call a 'wave' or 'flap' area. We will be returning to the region in a future chapter.[39]

CASE 35: On 21 August 1897, at Knock, a tiny village in the west of Ireland, a remarkable phenomenon took place. It is an example of the proto-entity phenomenon *par excellence.* The weather had been bad all day and was getting worse. At about

Bryncrug Chapel, near Towyn. The Bryncrug area was the scene of several sightings during the 1904-5 UFO wave (see Chapter 7), and also of the witness in case 34, who returning from this chapel saw a proto-entity. Bryncrug lies directly on the Bala fault. (*Author's photo*)

8.30 p.m. Mary McLoughlin set off to visit her friend Mrs Margaret Beirne. Her route took her past the village church. In a nearby field she saw several strange figures and 'something like an altar' with white light. As the rain was falling so heavily, Mary did not investigate any further and hurried on to her friend's house. Later on, while there was still some daylight, she returned home with her friend. Between the church and the two women, in a meadow, three persons seemed to be standing surrounded by an extraordinarily bright light. The figures formed a religious tableau, depicting the Blessed Virgin Mary, St. Joseph and a figure one of the witnesses felt must be St. John the Evangelist, who was depicted as a bishop wearing a mitre. Within a short while eighteen parishioners were assembled before the apparition. A diocesan commission later interviewed fourteen of these witnesses.

The three religious figures seem to have been motionless, looking almost like statues. They were clothed in dazzling, silver-like garments. Every detail on the figures could be seen, including a brilliant crown surmounted by a glittering crosses on the head of the Blessed Virgin. Behind the three figures was an altar with a cross on it; in front was a lamb with its head to the west. The whole phenomenon, in fact, was like a phantasmagorical hologram of traditional Catholic symbols. The tableau was surrounded by a golden, sparkling light, 'as bright as the sun', that illuminated the church gable 'like a wall of snow'. All the manifestations were located within the area of light and all the witnesses seemed to see the same forms. (Earlier in the evening an elderly man had been walking in the fields near Knock when he saw a large globe of golden light covering the whole gable of Knock church.) At one point a witness went to embrace the feet of the Virgin but her arms closed as if on empty air. The woman noticed that the ground beneath the images was dry.

The tableau was observed for several hours by the villagers, who got drenched to the skin. They all went home before midnight. Unfortunately, we are not told how the highly detailed images disappeared. The next day nothing was to be seen at the site of the phenomenon.[40]

CASE 36: The following event took place in Houston, Texas, on 18 June 1953. It was a hot night, and at 2.30 a.m. three people were still talking out on a front porch. One of them, Hilda

Walker, saw a huge shadow cross the lawn. This shadow seemed to 'bounce upward' into a tree. Then all three witnesses saw the figure of a man in the tree, swaying on one of its branches. The man had wings like a bat and was dressed in grey or black tight-fitting clothing. He was well over six feet tall and was 'encased in a halo of light'. Immediately after the sighting the witnesses heard and saw 'a loud swoosh over the housetops across the street. It was like the white flash of a torpedo-shaped object'.[41]

All the above cases refer to anthropomorphic figures forming within, manifesting out of or being closely associated with light forms. In some instances, however, it is zoomorphic figures or images that appear at the site of light phenomena.

CASE 37: In 1639 James Everett saw a great light three yards square near a muddy river in Charlestown, New England. The light suddenly contracted 'into the figure of a swine and ran off'.[42]

CASE 38: A Pennsylvanian woman heard a disturbance outside her house on the evening of 6 February 1974. Taking a shotgun, she went to investigate. On opening the door she was horrified to encounter a seven foot tall, hairy ape-like creature. In panic, the woman shot the creature in its midriff. To her utter amazement, the woman saw the entity disappear in a flash of light. A nearby relative came rushing over to see what the matter was and he also saw other ape-like creatures lurking on the edge of a nearby wood. A red, flashing light was seen over the trees.[43]

CASE 39: Periodically there are outbursts of sightings in southern England of a phenomenon known as 'The Surrey Puma'. It comes and goes inexplicably. In 1964 Bushylease Farm in Hampshire had a number of such sightings in its vinicity. While every odd footprint, night-time yowl and mauled farm creature was put down to the doings of this enigmatic cat-like creature, the farmer had noticed a strong smell 'with an ammonia tang' in the neighbourhood and had seen strange lights on the roofs of farm buildings at night.[44]

The following account does not mention a UFO-like event but is a particularly good description of a partially-formed event verging on the 'bear' or 'ape' type of entity. It is possible in the circumstances of this case that any light form connected with the genesis of the phenomenon would not have been observed by the witness.

CASE 40: In the dip between the two summits of the Glyder mountains in Snowdonia, North Wales, mountaineer and writer Showell Styles saw 'the only ghost I have ever seen on a mountain'. It was a heatwave day and there was not a breath of wind even at 3000 feet. Far down the southern slope of Pen-y-gwryd Styles saw what he took to be a figure coming up the slope. He soon perceived that the large brown shape was too big and moving too fast for it to be human. It passed within twenty yards of him, and Styles was able to see through the thing and hear the low roaring or rushing noise it was making. It was 'like a bear' and 'six or seven feet in diameter'. Styles felt no stirring of the air as it passed by.[15]

This case draws attention to a sort of sub-grouping of the proto-entity phenomenon: namely, that of incompletely formed creatures and 'entities' that bear little or no resemblance to any life-form we know, or else resemble some kind of simple-celled organisms. Many accounts of 'ufonauts' involve witness observation that beings moved in unnatural ways, that they had parts of the body missing or that they vanish or fade from sight even though previously seeming quite solid. The following accounts give a few examples of some of these aspects.

CASE 41: This is a case which has been widely recorded and is sometimes referred to as the 'Saltwood Horror'. On 16 November 1963 four teenagers were walking near Sandling Park at Hythe, Kent. They were alarmed at seeing a reddish yellow light descending at an angle from the sky. It seemed to slow down as it approached the ground, and became lost to sight behind some trees. Then a golden light appeared in a field near the witnesses, floating about ten feet above the ground. The light was oval, the teenagers said, about fifteen to twenty feet across with 'a bright, solid core'. This second light also disappeared behind some trees, but a few seconds later a dark figure shambled out towards them. It was 'all black', about the size of a human being but had bat-like wings on either side. Understandably enough, the young witnesses lost no time in making themselves scarce. Chilling as this description is, there was one other grim detail concerning the entity—it had no head.

CASE 42: Two teenage boys were coming home from work on a motor-bike on 20 September 1973. As they passed Stainland Woods between Huddersfield and Halifax they saw three triangular lights 'gliding' uphill through the woods. They decided to follow the shapes, which seemed to be speeding up their motion. A curious smell was in the air like 'burning oil'. When they reached the top of the wooded hill the yellow-white triangular lights had disappeared, but up in the sky the witnesses saw a small, round light. It was orange in colour. This moved away and was lost to sight within minutes. The triangular shapes had left no tracks that the boys could trace and they were hard put to find out how the lights had guided so smoothly through such dense woodland.[46]

CASE 43: In July 1975, Trevor P., then aged fourteen, was accompanying his parents in the viewing of a cottage in the Machynlleth area of Mid-Wales. Trevor decided to go for a ramble up a 250-foot hill nearby while his parents were busying themselves. On reaching the top of the small hill the boy saw a strange object resting on the ground a short distance away from him. He darted behind some boulders to observe it. It had a brilliantly illuminated hemispherical dome, which was transparent; this was resting on a silver coloured base which had large lights about its circumference. The whole thing was about forty feet across. Inside the dome Trevor could see a 'big metal' unit or irregular shape. Also inside the dome were two moving forms— large, odd-shaped pieces of jelly-like substance. These were a whitish translucent colour containing many white discs and were about seven feet tall. They were constantly *changing shape.* Trevor took all this in in less than a minute.

He then saw an opening appear in the base and one of the jellies 'floated' towards this and emerged from the UFO. Trevor ran off down the hill, babbled excitedly to his father and then ran back to the scene of the extraordinary events. By now the UFO was 'closed' again with both jelly entities inside and a constant noise was coming from it. The UFO's lights began to flash at an increasing rate until the colours seemed to 'blend' with the colours of the surrounding landscape and the whole object became invisible. Trevor ran back to his father shouting 'You won't believe me—come on!' and urging him up the hill. On the top the father was unable to see anything unusual but he

did hear a strange noise. Trevor subsequently suffered unfortunate after-effects: the following day his speech became
impaired; three weeks later his left eye became blind, then this
changed to his right eye and became almost total before easing.
He also underwent a personality change and up to 1978 at least
was still undergoing psychiatric treatment.[47]

These examples show quite clearly that there is a body of testimony which, when treated as a coherent type, identifies a
specific phase in some UFO events. The detailed observation in
Case 29 of a figure within a globe of light forming out of
coalescing dark patches gives, in my opinion, the true situation
with regard to 'UFO entities'—they are *not* occupants of a craft,
but are *further formations from the same material*. Were the
figures seen inside the transparent dome of the UFO in Case 25
really aliens inside a perspex cockpit, or were they more like the
little figure formed within a transparent bubble of energy that
haunts Lake Manchester?

The light phenomenon can partially form into figures—anthropomorphic, zoomorphic and indeterminate—in which case it
will be interpreted a a craft containing occupants. UFO light
phenomena can also transform completely into transient figures
which are mobile in their own terms.

Later on, we will consider where these various forms come
from, but the fact that a German engineer (Case 17) sees a UFO
in the form of a fantastic machine, for instance, or a small
Catholic community sees a light phenomenon form into
religious images (Case 35), hints at a possible explanation.

It is these sort of cases in which witnesses see the intermediate
stage between simple light ball and complex, independent entity
that I feel are crucial to the whole understanding of what is going
on during the occurrence of a UFO event. Bearing this approach
in mind, it becomes possible to cope with what are otherwise the
most bizarre, if not ludicrous, accounts of all UFO case histories.
Here is just one example out of several similar types from all over
the world:

CASE 44: A 64-year-old man in Milford Haven, Wales, was
getting up at about a quarter to five one morning in April 1977
when he became aware that there was a bright orange light
pulsating on his bedroom wall. Looking out of the window he
saw a large area of orange light enclosing two silvery objects.

The first of these the witness described as being like 'a very large Easter egg'. It was about four feet in diameter and was moving to and fro a little above and behind the chimneys of houses across the street. There was no sound. The other object was about forty feet above the witness' bedroom window: it was the figure of a 'man' in a silver boiler-suit type of garment, at least seven feet tall. The figure was quite stationary and on a level with the 'egg', in the position of a falling parachutist—motionless in the sky with arms and legs outstretched. The aerial scene apparently remained in this tableau for twenty-five minutes. The ellipsoid form finally moved up higher and glided sideways as did the humanoid figure, until both were out of sight.[48]

Only the proto-entity concept makes sense of a sighting such as this.

I have attempted to present a representative range of the rich UFO pageant collected from many sources and covering most of the main categories of UFO types. The two types of sighting I have not given examples of are cases where a radar echo has been recorded and where percipients claim to have been 'abducted' or taken aboard a UFO. I leave the latter cases out here because I shall be referring to them later (I think they are a different type of event altogether). Regarding the radar instances, there are few of these that are well-attested and there has been considerable controversy about the accurate identification of a UFO out of the multifarious echoes on a radar screen. Nevertheless, the evidence indicates that UFO phenomena can occasionally develop sufficient coherence, and I suggest that means increased density, that would result in a radar return if it happened to be scanned. A recent example of a radar-visual case occurred over New Zealand in December 1978 and was a widely publicized incident.

In summary, we can see that once we get past the carnival glare of the UFO pageant there are a few basic characteristics that can be identified about the whole phenomenon. The most important of these is the ability UFOs have to shapeshift. This is one of the most important clues UFO reports have to give us. I have put forward evidence to suggest that this process leads to the production of so-called entities in some cases.

Many UFOs exhibit motion that strongly indicates that they have a low mass. Even apparently solid 'metallic' UFOs frequently pass through a cycle in their manifestation that indicates a nature that is basically less stable and substantial. When observed closely or for a period of time, even what appear to be straightforward machines display non-solid characteristics such as transparency or anomalous chromatic effects.

A great many UFO witnesses report some form of electromagnetic disturbance in the vicinity of such objects. This can affect people and machines. This effect is too widely reported for it not to definitely relate to the process that produces a UFO manifestation. The fact that such ambient effects are not always reported does not mean that this observation has to be modified, as I pointed out in the analogy with magnetism.

UFOs sometimes appear to exhibit intelligent, inquisitive or evasive behaviour; but it has been suggested that this could be the result of an energy interaction between the phenomenon and the fields surrounding the body of the witness—*vide* the ball-bearing and magnet analogy. Marks left on the ground by UFOs mimic those reported after the appearance of natural phenomena such as ball lightning.

UFOs often appear *on the ground*—in the majority of cases in one type of sighting. Because of unproven assumptions, ground-based UFOs are interpreted as having landed. I have pointed out that I feel this need not necessarily always be the case.

Another basic pattern that can be discerned in UFO reports is that such phenomena tend to 'haunt' specific locations more than others and can often occur in temporal groupings—the so-called 'flap' or 'wave'. Whether or not there is some form of periodicity in this time/space pattern has not yet been established; but it means we need to consider the role of *place* in the overall problem.

An overview of the UFO pageant, therefore, seems to tell us that while we seem, by and large, to be dealing with an objective phenomenon, its nature is unlikely to be one of stable, dense matter (though if an energy process is involved there may be transient phases of coherence and tenuous material appears to be produced occasionally as a by-product). There is at least a hint that mental processes are involved with this objective phenomenon in some way, as well as location. UFO entities are not altogether convincing, and there is clear evidence that far from interpreting them as occupants of alien space craft it would be better to think of them as another form of the UFO phenomenon itself, composed by the same processes.

We are presented with a complex mystery, or one that appears complex, and before putting forward any further ideas it is necessary to consider briefly what explanations have already been put forward to account for the mystery and what can be learned from them.

3.
Interpretations of the UFO Problem

Three blind men came across an elephant. One felt
its trunk and thought it must be a kind of snake.
Another touched its legs and was convinced it was
tree-like. The third felt its ears and considered it to
be a form of cabbage.

The standard UFO 'explanation' encountered in our society is
the one offered by the Pavlovian response of orthodox science —
that the whole subject is just so much hokum. It would be
pleasant to be able to completely dismiss this attitude; unfortunately, it is to some extent correct! It is almost certain that
many, if not the majority, of UFO accounts are generated by
misperception of known objects, by the desire to deceive and, to
a much smaller extent, by various forms of mental aberration.

All serious UFO researchers know and accept that only a relatively small percentage of received sighting reports will turn out
to refer to genuinely unidentified phenomena. *It is the inability*
of the orthodox scientific mentality to apply itself to this very
important percentage that makes it culpable. Unfortunately, in
orthodox circles, the 'signal' of objectivity is too frequently
drowned out by the 'noise' of acceptability. When all the error
and hoax has been stripped away there remains a type of phenomenon being noticed on our planet, out of the corner of our
eye, so to speak, that does not yet come within the perimeters of
established scientific knowledge.

However, things are not a great deal better when we move
into the circles of those who believe in the actuality of UFO
events. Within such circles the dominant theory is that UFOs are
alien spaceships—this is the Extra-Terrestrial Hypothesis
(ETH). So strong is this idea (it is invariably the one picked up by

the media), and so applicable is it to our current cultural outlook, that it is difficult to get past it. I think it dominates not only our thinking on the subject of UFOs but actually *affects the perception of the phenomenon itself.* Witnesses will in most cases try to interpret their extraordinary experiences in ETH terms—probably the only UFO theory they have ever come in contact with. So a certain amount of conceptual modification may have gone on before their cases even reach investigators. These investigators themselves are then likely to involuntarily add ETH overtones, so that a phenomenon seen on the ground, for instance, may be automatically interpreted as having 'landed', or an entity seen in association with a UFO aeroform will be interpreted as an 'occupant'.

The famous film poster told us 'We are not alone'. That is reassuring. It gives us a cosmic-but-cosy feeling to believe that superior—and, of course, ultimately benign—beings are just around the corner to get us out of our boredom, out of our desecrated environment, out of the physical dangers which overhang our culture. A variant of the ETH theory is that 'We were not alone': the notion often ascribed to Erich Von Daniken, but put forward before him by the British writer Raymond Drake, that at the dawn of human civilization astronauts from an advanced civilization came and helped us on our way with the odd battery or two and a few battles employing tactical nuclear weapons. They seem to have been sufficiently human in form to be attracted by Earth women and so copulated around under the pretext of improving the human strain.

The ETH in its various guises is seductive: to counteract it you have to undergo the intellectual equivalent of a cold shower. Go out one starry night when you are feeling particularly brave. Look up at the endless heavens. Appreciate the stars as suns so distant from us and one another as to be *incomprehensibly remote;* so far away that the light from them left tens, hundreds and thousands of years ago. Out in that infinity there are probably a number of stars around which planets may exist in which the incredibly rare confluence of circumstances necessary to trigger conscious life has occurred. Accept that such planets, if they exist, are unlikely to have ever affected the planet on which you stand, which orbits one of a myriad stars in this galaxy alone, tucked away in a far-flung arm of the Milky Way. Put aside your mental toytown model of the cosmos and let your planetary ego dissolve away into the night. Alien civilizations with their time-warp or stellar-drive technologies would have to exist in their hundreds of thousands for the chance to come about of just one of them alighting on our planet. Judging by appearances, more than one civilization would need to have contacted us to explain the variety of entity types that have been reported. Quietly but audibly intone: 'We *are* alone'. Let it sink in. Turn, slowly go back indoors and pour yourself a large whisky.

ETH enthusiasts will naturally berate me for being flippant about their treasured theory and will doubtless go on to dismiss any alternative, less 'nuts and bolts' hypothesis as being airy-fairy. But, quite honestly, the concept does not warrant any more serious treatment. Indeed, enough time has already been expended on it over the last three decades.

One ETH exponent has said to me: 'But an alien civilization capable of travelling across interstellar space would have a technology appearing to us like magic, beyond our comprehension.' And yet it seems these interstellar wizards have to peer through windows to see what is going on; they need to pick up stones, soil and bags of fertilizer to analyze them just like our own crude astronauts on the Moon. Really hardened nuts-and-bolts UFO enthusiasts even talk of government conspiracies to hide the fact that UFOs have crashed and piles of alien interstellar junk have been collected by secretly knowledgeable Earth authorities. (Versions of Conspiracy Theory are often attached to forms of the ETH, which shows naivety in my opinion. It is a mistake to endow any government with superior knowledge.)

It is ultimately impossible to argue with ETH proponents. They can invoke any number of unknown possibilities when they are cornered. They *could* be correct, but the chances of the ETH being the right answer are so incredibly unlikely as to be beyond calculation. I suspect few adherents have ever bothered their brain cells with just how far beyond likelihood the ETH really is; and I do not think they sufficiently question the fact that their theory so coincidentally fits the conceptual level of our own culture's current technological development. Medieval UFOs were signs from God; late nineteenth-century UFOs were mysterious airships; the modern concept, the ETH, is a mental construct of mid-to-late twentieth-century Western society.

The ETH does not explain all aspects of the UFO enigma and what ETH researchers cannot come up with are eye-witness accounts of the time-warp mother ships leaving their highly advanced distant planets. Later in this book eye-witness accounts of where UFOs really come from will be presented — and it will have nothing to do with the ETH.

A theory that shares the idea of UFOs belonging to another civilization but at least brings speculation down to earth (indeed, into it) is that of the 'Hollow Earth'. The modern version of this old belief suggests that there is an advanced race living within our planet that sends UFOs out through holes at the poles to keep an eye on us. Satellite photographs in the 1960s apparently showing a hole at the North Pole helped to create a new interest in the idea. The fact that the effect of the 'hole' was created by mosaic techniques used in satellite photography combined with the polar winter has in no way deterred followers of this baroque fantasy. Fantasy it nevertheless is.

An original idea that also seeks to explain UFOs in Earth-centred terms claims that sightings are not of spaceships or aerial vehicles but of unknown *living creatures* frolicking in their natural habitat of the atmosphere. A well-known proponent of this idea was the late Ivan Sanderson, but perhaps the first person to speculate on the notion was Trevor Constable. In *The Cosmic Pulse of Life*[1] he gives an account, with many photographs, of his experiments with infra-red photography. He frequently obtained results that seemed to show odd shapes, usually organic looking, caught fleetingly in the atmosphere. I am no stranger to infra-red photography myself[2] and have used it to seek subtle effects, but I have never produced results like Constable. Neither has any other infra-red photographer with whom I have discussed the matter. Some of Constable's pictures look like the effects of poor processing and chemical damage to me, and a few are surely refractive effects (Constable did not always use filters). Nevertheless, apart from inadvertently using such probable infra-red herrings, Constable may well have captured some cases of an extraordinary atmospheric phenomenon which may one day lead us to an extended understanding of UFOs as natural phenomena of a currently unknown kind. I suspect that it is a geophysical answer rather than a biological one; but Constable seems convinced that what he has photographed are living aeroforms — 'critters' to use his terminology. This whole notion, though, ignores large sections of the collective UFO experience as it has been reported over the years.

Another explanation that keeps the enigma within the context of our own planet is that UFOs are time capsules occupied by time travellers from our own future. They drop back through the centuries and millenia to observe their own race as it developed and are analytical more in the way of tourists than scientists. This notion neatly answers problems such as the haphazard behaviour patterns exhibited by UFO entities and the failure of UFOs to put on a once-and-for-all, definitive 'landing'. A culture sufficiently advanced to cope with time travel would presumably be very conscious of the potentially uncontrollable problems that would be unleashed if there was any tampering with their own past. The serious problem against the hypothesis is the UFO pageant itself—the variety of aeroforms and the range of UFO entities. We are to undergo some major genetic mutations to account for some of the beings purportedly encountered by UFO percipients. Not only this, but humanoids are also witnessed that have a similar appearance to ourselves, which confuses the issue even further. The varied UFO shapes are explained away by adherents of this theory by referring to the many styles of vehicles used on land, sea and in the air today. This is acceptable, but the problem of entity types remains and renders the whole idea subject to suspicion—even before dealing with the apparent impossibility of physically travelling in time.

The time travel theory can be modified into the dimensional travel theory, which brings back hints of the ETH but in dimensional rather than spatial terms. It can also be used to explain entity types. In this suggestion, Earth of the third dimension is being visited by beings of other dimensional realms. Like the ETH, it is another easy, seductive theory— another 'fast food' type of explanation; but it is lacking in analytical content. It involves wholly unknown time/space mechanics. How supra-dimensional beings translate themselves into three-dimensional solidity becomes a mystery at the core of an unknown quantity. *Why* such beings want to bother employing these conveniently inexplicable mechanics simply to behave oddly in our world is anyone's guess. How they know of our dimensional existence is another problem: these beings not only have one universe to scan but whole other dimensions as well to find us! On closer consideration, even the theory's ability to explain away the variety of reported entity types becomes suspect: have beings from many different dimensions managed to master inter-dimensional mechanics? Why do they all congregate on our third dimensional world? Or do the supra-dimensional entities put on different forms at whim as if going to a fancy dress party? The idea could, again, be the right one; but it has to be said that it becomes increasingly unsatisfactory the more it is studied. I think there is sufficient evidence available to suggest alternative ideas that should be studied first.

One of the most dynamic and original of UFO researchers is John Keel. As far back as the 1960s he was questioning the reality of solid, physically real UFOs. In an article in *Flying Saucer Review*[3] he claimed that 75 per cent of all known sightings were of the 'ill-defined lights and formless blobs' type. He calls them 'soft' UFOs. His investigations into the metallic, physically 'hard' UFOs repeatedly failed to convince him. Hoaxes were uncovered after in-depth inquiry, and psychic effects frequently came to light in even the 'hardest' of UFO events. He explains that his ideal UFO landing would have to meet stringent criteria, such as the object appearing at all times as the same solid form; being seen first in the sky and then being seen to land conventionally; any occupants would have to appear as solid, biological creatures, no matter how bizarre, and witnesses would have to be demonstrably free of any pathological or mental aberrations.

Keel has become convinced that the UFO enigma is one that has always existed on Earth. It frequents 'window areas' of the globe, he maintains, where geological conditions cause electromagnetic conditions to prevail that possibly help the phenomenon to manifest. While I personally agree with all of this, and subsequent research by others has tended to confirm these aspects, I must confess to having been unable to find any 'hard' evidence published by Keel to demonstrate how he arrived at these ideas. On the face of it, he seems to have simply come up with his insight from an intuitive evaluation of data available to him.

Keel coined the term 'ultra-terrestrial' to describe UFO entities that he feels are 'elementals', other denizens of the Earth sharing it with us on another level and interacting with us through various geophysical gateways, perhaps influencing or even controlling the way we think and perceive reality. According to Keel, these entities appear not only as UFO entities but also as the sinister 'Men In Black', the bland-faced swarthy characters who are often reported as showing up in flap zones—often in curiously new-looking obsolete cars—questioning or threatening investigators and witnesses. Other researchers have considered these disturbing fellows to be government agents or messengers of some secret organization which rules the world in occult ways. Others feel that the evidence for the actuality of such Men In Black is questionable, to put it mildly. But Keel seems convinced that they are, in fact, parahuman elementals, the devils, faeries and even angels of former times.

Beings associated with the UFO mystery, Keel writes:

> are part of our immediate environment in some unfathomable fashion, and to a very large extent are primarily concerned with misleading us, misinforming us, and playing games with us . . . They may have watched other civilizations come and go. They may have sincerely helped us to preserve the memories of those lost ages and those past mistakes. Or it may all be rubbish, and we may be nothing more than pawns with which they play their mischievous games.[4]

In his classic *Operation Trojan Horse*[5] Keel tells us that somewhere in the vast range of the electromagnetic spectrum '. . . there lies an omnipotent intelligence . . . able to manipulate energy. It can, quite literally, manipulate any kind of object into existence on our plane.'

Along with many other researchers, I feel that Keel's ideas are nudging us in the right direction. He has begun to direct our attention towards telling aspects of the phenomenon. However, he still seems to assume that some 'other' intelligence is involved; he invokes loose concepts about 'rays', and has continued to find meaning in certain dark notions of 'conspiracy'. In the final analysis, he never seems to be really definite about the nature of his 'ultraterrestrials'. He would doubtless counter that that is part of the whole problem.

Another major UFO researcher is an American-based French scientist called Jacques Vallee. For many years he has produced books and papers exemplifying the leading edge of thought on the whole enigma, but it is in his *Passport To Magonia* that I feel he has achieved his most important insight into the UFO enigma to date. In this book he does not put forward a theory to explain the nature of UFOs—in fact he goes out of his way to avoid doing so: he simply but very effectively demonstrates that the basic motifs in modern UFO accounts parallel those to be found in ancient folklore. Like Keel, and at about the same time, Vallee pointed out that the faeries and elementals, devils and visionary personages of former times bear striking likenesses to today's UFO entities. Vallee writes:

When the underlying archetypes are extracted from these rumours, the saucer myth is seen to coincide to a remarkable degree with the fairy-faith of Celtic countries, the observations of scholars of past ages, and the widespread belief among all peoples concerning entities whose physical and psychological descriptions place them in the same category as the present-day ufonauts.[6]

There are three ways of interpreting the implications of this crucial observation made by Vallee: (a) modern UFO patterns match those of earlier folklore because UFOs and their entities have been visiting our planet for thousands of years; (b) the patterns match because today's UFOs and entities are merely repeats of earlier generations' encounters with Earthbound elemental beings that have subtly changed their appearance to correspond with current images of what other-worldly beings should look like; or (c) the archetypal, universal nature of UFO entities suggest that profound mental processes are somehow at work in the whole UFO phenomenon. In *Passport To Magonia* Vallee dodges the issue.

In the final chapter of his book, Vallee gets himself into some extraordinary tangles, as if in drawing the parallels between folklore and the UFO mystery he was left in a limbo of thought. He dismisses the ETH as 'naive', and then asks what the alternatives are. He lists three possibilities he patronizingly suggests 'imaginative science fiction buffs could perhaps look into'. For one of these theories Vallee proposes in outline what is, in my opinion, the correct way of dealing with the UFO problem:

> There exists a natural phenomenon whose manifestations border on both the physical and the mental. There is a medium in which human dreams can be implemented, and this is the mechanism by which UFO events are generated, needing no superior intelligence to trigger them. This would explain the fugitivity of UFO manifestations, the alleged contact with friendly occupants, and the fact that the objects appear to keep pace with human technology and to use current symbols.

This is in keeping with an earlier notion by C. G. Jung, as we shall shortly see. Vallee notes two other possible, though less effective theories. I first read *Passport To Magonia* in 1978, some years after starting on a similar line of enquiry, and was troubled as to why Vallee should bother to provide ideas for science-fiction buffs and not come up with anything for UFO researchers. I rather suspect that these ideas are all that are left if one accepts the powerful case proposed in *Passport To Magonia*. Trapped in an intellectual corner, Vallee found himself embarrassed.

He dismisses all three theories as 'unscientific', conveniently omitting to point out that the UFO *problem* is outside the boundaries of what we currently consider 'scientific'. So how can a prototype answer possibly be within those boundaries?

Vallee suggested that the ideas he had put forward ignore the principle facts of the situation as he understands it (one might well ask why he bothered to put them forward if that is the case): since World War Two there has been 'an extremly active generation of colourful rumours' concerning strange machines close to the ground in rural areas; these rumours share archetypal motifs discernible in faery-lore; the entities reported in some UFO events fall into various biological types, and the behaviour of UFO entities seems absurd, pointless, mischievous, like former accounts of faery and elemental behaviour. Actually, far from detracting from the idea put forward by Vallee that I have quoted above, these 'principle facts' only strengthen it.

It is difficult to understand how a researcher of Vallee's brilliance has been so able to bungle his thinking. It is my feeling that the most probable explanation for UFOs, the one I will be propounding in this present work and the one that Vallee blundered to the edge of despite himself, is so fantastic—far more so than the homely ETH—and so disturbing that he involuntarily, subconsciously, shied away from it. At all events, Vallee let himself off the hook by stating 'this is precisely the point where we must stop speculating' and hurriedly concluded his book with a few homilies of the 'it is better to travel than to arrive' type.

It could also be a factor that, deep down, Vallee yearns, like all of us, for there to be some form of intelligence exterior to the consciousness we share with our fellow human beings. This seems to be borne out by his more recent work in which he has gone on to investigate the 'conspiracy' approaches to the UFO problem.[7] Ironically, in this more recent material, Vallee states that 'only free speculation can open the door to an adequate understanding of what is happening around us', which is in contradiction to his stance in *Passport To Magonia*. Perhaps it is more comfortable to speculate in some intellectual corners than others?

I have a growing suspicion that too much immersion in the Western *milieu*, particularly in its prime form in North America, seems to encourage some researchers' preoccupation with the tangled, time-wasting infinitude of red herrings harboured by the various forms of 'Conspiracy Theory'. If there are Men In Black, and I stress *if*, if there are governmental, secret brotherhood or otherworld agencies trying to throw researchers off the trail of the UFO explanation, then the various versions of 'Conspiracy' represent the highest forms of their art.

Other groups of UFO researchers plump for even more elusive approaches to the problem. They tend to stand back from the whole pageant of UFO appearances and to look a little disdainfully at anyone trying to come to terms with whatever 'mechanics' are involved with the actual manifestation of UFO forms. Their overview of the phenomenon is usually articulate and informed and they correctly identify the archetypal nuances involved in the whole affair. They accurately perceive that to some extent the enigma is rather like a mirror reflecting back aspects of thought put into it by the human race. This is as good as far as it goes, but the failure of such researchers is their reticence in 'getting their hands dirty', in failing to identify the processes involved in the formal reality that expresses the content they have recognized. If it goes no further, there can only lie sterility beyond the elegant exterior of their approach.

There is a spiritual reality beyond time and space; there is a mental reality composed of many levels existing 'between' the spiritual and material realms which dips in and out of our reality, and there is the physical world where energy hits 'rock bottom' and appears deceptively as solid matter which seems to obey reliable laws—until one looks too closely. These are not separate worlds but, rather, one continuum. Patterns that move the stars also move in different ratios within human consciousness. The magicians understand this: from all time they have practised the art of correspondence—'as above, so below'. The archetype constellated in spiritual realms can fan out through mental levels and appear as an essentially transient spatial or temporal fact in the material universe. To such mysterious psycho-material mechanisms we doubtless owe the meaningful coincidence—synchronicity—amongst other effects, including growth itself. Geometry, symbolism, music and visual form are the only means of comprehending this ultimately transcendental process, for their truths operate at all levels in different ratios. The growth spirals confirm this: each arc is the same as the one before it and the one following it, only the scale changes;

twisting out of no-form into time/space reality. Magicians, alchemists and artists have been working on it for centuries, or, perhaps more accurately, have been struggling to remember it as the understanding has fragmented down the millenia.

My common sense and personal experiences tell me that something of this nature is so. But that does not stop me asking, when confronted with an actual UFO event (which most, if not all, these elegant researchers have never been), how the damned thing works at that stage of its manifestation. By answering that question, by *understanding the form as well as the content* of the UFO experience, we will learn more about the world, ourselves and the information the UFO medium imparts.

By stark contrast, there are those who seek to explain UFO occurrences in strictly physical, electromagnetic terms. They eschew the nuts-and-bolts ETH approach but feel sure the UFO phenomenon is essentially some form of natural, objective event. This approach turns up in different forms from time to time in the UFO literature; the most recent idea, and one of the better ones, that I have seen at the time of writing occurs in an acclaimed article by Stuart Campbell in the *Journal of Transient Aerial Phenomena*.[8]

Campbell suggests that the basic UFO shape, the ellipsoid or oval form, has remained remarkably consistent over the years since 1947 when the term 'flying saucer' was coined in the West to describe the phenomenon. Campbell points out that prior to 1947 the West had a clear idea in its films, comics and magazines that spacecraft, even alien ones, were going to look tubular with stabilizing fins. Only after the discoid phenomena had erupted on our awareness did film makers and other dream merchants introduce the idea of alien space vehicles in terms of discs and spheres. Campbell concludes that it was a real phenomenon that was perceived and not some form of collective hallucination. He dismisses the early stories of contactees and of those who claimed to have travelled on the alien spaceships simply as the products of 'notorious opportunists'. Campbell writes:

> Ufography (the descriptive science of UFOs) tells us only that there exists in the skies of Earth a phenomenon which manifests itself mainly as an anomalous discoid; it does not tell us that the phenomenon is either extraterrestrial or alien. The consistency of the reports and their universality suggests that the phenomenon is both consistent and universal.

Finally, Campbell opts for a theory that invokes the presence of a natural phenomenon to explain the appearance of the UFO aeroform: he feels this is predicted by the essentially discoid shape of the UFO appearance and gives many examples in nature where this shape has been selected by natural processes. Studying planetary forms, he realized that each possessed an invisible discoid shape around it—a dipolar magnetic field. Not only planets, but stars and galaxies probably have such fields, so their form is not a function of size but is an inherent feature of rotating magnetic dipoles. Campbell maintains that it is the discoid form of rotating dipolar magnetic fields that produces the traditional UFO form within our atmosphere. He describes a mechanism that could produce a contracting and rotating mass of air, the rotation producing ionization and therefore, ultimately, the production of light. The areas where air has the optimum ionic properties for this mechanism are rural, mountainous and coastal regions—the very ones preferred by UFOs. 'As the ions contract with the air,' writes Campbell, 'then the local field must contract with them.' This process would lead to a 'pinch' in the local magnetic field of the Earth, which in turn would create a singularity with dipolar characteristics. He proposed that this concentration of air ions must lead to a local concentration and intensification of the field. The energy and radiation pressure of the singularity expels air molecules creating 'an evacuated cavity inside the ionized shell'. This would make the feature lighter than the surrounding air allowing floating capabilities. A full development of the rotating dipole would create a discoid form as 'loops' created in the dipolar field struggle to accommodate themselves to the surrounding field lines of the Earth's magnetic field.

At low strength this singularity would be visible as only a small, ball-shaped object—ball-lightning. At full strength the discoid shape would manifest. Intermediate strengths would produce varied forms and help explain the shape-shifting characteristics so often reported by UFO witnesses. Campbell goes on in detail to explain further effects possible from his suggested mechanism. An important one of these is that the phenomenon could produce a reflective, metal-like surface in the manner a bubble does in glass or under water, because it is essentially a vacuum bubble in air with an interface defined by a tenuous plasma layer.

Campbell's theory very neatly explains many of the objective

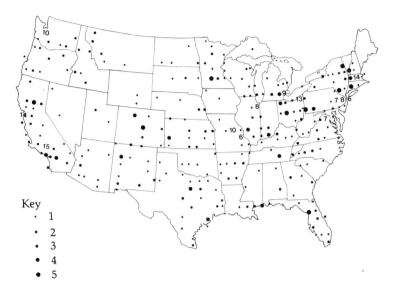

Key
· 1
· 2
· 3
• 4
• 5

Distribution of all UFO report categories in the United States for all years. (*after Persinger & Lafrenière*)

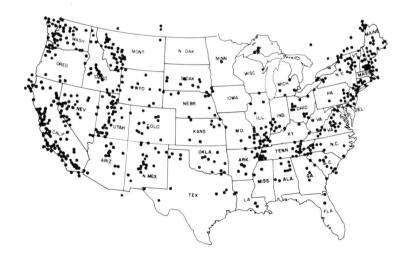

Distribution of mid-range (V-IX) earthquake intensities (Mercalli Scale) in the United States. (Modified from E.S.S.A., 1973). (*after Persinger & Lafrenière*)

elements in UFO manifestations, and should be borne in mind. It does not, though, account for the link between UFO forms and the motifs of human consciousness so clearly indicated by Vallee, nor does it explain the appearance of humanoids—as Campbell admits. So it is a good theory as far as it goes, but it clearly misses something out.

A vaguely similar but far more comprehensive theory has been put forward by the Canadian scientists Michael Persinger and Gyslaine Lafrenière in their *Space-Time Transients and Usual Events*? Their hypothesis is perhaps the most satisfactory one that yet exists; the fact that it is not as widely known as it ought to be must to some extent be due to the opaque, semi-scientific jargonese in which their case is couched, rendering it virtually unreadable. But the effort made to penetrate this is well worth while.

Persinger and Lafrenière begin their study by analyzing a range of UFO and 'Fortean' events (anomalous happenings outside the normal casual explanations as collected and categorized by the American researcher Charles Fort). Their UFO sample amounted to a total of 1242 reported events. They displayed a distribution pattern of the U.S.A. material.

Graphs of U.S.A. cases and non-U.S.A. cases showed remarkable simularities in monthly distribution, with both patterns showing UFO-sighting peaks in April and July, August and September, with a preponderance of UFO 'landings' occurring in November. UFO sightings seemed to display a correlation with the distribution of population in the U.S.A. but did not show a marked relationship with population *density*. Their data suggested that UFO phenomena did tend to cluster in areas, Keel's 'window' concept, but they discussed at some length how big such window areas could be. They tested unusual event (Fortean as well as UFO) clusters in the state of Illinois and found that there was a particular area that over the years exhibited a relatively larger incidence of unusual events than elsewhere in the state. Their data showed a marked similarity between UFO distribution patterns in the U.S.A. and certain other types of Fortean events in the U.S.A. This correlation also occurred in England, the researchers claimed. But they admit to the 'confounding involvement of population' in fully evaluating such patterns.

The Canadian researchers discuss many potential trigger mechanisms—stellar, planetary, solar and lunar and how these might effect human bioelectrical systems and seismic and mineralogical features on Earth. These probably result in electromagnetic anomalies that might be contributory elements to a mechanism capable of producing unusual events, of which UFOs comprise one category.

After considering a large number of possibilities, Persinger and Lafrenière state that *'the data consistently point towards seismic-related sources'*. Their core theory for explaining UFOs involves seismo-electricity. They point out that mankind lives on a thin shell beneath which 'mammoth forces' operate, a situation which they feel cannot be over-emphasized. As their data, when closely analyzed, reveals that the majority of transient events seem closely linked with seismic movement, the researchers ask:

> Could it be that unusual events are produced by the forces exponentially accumulating in seismic-prone areas? Are unusual events transient by nature because the accumulating pressures on subsurface structures pass through several *qualitatively* different expression modes until the structures finally break, and the earthquake it felt? Are the periodic manifestations of unusual and transient events in earthquake prone areas . . . results of the seismic pressures waxing and waning below the surface?

They state that research has shown that during the strain of seismic unrest pressure on rock crystals in a large area produce electric fields through a modification of the piezo-electrical effect.[10] These pre-fracture electric fields can reach values of several thousand volts per metre—'intensities capable of ionizing the local area into visible luminosities'. In some cases such fields could perhaps reach up into the ionosphere. It is possible that sonic energy could also be produced during periods of seismic stress, producing audible as well as infrasonic and ultrasonic effects.

Stress may come to bear on a geological fracture—a fault— quite slowly so that forces in a seismic area accumulate gradually. As a result, a localized 'electrical column' could be produced over the area. It is *while the stress is present* that such an effect would be created and during which period transient phenomena would be likely to occur. When the earthquake happens, or, conversely, when the trigger mechanisms causing the stress begin to subside, the column would disappear.

During the presence of the column, Persinger and Lafrenière

postulate, low level ionization of the air within and adjacent to the column would take place. This could cause several effects associated with unusual events, and if the field strengths reached sufficiently high values luminous phenomena would be produced.

The researchers make the important point that as stress moves along a geological fracture the localized column would move with it giving any unusual phenomena produced in association with it the same mobility. They underline the fact that an earthquake is not necessary to produce such phenomena; indeed, such an event would relieve the stresses causing the conditions favourable to the production of the manifestations. Every day in many parts of the world geological structures build up tension and relieve it quietly. But since certain areas are particularly prone to such effects 'when the forces reappear later, and the cycle waxes again, another burst of phenomena takes place in the same area and the concept of a "window" is recognized'.

An important aspect of the theory put forward by the Canadians is that they claim the human element is also encompassed in the model. They explain that the existence of electrical columns produced by accumulating tectonic stress would affect living electrical systems as well. They refer to research which has shown that when parts of the brain are electrically stimulated dreamlike states can be induced and vivid imagery unleashed even in waking consciousness. Such stimulating currents are not large and could conceivably be produced by transient currents associated with tectonic stress. Imagery stored in an individual's mind, perhaps primal fears and desires dressed in imagery donated by films and television, could be released at the same time and by the same forces producing the objective, luminous globular effect in the atmosphere, thus affecting the perception of the event. Hence truly phantasmagorical elements could become welded into the witness' experience of the atmospheric ionization.

Most of this theory propounded by Persinger and Lafrenière provides a satisfying model. Nothing is being claimed that is necessarily beyond the bounds of known science, and if not all the effects associated with UFOs are explained, then most of them are.

The Canadians add that while the major source of energy for such a phenomena-producing mechanism would come from fields associated with geological stress, smaller displays might be triggered by electrical fields generated by meteorological events such as thunderstorms. Other effects could add to these sources, such as impulses from the sun and moon contributing to the energies in existing Earthly systems. They record that researchers have already shown that magnetic anomalies can be produced at the Earth's surface above appropriate mineral deposits during times of geomagnetic storms.

The study as presented by Persinger and Lafrenière can be criticized for being derived from a weak data-base: less than 1300 UFO cases over the entire U.S.A. is really not enough. It is true that they incorporated many more cases of unusual events, but this constitutes a criticism in itself: why attempt to explain other, possibly more complex and perhaps unrelated mechanisms under the same conceptual umbrella? In the final analysis, their theory is only really satisfactory for dealing with UFOs and associated phenomena. This approach to the UFO problem cannot sensibly be conducted over the entire USA in any case—the area is so vast that untenable numbers of UFO events would have to be involved. And how would one cope with the *detailed* geological data of such a continental area, even if it is available? While I feel that these researchers are probably correct to a large extent in their findings, I have a sneaking suspicion that despite all the scientific trappings their work displays, the conclusions drawn owe as much to intuition as to the computer to which they dedicated their book.

Ideally, a smaller country, well-mapped in both topographical and geological terms, with good communications, a substantial population-to-area ratio to provide meaningful perceptual cover and excellent archival resources is required. European countries lend themselves best to this approach. Because of their precisely *and naturally* defined area, wide range of geological terrain, long recorded history and ubiquitous UFO reporting facilities the British Isles are perhaps the most ideal 'laboratory' anywhere for this type of ufological analysis. I am not being jingoistic here but simply observing where the necessary requirements are best deployed. Later in this book I will present preliminary material along these lines associated with England and Wales, but the full job of work will have to be undertaken by someone with greater resources at their disposal than my colleagues and I have had up to the present time.

American material dealing with the sort of associations studied by Persinger and Lafrenière may well be best provided by research groups such as the Michigan Anomaly Research Bureau,[11] which is undertaking a multi-disciplinary study of that state. However, the land area is artificially designated, and with an area almost precisely the same as that of England and Wales has only about nine million inhabitants.

Despite all the criticisms that can legitimately be levelled at them, I am personally convinced that Persinger and Lafrenière are on the right lines in making the crucial association of UFOs with seismic features. The fundamental problem with their model, I find, involves the part that relates to how the UFO *imagery* is generated. It seems hard to accept the coincidence of mental imagery being triggered in synchronization with an objective effect to such a perfect extent that the two unrelated systems become as one to the witness' perception.

In their various ways all the approaches aimed at explaining the UFO phenomenon so far discussed rely on some form of 'out there' mechanism. On the other side of the coin there are those who see the UFO as a psychological product in essence, even if that product can somehow be transferred into exterior reality.

One of the earliest and most distinguished exponents of the 'psychological' approach was Carl Jung. He published an essay in the late 1950s entitled: *Flying Saucers—A Modern Myth of Things Seen in the Sky.*[12] It is the *rumour* of UFOs that Jung primarily deals with. If UFOs are real, he asks, what are they? If they are fantasy, why should such a rumour exist? He goes on to point out that the rumour itself *is* real. He called it a *visionary rumour*, and associated it with the end of an era in human affairs and the hesitant dawn of a new period of collective mental change, one that possesses the threat of almost total destruction. referring to UFOs he wrote:

> If these things are real—and by all human standards it hardly seems possible to doubt this any longer—then we are left with only two hypotheses: that of their *weightlessness* on the one hand and of their *psychic nature* on the other. This is a question I for one cannot decide. In the circumstances, however, it seemed to me advisable to at least investigate the *psychological aspect* of the phenomenon, so as to throw a little light on this complicated situation.

This Jung did by studying the dreams of patients and acquaintances in which UFO imagery was involved, even though most of the people concerned knew little or nothing about the subject of UFOs. Jung concludes that the UFO disc or sphere is a symbol of order, a mandala, a magic circle which organizes and encloses the psychic totality. It expresses the archetype of the *self*—a term Jung used to mean the totality of the conscious and the unconscious, not merely the ego. The UFOs are 'an involuntary archetypal or mythological conception of an unconscious content, a *rotundem*, as the alchemists called it, that expresses the totality of the individual'. Jung felt that the threat of nuclear war, a whole new traumatic vision that opened on the world after World War Two, could be one element causing mass tension and deep-seated fear.

Throughout his essay Jung stresses the *autonomous* nature of the unconscious and how its actual nature is unknown to us except in terms of symbolism. He emphasized how conscious human awareness depends on the whim of the unconscious despite the inability of rationalists to appreciate this fact.

> Modern man . . . depends on and is sustained by an entity he does not know, but of which he has intimations that 'occurred' or—as we can fitly say—revealed themselves to long forgotten forebears in the grey dawn of history. Whence did they come? Obviously from the unconscious processes . . . The unconscious depicts itself in dreams and visions, as it always did, holding before us images which, unlike the fragmented functions of consciousness, emphasize facts that relate to the unknown whole man.

Jung skirts the problem of the apparent objectivity of UFOs, but states that it is possible that some unknown natural phenomenon occurs onto which the mandalic imagery so needed by the psyche at this time becomes mentally projected. He suggests that the real nature of UFOs and its symbolic content could be separate elements brought together by synchronistic convenience. But at the end of his ruminations Jung felt himself obliged to return to this problem of how a possibly objective phenomenon was able to display psychic motifs. He admitted unease with the hypothesis of 'psychophysical parallelism'. He toyed with the idea of an 'as yet unknown substrate possessing material and at the same time psychic qualities. In view of the trend of modern theoretical physics this assumption should arouse fewer resistances than before'. This might be from where Vallee obtained his 'medium in which human dreams are implemented'.

One of the fundamental aspects of UFOs that had to be taken

into account, Jung contended, was their 'psychic relatedness'. Mythic images from antiquity, as Vallee has shown, and deep-seated archetypal motifs, as Jung demonstrates, are embroidered into the UFO pageant. *No theory which fails to account for this element can be correct, or, at least, complete.*

If not such a substrate, if not an internal projection onto an unknown, coincidentally occurring objective phenomenon, then how are UFOs to be explained? Jung was one of the earliest researchers in the subject to pick up on, and not necessarily dismiss, the idea that UFOs were living creatures of some unfathomable kind. But what of a psychic projection that actually exteriorizes and takes on material attributes? 'The notion of a materialized psychism,' Jung writes, 'opens a bottomless void beneath our feet.' It is important to note this attitude by Jung, because some ufologists actually believe he championed the notion of externally projected psychic material. He did no such thing. He admitted that mediums are reported to be able to create materializations, but 'this phenomenon depends on the presence of one or more mediums who exude a weighable substance, and it occurs only in their immediate environment. The psyche can move the body, but only inside the living organism. That something psychic, possessing material qualities and with a high charge of energy, could appear by itself high in the air at a great distance from any human mediums—this surpasses our comprehension.'

Nevertheless, I cannot avoid a suspicion that Jung was deliberately floating such concepts for them to perhaps take root at some later period: he was already 'sticking his neck out' enough, as he himself indicated. In the end, despite his obvious dissatisfaction with it, Jung seemed prepared to accept 'psycho-physical parallelism' in that UFOs could be material phenomena of an unknown nature 'presumably coming from outer space' that had long been visible to mankind but otherwise have no connection with the Earth or its inhabitants. But just at this time, when our cultural attention is directed skywards with regard to spaceships, and figuratively because our Earthly existence seems under threat, 'unconscious contents have projected themselves on these inexplicable heavenly phenomena and given them a significance they in no way deserve'. It is important to realize here that Jung was referring to an *internal* projection from the unconscious onto the conscious awareness. No externalized process is being suggested. It is merely that the inexplicable natural phenomena hypothesized by Jung provide the suitable external vehicle or trigger for this internal traffic. I am one of those people who frequently sleep with my eyes open and have often awoken to experience an element in a dream fade into the contours of some object in the room . . . eagles into doorknobs, and so on.

More recent researchers have felt less shy than Jung about proposing psychisms as an explanation for UFOs. A precedent often quoted is the alleged existence of the *tulpa*: a practice carried out in Tibet, we are told, in which mental procedures can create a material being that can move independently while having a somewhat disturbing relationship with its mental progenitor. If not kept an eye on, apparently, such materialized entities can subtly change and take on sly and more self-motivated characteristics. The evidence for the reality of such thought forms is, however, somewhat slim. What is being suggested in this idea in any case is that untrained Western witnesses can provide involuntary tulpic displays of awesome magnitude overshadowing the more modest productions of highly-trained Tibetan shamans.

Other researchers choose the 'mixed bag' hypothesis in which it is claimed there could be actual extraterrestrial craft visiting Earth while at the same time there are collective hallucinations or exteriorized psychisms that happen to echo the visiting spacecrafts' forms. Such a scattergun explanation seems pretty scatterbrained to me. It reeks of mental bankruptcy and relies on the existence of a cosmic coincidence of unmanageable proportions. The human brain can come up with better options.

Certainly in British ufology, and probably elsewhere, there seems currently to be a quite dramatic split between those who insist the UFO phenomenon is a strictly material, objective problem and those who feel that psychic or psychological elements have to be given priority in any attempt to answer the riddle. I have met and talked with researchers of both camps and it is sometimes difficult to believe that one is dealing with the same subject. It is possible to be talking to one research group one day, surrounded by oscilloscopes and a 'club' atmosphere more associated with model train enthusiasts, and to be deep in psychological jargon with another group the next day.

One of the most prominent of the 'new wave' of British ufologists is Jenny Randles. In a recent book[13] with Peter Warrington she brings, to some extent, a breath of clear, objective air into the whole business. Randles and Warrington distinguish between what they call *true* and real UFOs. In their terminology a *true* UFO is an actual atmospheric phenomena of a revolutionary nature. They consider such phenomenon could account for certain types of UFO sighting, particularly the low definition LITS sort of report. But their research indicates that the greater definition a sighting has—when more details are seen or greater contact is had with the UFO—the more subjective elements arising from the witness come to the fore. This is a *real* UFO. If *true* UFOs account for only 10 per cent of the total number of UFOs reported, then Randles and Warrington feel that *real* UFOs can account for only about one per cent. A rare phenomenon indeed.

These researchers argue that very close encounter, high definition cases seem to be different to the *true* UFO phenomenon of lights seen at a distance *and require a different explanation*. Witnesses to *real* UFOs seem to display psychic tendencies in many cases; other people nearby do not always see the phenomenon, and such witnesses sometimes have a history of repeated UFO encounters or of poltergeist or other psychic manifestations. This sort of information usually only comes out when such cases are investigated in depth: on the surface the close encounter experience simply seems to be a higher definition version of aerial phenomena seen at a distance in the more run-of-the-mill sightings, but deeper research does not seem to bear this out. These researchers consider that the evidence demonstrates that 'contact witnesses were of a *different type from those who experience all other kinds of UFO event*'.

Randles and Warrington make the eminently sane suggestion that the term 'UFO' should be replaced by the more accurate one of 'UAP'—Unidentified Atmospheric Phenomenon', which would cover both airborne and grounded phenomena. These investigators also expand and modify the UFO classification system developed by Hynek which is referred to in Chapter 2. One of their more significant alterations is to add a category to the Close Encounter type of report, namely, CE4—close encounters with psychic effects: 'They include all reports of a highly subjective nature where effects of a psychic (here defined as "apparently non-physical") nature take place. This often means abduction claims, where there are time-lapses and other "non-real" elements.' Randles and Warrington point out that in many cases only the investigator concerned can determine whether a case is a 'normal' CE3 or a CE4.

They observe that CE4 cases involving *real* UFOs often seem to have a 'sphere of influence' aspect: huge aerial phenomena reported by the principle witness may not be observed by other potential witnesses. We can think here perhaps of the occasional cases of young girls who apparently experience the presence of the Blessed Virgin Mary while those looking on are unable to see or hear anything. An example in the UFO literature is the case concerning one Maureen Puddy of Australia. She claimed three UFO encounters and on the third of them she experienced seeing an alien and going aboard its UFO, observing considerable detail 'on board'.[14] These events seemed to cause her genuine and considerable emotional upset, yet it all happened in the the presence of two UFO investigators who saw nothing! Even when Maureen was 'aboard' the UFO her physical body was still in the car with the other two people. It can hardly not be mentioned that she was clearly under personal, domestic stress with two young children and an invalid husband (who died about six months after the supposed 'abduction').

Randles and Warrington conclude that psychological processes must be considered to play a major role in such cases. Interestingly, they do not seem to concern themselves with the possibility that those who do *not* see a phenomenon might be the ones experiencing the psychological abnormality: is it not possible that at least in certain cases some internal censoring cuts in, shutting off the 'offending' sight of a UFO in those inherently unable to withstand the trauma of witnessing such a thing? A sort of real time amnesia? Such 'negative hallucinations' can be induced under hypnosis, in fact. Such people at the scene of a UFO event may be experiencing a missed perception as opposed to a misperception!

Nevertheless, despite this oversight on their part, it is impossible to disregard the overall case Randles and Warrington put forward for separating at least some of the close encounter types of case from the more numerous accounts of LITS. To identify the abduction cases and some other types of close encounter reports as being probably 'fifth column' aspects in ufology is perhaps the greatest service done for the subject in recent years. Such psychological events are, of course, extremely interesting in themselves and might help to build a bridge spanning the understanding of more generalized psychic, psychological and religious experiences. *But they can confuse the understanding of genuine UFO events.*

Unfortunately, these two researchers attempt to take this valuable distinction further. With them the required pendulum swing away from the ravages of the ETH becomes perhaps too pronounced. For example, they quote the case of the Hill family who witnessed a phenomenon over Wellingborough, Northamptonshire, in 1966. Three members of the family saw an orange-red cylindrical shape hovering in the sky. It vanished after a few minutes leaving an orange-tinged cloud that gradually disintegrated and drifted down wind. I am particularly interested in this case as it so closely parallels the Ravensbourne sighting just over a year later (this case was not known to me at the time). But Randles and Warrington allow themselves to become confused: they report that the following night a television news item showed a fragment of movie film shot by a woman in an aircraft which was flying over Staffordshire. She suddenly saw a cigar-shaped object in the window frame. It altered shape then vanished. This publicized event encouraged the Hills to come forth publicly with their account. Later it was conclusively proved that the woman in the aircraft had filmed a simple refractive effect. 'So what indeed did the Hills experience?' Randles and Warrington ask, rather oddly. What they said they did, of course! Why should a refractive effect over Staffordshire producing a dark, non-luminous blob (I saw the film) have anything to do with the experience of a luminous orange cylinder over Northamptonshire? The two researchers seem to be hinting at some dark, mysterious psychological process. Nonsense. The Hills had had a remarkable and disturbing experience. It produces a kind of shock afterwards, as I pointed out in Chapter 1. UFO witnesses actually require professional counselling after their experience, because they have undergone conceptual rape. In actuality, a UFO witness is more likely to attract abuse which deepens the trauma already experienced—and to witness a UFO *is* to undergo trauma. Non-witnesses are too blasé about the whole experience. In this case the television item obviously gave the Hills the necessary encouragement to speak publicly about their sighting.

It sometimes annoys me that UFO researchers, even the best of them, concentrate so much on the subjectivity of the UFO witness. As a witness myself, I know that the single most detrimental factor in UFO investigation is the *subjectivity of the non-witness*, whether that person is a sceptic, a balanced investigator or an out-and-out 'believer' (UFO witnesses are not believers; they are experients). If more such people witnessed major UFO events themselves there would be far fewer 'ifs' and 'buts' about the enigma. But then, they would no longer be non-witnesses—they would have joined the unfortunate elite of UFO witnesses who, in fact, have *less* recourse to the luxury of subjective response than the non-witnesses.

Randles and Warrington go on to refer to the precognition some witnesses have that a UFO is about to appear. Is this purely psychic? What if UFOs are the product of some form of electromagnetic process—could not the change in the immediate electromagnetic environment affect the electrical processes of the witness' brain generating a sense of an impending event? Some people experience this before a common-or-garden thunderstorm, and animals can sense an imminent earthquake, before any effects can be noted by humans.

These researchers finally conclude by saying that 'there are no clear cut answers'. *Real* UFOs must, they say, be the result of hoax, of 'beings' flying remarkable craft occasionally making contact with humans, or of 'a mechanism which is basically a stimulus, but which is personally experienced in many different ways due to the individuality of the observer'. They feel this stimulus must either be a certain psychic ability possessed by a few individuals to a high degree and by all of us subconsciously and which can be triggered by the appropriate circumstances, or it is the machinations of another intelligent species existing 'contemporaneously with ourselves on the Earth, but on sensory planes of which we are not normally aware'.

They advise that ufologists should be more concerned with 'repeater' witnesses. Such people may have the ability to manipulate energy with their minds, they suggest, and to make this appear briefly on the physical plane. The researchers remind us, as did Jung, that mediums seem able to perform such feats with the semi-physical material called ectoplasm.

In a later piece of writing[15] Jenny Randles defines her position to some extent. She explains that low and medium definition sightings seem to refer to essentially objective sightings but the experiences closer to UFOs, the CE3 and CE4 experiences, refer to 'essentially subjective experiences'. She goes on to state that there is an overlap between the two sets of data and that there is some residue in the objective data of unknown phenomena 'remains a possibility, but only a possibility'. What she clearly wants to believe is that after subjective factors and misperception of known objects have been taken out of the situation there may be no objective UFO phenomenon at all. Apart from being simply wrong in this, Jenny Randles is here pushing a necessary corrective perspective to the point where it could be self-defeating.

All this is important, because there is a growing iconoclastic mood amongst some ufologists on both sides of the Atlantic at this time. While they are undoubtedly pointing out weaknesses in earlier UFO research, some of them are tending to act like over-enthusiastic new brooms sweeping just a little too clean. Careless sweeping can cause the loss of a pearl dropped in the dirt.

★   ★   ★   ★

We have here considered the principal interpretations of the UFO problem as it is understood today. There are other notions, of course, such as the underwater base concept, but they tend to be variants on the major explanatory themes.

Essentially, the UFO problem is like a coin according to the spectrum of current thinking: heads, it is a physical phenomenon of some kind; tails, it is psychic or psychological. Sceptical explanations can be found on both sides of the coin: on the physical side UFOs are misperceptions of actual but known objects; on the other side UFOs are hallucinations or hoaxes. Some ufologists—the ultraterrestrial school, the projected psychism theorists and so on—balance the coin precariously, but it inevitably falls on one side or the other.

No one, it seems to me, is prepared to sit back and see what the data are actually saying. Researchers and sceptics constantly toss the coin, trying to arrange for it to come down on the side of their choice. In reality, the data do not allow that luxury. The information non-witnesses receive, when considered *in toto*, says one thing quite clearly—UFOs are objective but can occasionally 'carry' subjective material. A hypothesis has to be forged to accommodate the facts as they are known.

Despite their apparent diversity, I think some of the UFO interpretations offered to date do show that the human mind has got the measure of the problem, but because of fragmentation and non-witness subjectivity the whole answer has become scrambled.

There *is* an objective element to UFOs: to that extent the ETH people are right. Where they perhaps go wrong is to then speculate that the only source of such objective phenomena must be from some other physical location—the stars, inside the Earth, under the sea, and so on. Sentience does seem to be involved with the appearance of UFOs—all theorists agree on this. The failure here, possibly, is to assume that such intelligence must originate *outside* the perimeters of human consciousness. But then we have the 'psychological school' who correctly point out that there is a high degree of mental imagery tied up with the UFO sppearance. The 'objective school' becomes angry at this, but knowing they have correctly identified a genuine aspect of the enigma the psychological school dig in their heels and are sometimes prone to overstate their case, casting doubt on *any* objective element to UFOs. And so the soap-opera proceeds, with interpretations becoming ever more polarized.

They are surely all correct—partially. They are surely all wrong—to some extent. But the whole answer is in there somewhere, in amongst the ideas presented in this chapter.

The first stage in disentangling the mess is to clarify what types of UFO appearances are to be provided with what hypothesis. I feel that all types of UFO appearance can be explained under the umbrella of a single concept except, possibly, for one: the abduction type of case. It is therefore important to stress that some of today's most experienced researchers, as we have seen, feel that such cases have a high subjective content.[16] Percipients involved in them seem to have a history of or propensity towards psychic or hallucinatory episodes. It is essential that we now learn to differentiate between those who have witnessed some form of objective event and those who have suffered some form of internal, mental manifestation. *There is only one set of stores of human imagery, the human mind, so appearances are likely to be similar even if mechanisms are quite different.*

There are certainly liars amongst those who claim contact and abduction experiences. In some cases, though, it seems that some percipients are telling the truth as they know it. One such case is the so-called 'Aveley Abduction' which took place in Essex in the early 1970s and involved a family I shall call Smith. Shortly after seeing a blue light in the sky as they were driving home one evening they ran into a greenish mist which was straddling the road. On reaching the end of their journey they discovered that they were 'missing' an hour or two. Much later, regression hypnosis on the husband, John, provided apparent information as to what had happened to him in the missing time. As his experiences came forth, session after session, John's wife began to involuntarily recall what had happened to her as well.

Apparently, when they had driven into the green mist their 'astral bodies' left their physical forms (an event seemingly observed by one of the children) and they found themselves 'aboard' a mistily illuminated 'spaceship' peopled by tall humanoid beings and another group who were short and animalistic in appearance. The husband and wife were taken off different ways and each experienced a sequence of events separately. These events, apart perhaps from the obligatory 'medical', can only be described as archetypal in nature. It was the inner, visionary experience described by abductees and religious visionaries alike. Jung could see this in the early contactee material.

I have questioned John closely and happen to believe he is genuine in his recall of his experiences. But was it a UFO experience? Some researchers are becoming increasingly dubious about imagery invoked by regression hypnosis. Also, John did say to me that to this day he could not swear that the 'spaceship' was a solid structure. What these people seem to have undergone is an 'out of the body' experience (OBE) or 'astral projection', as it used to be called, in which the waking consciousness seems to be located outside the physical body. This is a well-known and widespread experience and explanations vary from the orthodox scientific one that an aberration creates the illusion of displacement of consciousness to the straightforward one that consciousness *does* leave the body. Anyone with any grasp of what consciousness is, of course, realizes that it inhabits the body and is not dependent on it, so the psychological explanation is likely to be wrong.

There is a considerable literature on the subject of astral projection and OBEs going back many years. Experiences undergone decades before the post-war flying saucer era contain elements similar to abduction scenarios. People undergoing OBEs can find themselves in their normal physical environment, which they can 'fly' around in, passing through solid objects, or they can be projected into various types of 'astral' worlds. These seem to be dream states which, from the point of view of the exteriorized consciousness, take on a transient tangibility. Thought forms become plastic. Most OBE percipients find themselves alternating between these mental environments and their physical surroundings. We would expect today that some elements in the mental states would echo UFO type of imagery.

The triggering mechanisms for OBEs vary. It is quite possible to train oneself to have the experience, and moments of extreme physical and emotional stress also seem able to promote involuntary experiences. Drugs, particularly cannabis, can induce it. I think it is also feasible that certain electromagnetic phenomena could promote OBEs. I rather suspect that in the Aveley case the green mist might have been an actual phenomenon that wreaked its powerful effects on the Smith family.

Whatever the trigger, I have no doubts in aligning myself with those UFO researchers who consider the abduction type of case to be a different animal altogether to the actual UFO experience. It could well be a mistake built on deceptive image content that has brought the so-called abductions and similar close encounters into the spectrum of UFO sightings.

It is also possible that accounts of Men In Black and the like are the products of the involuntary myth-making that the human mind goes in for when contemplating phenomena it does not understand. Our brains are as adept as spiders at spinning webs. It is a shadowy area where the hoaxers, the pseudo-religious fanatics and the demented can feel at home. It is all of great human, psychological interest, of course, but it has seriously detracted from the sober observation of actual—but possibly more remarkable—UFO phenomena.

Apart from distinguishing this particular type of UFO report, however, it does seem to me that probably all other UFO manifestations can be put under the influence of a single explanation. Where there are several witnesses to a genuine UFO events we can expect discrepancies in accounts: some will exaggerate, some will forget details, some will be shocked. All of them will interpret what they saw through the filters of their own personalities and previous experiences in life. But this happens in all kinds of witness testimonies, from car accidents to bank robberies. This annoying but mundane psychological fact should not be elevated into a mysterious mechanism. While there are undoubtedly psychic elements involved in major UFO events, it is important not to confuse the mundane with the extraordinary.

We have studied the nature of the beast; now let us seek its lair.

PART TWO
Signs in the Earth

4.

The Secret Side of Nature

When we stroll along a beach in the moonlight and watch the tide coming in or going out, we are witnessing a visible phenomenon of extraterrestrial origin at close quarters. Peaceful as the scene may appear, how many of us are aware of the tremendous forces at work?

Guy Lyon Playfair and Scott Hill,
The Cycles of Heaven

The supernatural is usually defined as that which is not explicable by the known forces of nature.

Lyall Watson, *Supernature*

It is being suggested in this book that the objective component of the total UFO event is a form of natural phenomenon currently not identified as such by establishment science. This is hardly surprising as there are many natural phenomena undoubtedly occurring within the Earth's atmosphere that are not formally accepted by science. Meteorites and ball lightning, for example, had to wait an inordinately long time for scientific acceptance. Establishment science is a little like a dinosaur—its tail can be bitten fiercely for a considerable time before the message makes it way to its brain.

Nevertheless, if a hitherto unrecognized phenomenon is to be postulated, it must be shown that there is a geophysical matrix of influences and events that could accommodate it. Many of the sources quoted at the end of this chapter will give the reader a much broader insight into the secret side of nature than I can afford the space to provide; here I can merely outline some of the facts and accounts that demonstrate quite clearly that such a geophysical matrix does actually exist.

The Sun provides as logical a starting point as any for our whirlwind tour of Nature's more subtle processes. Nothing could seem more simple and understandable than our local star. It rises, it sets. It is the source of life and energy, of light and warmth. Yet only with the advent of space technology and other sophisticated technical advancements have scientists come to learn that the Sun is far from a stable, simple body.

The Sun is a modest star, about 865,000 miles in diameter. It seems to be powered by nuclear fusion—in effect, a cosmic hydrogen bomb explosion without end or, at least, an end only in time scales beyond our comprehension. The Sun's output of energy is equally beyond conception—the equivalent to the burning of about '11 billion times the world's annual coal output *every second*'! Although thought to sit at the centre of its planetary system, the Sun does not coincide exactly with the centre of mass of the solar system. At certain times this centre of mass can move completely outside of the Sun itself. Within the surface layers of the solar atmosphere darker, because cooler, patches of turbulence are sometimes observed. They are called sunspots. These appear and disappear usually in a total cycle of around twenty-two years—eleven years from peak to trough in sunspot activity. There have been variations in this cycle. Surrounding the Sun and extending thousands of miles beyond it is the solar corona. Streamers from the more dense levels of the solar body penetrate this layer; these vary in appearance with the Sun's inconsistent output of energy and seem to conform to the lines of the solar magnetic field. Sometimes there is a sudden outburst of solar energy in the form of solar flares which can leap many thousands of miles into space, emitting increased X-ray, ultraviolet and visible light energy.

The Sun emits a stream of particles called the solar wind which gusts past the Earth and on into deeper space. This 'wind' of highly charged particles reveals the structure of the solar magnetic field which is divided into four sections, each one charged opposite to the next segment. The Earth's orbit takes it through these segments, of course, but the rotation of the Sun also spins the magnetic structure every twenty-seven days so that each segment boundary passes across the Earth in that period of time. The solar wind and magnetism are thought to be the media through which changes in the Sun can affect many different mechanisms on Earth.

Each time a solar magnetic segment boundary passes across our planet 'it produces a sharp jolt in geomagnetic activity one or two days later'. An increase in particles emitted by a solar flare causes disruption of terrestrial radio signals, disruption in the ionosphere and probably affects our weather and geomagnetic activity[3] [4]

The sunspot periodicity has been linked to many terrestrial effects: disturbance of the Earth's magnetic field; extreme weather conditions; incidence of thunderstorms; the length of the crop-growing season; admissions to mental hospitals; the blood-clotting rate in humans; the outbreak of diseases; plagues, and even social unrest! Some of these 'coincidences' are more confirmed than others, but enough data exist to indicate that sunspot activity, not to mention other solar effects, holds enormous sway over terrestrial mechanisms in a multitude of situations.

Perhaps one of the most startling and significant solar effects was proven by the decades of work on water by the late Professor Giorgio Piccardi. By intensively measuring screened and unscreened test tubes of distilled water Piccardi found that certain chemical reactions were significantly different between the two sets of water samples. He was able to discover that solar activity, lunar phases and cosmic radiation all affected processes in water. The medium through which these cosmic influences got through to the water molecules was by alterations in the Earth's own magnetic field. This discovery means that vegetable, animal and human systems—all heavily composed of water—must be susceptible to cosmic influences. And if the Earth's magnetic field is altered by these influences, then the terrestrial atmosphere and geological body must also be affected.

In the late 1940s John Henry Nelson of RCA Communications Inc. was given the task of studying sunspots and their relation to

magnetic storms which greatly disturb radio communication on
Earth. Nelson's studies led him to discover that certain be-
havioural characteristics of sunspots could be associated with
planetary positions. It seemed that when certain planets were in
certain positions relative to the Sun their combined influence
was sufficient to cause effects on the great solar body itself.
These in turn had effects on Earth. Using this observation,
Nelson was able to vastly improve the prediction of bad radio
days. The planets, it seems, can affect Earth through the
mediumship of the Sun—and perhaps directly. Certainly all the
planets, particularly Jupiter, emit radio signals, for example,
which impinge directly on the Earth.

If the planets can affect the Earth, through whatever medium,
they can presumably affect human beings on our planet as well.
This, at least, is the finding of French researcher Michel
Gauquelin. 'The Sun, planets and satellites are constantly
exchanging energy and matter', he writes[5] He refers to the
magnetic 'tails' carried by the planets. These are caused by the
presure of the solar wind compressing the magnetic field on the
sunward side of a planet but not on the opposite side: the
magnetic tail of the Earth has been estimated to extend for at
least twenty times the distance between the Earth and the Moon.
All planets, and their satellites, have these tails—and that of
course includes our own Moon. There is a drop in the Earth's
magnetism when the Moon is full; this may be because the Moon
is crossing our magnetic tail at that phase. When the Earth shares
certain positions relative to other planets—such as Venus, Mars
and Jupiter—magnetic changes are noted on our planet. 'The
silent ballet of the planets around the Sun and the satellites
around the planets is complex and alive', Gauquelin remarks.
'Through this "cosmic" conception of the solar system, we
perceive a new dialogue which has always existed but which,
until now, we had no means of understanding.'

The main thrust of Gauquelin's personal research has been to
show statistically that certain planets seem able to somehow
influence the lives of human beings. By obtaining hundreds of
birth times and relating them to planetary configurations
Gauquelin perceived some staggering statistical correlations.
Children born as Mars or Saturn were rising, for example,
seemed destined to attain success in medicine. Mars also seems
to 'influence' the development of scientists. On the other hand,
soldiers and politicians seemed linked to Jupiter at their births.

Gauquelin found that no famous French writer was born with Saturn in the ascendant.

Gauquelin has done a vast amount of research along these lines. His results have ben challenged but his work remains the best on the subject, and that work says some planets do seem to have an effect on human activity. We are a long way yet, however, from unravelling the full implications of the interplanetary 'silent ballet'.

The Earth's magnetic field protects the surface of the planet from the gross effects of the solar wind; if it did not, then life would have been unable to develop here. More solar radiation 'gets through' at the poles than elsewhere, creating northern lights or aurora effects in the upper atmosphere (although there have been reports of such effects reaching the actual surface of the Earth on rare occasions). But we have already seen that highly energetic solar particles do wreak their effect all over the Earth and interfere with terrestrial activity. The actual body of the Earth is also affected by the Sun. A solar storm, for example, can affect the Earth's rate of spin, in a sense braking the rotation of our planet. This effect would seem to be minute, yet research into earthquake events of magnitude 7.5 or more 'throughout a complete solar cycle suggest that there is indeed a correlation between Sun, length of day, and earthquake incidence'.[6]

The Moon also has a great part to play in the pulling and shoving of Mother Earth, for though it is a small body in planetary terms its proximity to us makes its effects important from our point of view. The effects of lunar gravity in terms of ocean tides are, of course, well known. But the Moon also pulls at the solid ground as well, raising land masses by several inches when it is overhead. This is bound to contribute to the pressures and strains at weak points on the Earth's surface such as geological fault lines. The Moon combined with the Sun puts the terrestrial body under continual massage. These pressures might not always trigger earthquakes—although this might be the case in some instances—but they must provide the 'last straws' in some events where internal geological pressures are already building up. A Russian scientist, Dr N. Kozyrev, considers the Moon's effects to be so closely associated with terrestrial activity that he says it is 'as if the Moon were in direct contact with the Earth; as if it were its seventh continent'.[7] Studying many hundreds of major earthquakes between 1904 and 1967 and comparing them with hundreds of transient lunar events (odd

glows and clouds that appear on the Moon's surface from time
to time) he has found evidence that Earth and Moon are
mutually linked, though they show a time lag of up to three
days.

It must be remembered, too, that there are tidal effects not
only on land and water but in the Earth's atmosphere as well.
Playfair and Hill, the authors of *Cycles of Heaven*, point out
that while tidal effects are to be expected when Sun or Moon are
overhead, the 'shear forces' on geologically weak points are to
be expected when these cosmic bodies are crossing the horizon.
They also present evidence suggesting links between solar
activity and earthquakes, possibly through the medium of
terrestrial magnetism.

The Moon is commonly associated with effects on the human
mind, as the very term 'lunatic' suggests. Dr Arnold Lieber's
theory of 'biological tides'[8] states that the human body is susceptible to the same cosmic influences as the Earth itself and that
body processes ebb and flow with gravitational and electromagnetic influences. If the seas can be moved by the Moon, for
example, why not the fluids in the body? Equipment actually
exists that can measure tidal effects in a cup of coffee.

The now well-known work of Frank Brown of Northwestern
University, U.S.A., has shown that simple marine creatures,
deprived of all visual cues, still respond to lunar tides. He and
other have demonstrated, too, how living creatures are sensitive
to terrestrial magnetism. All these effects were once thought to
be too subtle to be detected by living organisms.

Drs. Burr and Northrup have shown that electromagnetic
fields seem to surround living organisms; they call them L-fields.
These dynamic fields, internally generated and which may be
connected with the 'aura' perceived by sensitives and possibly
recorded by Kirlian photography, respond to lunar phases and
many other external stimuli. The Moon affects the Earth's electromagnetic field and Lieber is convinced that it also affects the
human field. Mental illness is apparently accompanied by a
change in the patient's electrical field and Lieber effectively
suggests that there may well be truth in the old wives' tale of the
Moon affecting our mental state. Police forces have certainly
noted the incease of violent crimes associated with lunar phases.

Apart from the gross effects of violent and psychotic mental
conditions, a lunar association has been noted with the subtler
functioning of the psyche. Many years ago Andrija Puharich

conducted a series of telepathy experiments for a full lunar month.[9] It took him five years to arrange a series of tests where all conditions were controlled except the test condition—the effect of lunar phase on ESP performance. Puharich's graph in Figure 2 speaks for itself on the results he obtained. The two key peaks of telepathic scoring occurred at the times of full and new moons—the key phases in so many other effects, too, it seems—the times when the range of tides is increased: perhaps further, and subtler, evidence of Lieber's biotides idea.

Puharich has also noted the effect of atmospheric ionization

Lunar Day	Hit Scores/50	0	5	10	15	20	25	30	35	40	45	50
1	28											
2	17											
3	10											
4	8											
5	11											
6	10											
7	9											
8	9											
9	8											
10	9											
11	16											
12	28											
13	32											
Full Moon	46											
15	Subject	Could Not Complete Test—Due To Trance										
16	44											
17	22											
18	8											
19	10											
20	9											
21	10											
22	10											
23	9											
24	9											
25	11											
26	20											
27	31											
28	18											
Total	454											

Hit Av. = 16.8/50

Graph of telepathic scores of lunar phases during a full lunar month, as recorded in the experiments of Andrija Puharich.

on *psi* performance. An air ion is created when an atom in the atmosphere gains an electron (becoming a negative ion) or loses one (becoming a positive ion). Most atoms in the air are electrically balanced—neutral—unless charged in these ways. The process whereby electrons are 'broken off' atmospheric atoms and float free before becoming attracted to other, neutral atoms is called *ionization*. Ions are the means by which electric charge is distributed in the atmosphere. The process can be generated by various forms of cosmic bombardment, geological radiations and meteorological phenomena such as thunderstorms. A waterfall and other examples of running water are also good generators of ionization. Negative ions have a beneficial effect on humans; with 'healthy' or 'bracing' locations such as mountainous and coastal regions being usually relatively rich in negative ions. Negative ions seem able to help relieve certain ailments such as hay fever, asthma and some allergies. Positive ions, on the contrary, seem to aggravate some disorders and lead to irritability and an unsettled frame of mind. Puharich has carried out experiments which show that an environment with an excess of negative ions provides more favourable conditions for the performance of at least some forms of ESP activity. Puharich points out that an ancient magical text, *The Key of Solomon*, instructs that calm weather is required for certain magical acts, and dowsers have noted their ability to divine water or minerals is adversely affected in poor or thundery conditions. On clear, bright days ions tend to be more highly concentrated than in unsettled weather conditions. The burning of fires also produces ions (of both charges), which can augment the preponderant electrical conditions of a given environment. Thus the use of ritual fires in conditions suitable for ESP performances, such as shamanistic rituals, could add their negative ions to enhance the suitable electrical conditions.

So it would appear that lunar and ionization effects can alter mental states. On the grand scale, there is evidence to indicate that the Moon may somehow influence the incoming rate of meteors into the upper atmosphere, which in turn may affect the production of rain in the lower atmosphere.

But whatever scale we look at, it is clear even from this glimpse at the secret processes of Nature that behind the more obvious effects of our terrestrial environment there are fantastic, wheeling forces acting on or interacting with many processes taking place on our planet, sometimes directly and sometimes by devious routes that are hard to pin down. We can assemble a necessarily crude picture of Earth being buffeted by all manner of cosmic forces, emanating from Sun, Moon and planets and perhaps from sources far out in interstellar—perhaps even intergalactic—space that affect its atmosphere, its electromagnetic processes, its geology and its inhabitants. The Earth itself responds to these influences and puts out changes of electromagnetic fields which in turn add further inputs for the atmosphere and organic life to respond to.

It is entirely wrong for science to consider that the study of the Earth can be divided into disciplines such as geology, biology, meteorology, astronomy, and all the rest. The Earth is one *whole*, living system: aspects of its cosmic environment impinge upon it, and effects in the terrestrial geology create further effects in its meteorology. Changes in its magnetic envelope can funnel further influences back to its geology. The whole system, as it were, *resonates*. All these forces and reactions play back and forth, creating responses, changes and echoes in all terrestrial structures and processes, from the most dense to the most subtle.

Perhaps the chief battlefield in this gigantic interplay of forces is the Earth's atmosphere, as it is the buffer zone between outer space and the dense surface of the Earth. If this great hinterland of cosmic and global physics manifests any anomalous effects anywhere it is probably in the atmosphere that they are most likely to appear. I consider that the objective component of UFO events is likely to be one such effect, but there are many others that may belong to the same general 'family' of phenomena, even if some are distant relatives.

Possibly amongst the most commonly reported atmospheric effects about which virtually nothing is known are those labelled 'earthquake lights'. These are curious luminous phenomena sometimes observed in the skies near or adjacent to areas of seismic activity. They can appear as 'slow sheet lightning' or as auroral beams, streamers or columns, sometimes as individual lights. Just before the 1957 earthquake in England, epicentred on Charnwood Forest in Leicestershire, for example, people in several counties reported seeing lines of 'tadpole-shaped' lights in the sky![10] During the Japanese Idu Peninsula earthquake of 1930 a straight row of round masses of light was seen![11]

By the nature of their circumstances most earthquake lights

tend to be reported by untrained observers, so they have been easy targets for the blind eye of science. The first serious investigation of the phenomena seems to have been carried out by Terada and Musya who studied some 1500 reports of aerial lights from the Idu Peninsula quake. These lights were reported up to 112km from the quake's epicentre. More recently, another Japanese researcher collected photographs of lights seen during the Matsushiro 'earthquake swarm' in Japan from 1965 to 1967 (a most intense period of worldwide UFO sightings, incidentally).

During an earthquake at Santa Rosa, California, in October 1969, there were many sightings of earthquake lights which reportedly took the forms of lightning, electric sparks, St. Elmo's Fire, fireballs and meteors. There were also reports of explosive sounds. A leading British politician also heard aerial explosions during the terrible T'angshan earthquake in China in 1976. This quake also produced intense displays of aerial illumination.

Curious sounds have been associated with meteorite strikes as well: on Christmas Eve 1965, Britain experienced its largest recorded meteorite fall at the village of Barwell, Leicestershire. Loud acoustic phenomena accompanied its fall, breaking glass

Earthquake lights photographed during the Matsushiro earthquake swarm (1965-67). (*Photo: T. Kuribayashi*)

many miles away but, more remarkably, its arrival was *preceded* by curious hissing sounds issuing *from the ground!*[12] (It is, incidentally, interesting to note that many *major* meteor-fireball events occur over Britain around midwinter. There was the 'great Christmas fireball' which lit up most of the northern British Isles in 1973 and which may have landed in Northern Ireland; and on Christmas Day 1980 a spectacular multiple fire-ball event lit up the skies over the southern half of Britain. There have certainly been other such events near Christmas time in recent years. What patterns hidden within the secret side of Nature are at work here?)

Explosions and earthquake lights in the form of 'a brilliant reddish object like a huge globular lightning'[13] were witnessed during an earthquake in Cyprus in 1941.

The accounts could go on: earthquake lights have been reported worldwide. No one knows how they are occasioned, but probably the best theory so far puts their appearance down to a result of piezo-electricity generated in quartz-bearing rocks subjected to pressure during seismic disturbance.

A phenomenon probably closely related to earthquake lights is that known as 'mountain-top glow'. This effect has been reported particularly in the Andes region of South America, also, to a lesser extent, in the European Alps. This phenomenon appears as beams or sheets of light which emanate from mountain peaks and stretch away up into the atmosphere. Such effects can be visible hundreds of miles away. In the Chilean Andes, *where thunderstorms are said to be rare*, mountain-top discharges are visible from late spring to early autumn and usually come from certain points. A constant glow around a mountain summit can give way to occasional outbursts which have the appearance of great searchlight beams. It has been noted[14] that such light displays have been reported under cloudless skies.

At the time of a great earthquake in Chile, in August 1906, these mountain-top discharges were particularly brilliant—the 'whole sky seemed to be on fire'![15] This may give us a clue that the phenomenon is subject to similar generation principles as those pertaining to earthquake lights. Mountainous regions are fault regions, so pressures building up tectonically (not nece-ssarily always triggering an earthquake) could affect mountain masses, perhaps producing a piezo-electrical effect, as the rocks in the mountain were squeezed, which is discharged from the relatively sharp mountain peak.

An example of ball lightning. The dashed form of the light trace indicates that the phenomenon was pulsing. Close examination of this picture shows that it is one of the few authentic photographs of ball lightning in existence. (*Photo: R. C. Jennings*)

What these type of phenomena show is that seismic events can produce luminous phenomena in the atmosphere, whatever mechanism is involved. Such phenomena can sometimes be produced at a considerable distance from the centre of seismic activity. As will become apparent in Chapter 7, I feel these types of manifestations, earthquake lights and mountain-top discharges, to be closely allied to the UFO mechanism.

Another well-known but poorly-understood phenomenon is ball lightning. Although there are reasons for believing this is a little more distantly related to UFO manifestation it has frequently been invoked to explain UFO sightings.

Ball lightning, or Kugelblitz, usually appears as a luminous spherical form measuring between 10 to 40cm. However, it can vary in size from that of a pea to several feet across and assume non-spherical shapes such as ellipsoids, cylinders and dumb-bell shapes. It is hardly a standardized phenomenon. It usually accompanies thunderstorms—in about 70 per cent of the cases in a particular study[16] —but has been reported in clear sky conditions as well. One researcher[17] has stated that 'all that is required for the formation of at least some types of ball-lightning is an intensification of the local electric field'. So even the thunderstorm connection is far from standard: it is presumably simply one of the most common ways in Nature for the local electric field to be intensified. The phenomenon has appeared in all colours, though green seems to be the least frequently reported hue. If often gives off a smell of ozone or 'sulphur'. Ball lightning appears out in the open and in closed areas—even the interior of an aircraft in flight. It can disappear like a bubble without a sound on some occasions, while on others it explodes with an accompanying detonation. Ball lightning has rarely, if ever, killed anyone but does often seem attracted towards a witness, following the person around, or moving up to the startled observer then gliding away. Could this attraction be due to the electric fields surrounding human beings? The phenomenon thus sometimes appears to be semi-intelligent. Perhaps the UFO reports of balls of light approaching witnesses, high tension cables and cars might also be due to some electromagnetic reaction, rather than sentient piloting by occupants of such fiery spheres. There follow a few eye witness accounts of ball-lighting.

In March 1977 in Newgate Street village, Hertfordshire, a white light about 10cm across was seen through a window hovering at ground level. It was about as bright as a cycle headlamp, and disappeared after four to five seconds. The grass where the phenomenon had been seen was found to be burned yellow-brown, and there was a burning smell. There were no thunderstorms in the vicinity at the time of the sighting.[18]

During a thunderstorm one afternoon in July 1937, near Llangollen, North Wales, two men witnessed a yellow, spherical light about 20cm in diameter with a soft outline rolling slowly down the roof of a building. It had almost a 'hopping motion' until it met the gutter. It then turned at right angles and rolled along the gutter until it reached an ornamental spike where it disappeared in a bright flash accompanied by a clap of thunder.[19]

The following French case, which took place next to Val-de-Grace church, was reported in 1852 and is a good example of the almost intelligent behaviour of some ball lightning. There was a strong flash of lightning and shortly afterwards the firescreen covering the fireplace in the witness' room was knocked inwards and a fireball 'the size of a child's head' gently entered the room from the fireplace aperture. The phenomenon wandered slowly around the room before it approached the witness' feet, where-upon it rubbed itself against the man's legs 'like a young cat'. The man felt no heat from the ball, but carefully withdrew his feet and avoided further contact. The ball of light eventually rose up to the level of the man's head (he was seated) whereupon it became somewhat elongated and made its way towards a hole for a stove pipe above the upper cornice of the fireplace. This hole was obscured by wallpaper which the ball peeled away 'without tearing' and disappeared up the flue. It exploded near the top of the chimney causing some damage but no injury.[20]

Not all ball lightning is luminous. On 19 March 1887, Captain C. D. Swart on a Dutch vessel saw a curious 'meteor' during a fierce storm. The meteor was in the form of two balls, and though one was luminous, the other was 'very black'. The 'illuminated ball was oblong' (sic) and hovered over the ship. The atmosphere became dark and dense and the phenomenon fell into the sea with a roar, creating a huge surge of water that washed over the vessel. A suffocating atmosphere prevailed making everyone on board gasp for breath. Immediately after the event solid lumps of ice fell on deck and the rigging of the ship also became iced up. The account does not mention what became of the 'dark meteor'.[21]

Ball lightning can take on forms as intricate as many described in UFO accounts. Take this incident in Dublin in 1919, for example. A Mr Gilmore went outside one evening after a thundery shower. He suddenly saw a luminous ball lying in the middle of the street. It was about eighteen inches in diameter and blue in colour. What was particularly remarkable was that the sphere had 'two protruberances of a yellow colour projecting from the upper quadrants'. It vanished after a second or so, a loud peal of thunder occurring at the same time. No trace was left on the roadway.[22]

Just occasionally there are hints of some relationship between ball lightning and meteorites. This, however, would require connecting mechanisms which are currently outside the scientific imagination. Here are two such coincidences. On 18 March 1979, there was a powerful explosion in Marlborough, Wiltshire. A large ash tree was found with a crater at its foot, the hole penetrating the main sewer. The explosion had been caused by something igniting the methane in the sewer. But what was the something? The bursar of Marlborough College saw a 'tremendous flash of lightning which zipped across the river Kennet right up to the Bath road'. Another witness was Keith Lovatt who was walking his dog at the time. 'There was this ball of blue,' he said, 'just like the arc of an electric welder. It rolled over the ground and I thought it struck me. It seemed to hit all round me. I didn't realize at the time exactly where it had struck.' Certainly the effects on the tree were characteristic of ball lightning—all the bark was stripped off without being scorched. A shrub at its base was withered. Just over five hours after this incident hundreds of people saw a huge meteoric fireball speed through the sky over Wales and the West Country. It was a blue-green colour changing to orange.[23] Just a remarkable coincidence? Perhaps. But it calls to mind a similar coincidence Andrew York and I noticed when we were undertaking our wide-ranging study of Leicestershire (Chapter 7) in central England. On the night of 11 September 1975, a fierce electrical storm swept across the county. During the course of this a 'three foot wide ball of fire' was seen moving down a street in the village of Barwell. It came in contact with a house and blew its roof off, and the building had to be shored up the next day. A man inside was uninjured but had the cap he was wearing blown off his head as he sat watching television. The area was reported as reeking of sulphur. Any ball lightning, but especially one so large as this and causing so much damage, is a rare event. Yet Barwell, a tiny, insignificant village in west Leicestershire played host to another incredibly rare geophysical event—Britain's largest recorded meteorite fall ten years earlier, as mentioned previously in this chapter. It may just be a coincidence, and orthodox scientists would undoubtedly dismiss it as such, but more thoughtful people might be forgiven for wondering if such coincidences were actually manifestations of some unknown mechanism operating within the secret side of Nature. If science was what it claimed to be, it would pay more heed to such patterns of events, however unconnected they may seem in our present state of knowledge.

'A unique meteorological phenomenon' observed on the Fuch's Ice Piedmont, Adelaide Island, Antarctica, by Ulster explorer Eric Wilkinson, late of the British Antarctic Survey, who commented 'the cloud emitted a thick black ray of light which hit the ice at an angle of 45° and churned up a "snow devil"'. (*Photo: Eric Wilkinson*). Totally inexplicable phenomena like this prove that scientists do not yet understand all the mechanisms occurring in our atmosphere.

The list of ball lightning sightings could be extended by thousands—it has been a widely-observed phenomenon. But what explanations have been put forward for it? None that completely copes with all its manifestations. A common explanation is that ball lightning is an area of plasma (a superheated gas which is completely ionized) produced under thundery conditions. Lightning creates plasma, but plasma is about as stable as 'a jelly held with rubber hands'[24] and it is difficult to imagine where sufficiently strong magnetic fields would come from to bind it together in the odd but coherent forms that have been ascribed to ball lightning. The Earth's field is not strong enough. Also, numerous witnesses who have come in contact with ball lightning have stated that the phenomenon was not giving off any heat—as we have seen in an example already quoted.

Another suggestion is that ball lightning is a somehow detached 'step leader' (the first pulse of a lightning leader stroke from cloud to ground which opens up a typically forked conductivity channel within the air that allows the return stroke back up from the earth). But what about ball lightning events when there is no thunderstorm about? Various chemical theories have been put forward and have been found wanting. There has even been the startling theory that ball lightning results from the presence of anti-matter dust particles![25] Apparently this hypothesis has some flaws as well. One of the big problems with ball lightning being some form of electrical phenomenon (which it nevertheless must be) is its ability to appear in closed rooms and sometimes to enter closed metal boxes or pass through wire mesh without instantly discharging. An attempt to answer this conundrum has been made by Russian researchers Kapitsa and Cerillo, who suggest that the phenomenon is associated with a standing wave of electromagnetism produced in a thunder storm, in which waveforms assuming stable parameters could contain pockets of ionized gas between their 'links': the standing wave would move, the glowing form would appear to move but would in fact be different gas at different points in the waveform's journey. This explanation accords well with some reported incidents but, again, can hardly account for all the ball lightning manifestations on record.

The truth of the matter may be that there is a whole spectrum of closely-related phenomena that have been grouped together simply as 'ball lightning'. From the point of view of this book it is sufficient to note that this group of phenomena can glow, change shape, appear on land or in the air, behave in what could be construed as a vaguely intelligent manner and can leave ground traces such as burn marks and furrows in the soil. UFOs and ball lightning clearly must have some mechanisms in common, and it would be a rash ufologist who would deny it. Nature *can* produce mobile, coherent if transient glowing forms that can leave energetic effects.

A phenomenon that seems to be a cross between mountain-top discharge and ball lightning was reported at the beginning of this century.[26] During a geological expedition that took him through the Euphrates Valley, Ellsworth Huntington heard from a local man that two mountains in the area, Keklujek and Ziaret mountains, 'fought' with each other using balls of light. Huntington followed the story up with numerous other witnesses widely separated along the valley. The reports agreed: two or three times most years, but never when the sky was cloudy, balls of light would be seen flashing between the two mountains accompanied by a sound like thunder. The balls of light could be seen only at night. The phenomenon usually occurred during the autumn, after the long dry season.

But reports of odd light phenomena at sea or on land, small events or sometimes effects on a vast scale, abound in captains' logs, in scientific papers, in the accounts of explorers and as anecdotal accounts from ordinary people the world over.[27] *Planet Earth teems with unexplained phenomena*. I recall, myself, when a young teenager, seeing a strange light phenomenon from the upstairs window of my home in Leicester-shire: a little before midnight I saw two fan-shaped displays of light, appearing one after the other, emerge from a point apparently on the ground behind a lone tree situated in a hedgerow some distance away in the middle of the countryside. The fans of whitish light reached up beyond the height of the tree which stood at leasty sixty feet tall. The events were soundless. After a period of ten minutes, the same thing happened again. I continued to watch for the best part of an hour afterwards, but nothing untoward took place so I went to sleep. This really happened—but what is the point of telling anyone? It does not fit into any currently acceptable scientific pattern and so, from the point of view of science, such events do not exist.

There are enough problems with recognized phenomena: take thunderstorms for instance. Lightning is produced from a build-up of electric charge in clouds (usually cumulonimbus). The arrangement is usually that the upper part of the cloud has an overall positive charge while the lower regions of the cloud possess an overall negative charge. No one really knows how storm clouds build up these electric charges. It is also not understood why the leader stroke of lightning follows a zig-zag path to the ground. One theory proposes that as cosmic rays hit the top of our atmosphere, the secondary, less energetic rays produced by this impact within the atmosphere, cascade down through the storm cloud causing ionization as they pass through. When sufficient charge has been produced to form a lightning stroke, the step leader follows the path of least resistance to the ground, following segments in which the air has been ionized by the passage of the secondary cosmic ray particles.

Perhaps. A recent theory suggests that it is the collisions of forming hailstones within the thunder cloud which 'knock' electrons free, causing ionization to produce the required charge within the clouds.

And if scientists struggle to understand the mechanism of lightning they are a long way indeed from fathoming the nature of 'superbolts', which are incredibly more energetic and longer than conventional lightning. They occur on average about once in every ten million lightning flashes and have been observed from space satellites.

And if hailstones are used in one theory to account for thunderstorm electricity, then it has to be remembered that hailstones themselves display inexplicable characteristics at times. Anomalous blocks of ice falling from the skies have been reported on many occasions, but have been either dismissed by the inherent subjective tendency of science, or else explained away as having fallen from aircraft wings even when investigation has shown this to have been impossible. One ice fall scientists cannot dismiss, however, is that which occurred in Manchester in April 1973. After one long, isolated flash of lightning a huge block of ice crashed to the ground barely ten feet away from the feet of . . . an atmospheric physicist. The man, R. F. Griffiths, said: 'The object fell fast enough to be shattered into many pieces on impact.' He picked up the nearest fragment which weighed 612g and was about four-and-a-half inches long. Later analysis showed it to have the layered structure typical of hailstones, containing fifty-one rings of cloud water. The sample was preserved—proof of the meteorologically impossible. The original ice chunk was estimated to have weighed around 2kg, an untenable size for a hailstone, defying the laws of physics as they are currently known. Only two aircraft were vaguely in the vicinity and they reported no ice-formation and physical examination of them afterwards also failed to reveal any evidence of icing.

When regularly observed and studied events like thunderstorms and their attendant phenomena can still present such problems and mysteries for the scientific mind, any dismissal of UFO phenomena by scientific 'experts' should be treated with the gravest suspicion. When scientists can explain the precise nature of earthquake lights, ball lightning, thunderstorms and ice falls, *then*, perhaps, we can consider it safe to listen to their pronouncements on UFOs. It is my guess that when such a level of understanding of the goings-on in our atmosphere has come about, connecting mechanisms will have been uncovered that will render the occurrence of UFO-type phenomena to be far more accepted by the establishment scientific mind than is the case today.

The air may seem clear enough, and fluffy white clouds on high seem innocent enough; but it is an arena in which parade extraordinary—if rare and transient—phenomena which are currently inexplicable. They are none the less real. The thunder god Thor is a powerful deity and it is from his strange and awesome kingdom that UFOs come forth to confront us.

In this chapter we have seen that there are enormous, unexpected interactions going on within and around the Earth against a backdrop of primordial forces on a scale so vast that phenomena we have barely observed, let alone explained, are bound to result. Events have been described that bear great similarities to UFO appearances. The likelihood that UFOs are related in one way or another to such phenomena cannot reasonably be denied.

The fundamental geophysical processes exist. Resulting events have been repeatedly observed. UFOs do not come from holes at the poles, from some planet near *Alpha Centauri* or from a parallel universe. UFO events emerge from the processes taking place within the secret side of Nature.

5.
The Earth's Body Language

*The existence of man upon a thin shell beneath which
mammoth forces constantly operate, cannot be over-
emphasized nor is it exaggerated in perspective.*

Michael A. Persinger and Gyslaine Lafrenière,
Space-Time Transients

It is necessary to briefly consider the geological nature of our
planet if it is being claimed that UFOs are products of the interactions between the Earth's physical body, the surrounding
atmosphere and the welter of ambient cosmic and terrestrial
forces. In this part of the work I acknowledge and express my
appreciation of the major contribution of Paul McCartney, a
trained geologist, and his co-research with me on some of the
correlations to be presented in following chapters.

The physical body of the Earth is not a dormant lump of
matter but, rather, possesses a dynamic nature. It is the key one
of the several elements that go together to produce the UFO
phenomenon.

Most people would visualize the crust of the Earth as a contin-
uous shell housing the familiar outlines of our continents and
oceans. This impression is reinforced nowadays when we can
'see ourselves' through the medium of cameras in orbiting
satellites. A hundred million years ago, however, the pictures
such devices would have taken would have been very different.
The Atlantic Ocean, now a vast barrier between the Americas,
Africa and Europe, would have been merely embryonic in
nature! The giant mountain chains of today, the Alps, the
Rockies, the Andes and the Himalayas would not have existed.

How then did the surface of our planet change? Early theories were of a stabilist nature: continental/oceanic outlines changed by vertical movements of the sea or land relative to each other, it was thought? It was not supposed that continents could migrate about the globe. But Britain, for example, was once in the tropics; there is plenty of evidence in the rocks to inform us of that truth. The paleontologist, who studies fossils, the evidence of past life, had long wondered how past and present distribution of species could be accounted for if the continents had never been nomadic. They postulated the existence of enormous land bridges joining widely-separated land masses along which animals could migrate? If so, why is there no evidence of their existence now? Surely they are still there, covered by the waves of the great oceans?

But they are not. Their absence, together with many sophisticated advances in research methods led, in the early 1960s, to a radically differing viewpoint. The theory of Plate Tectonics was born. Essentially, this states that the Earth's crust was composed of a number of saucer-shaped plates each in continual motion? This is a dynamic picture; the surface features of our planet are merely transitory with large-scale horizontal movements of the plates performing never-ending surgery, forever redefining the land and water boundaries of the globe.

The most violent effects of this tectonic motion occur round plate margins. It is here that material is devoured and carried into the deeper levels of the crust, to be reborn in the guise of violent volcanic eruptions, such as those that resulted in the formation of the island of Surtsey in November 1963? They may occur in more subtle ways. Rocks melted at very high temperatures and pressures deep in the crust form molten magma, which may solidify before it has been able to force its way back to the surface. Coarse-grained igneous intrusive rocks result and these may subsequently be exposed at the surface after aeons of weathering and erosion have removed the younger cover above. The daunting landscape of southwest England with its huge granitic outcrops of Dartmoor, Bodmin Moor, Exmoor and Land's End reflect the exposed parts of one gigantic intrusion injected into the crust hundreds of millions of years ago.

Rocks around the plate margins also suffer other alterations. Some are redefined as the large-scale earth movements— creating formidable compressional forces—produce temperatures and pressures sufficient to recrystallize rocks without taking them through a molten or mobile phase. These are the rocks subjected to metamorphism. The earth movements themselves are responsible for the building of mountain chains, formed by the head-on collision of two plates.

The clash of two immensely large moving bodies, such as two plates, requires that huge quantities of rocks are dislocated and moved along fracture planes. This is faulting and faults are a common and widespread consequence of plate movement. The dislocation of two rock bodies relative to each other produces powerful shock waves which pass through the masses of rock, transmit energy and frequently cause more earth movement.[7]

We call them earthquakes and their intensity depends upon the degree, the scale and the suddeness of earth movement. Compression of the crust in the region of two converging plates must lead to the buckling or folding of the rocks on either side of the plate margin. Material is often uplifted in this way and culminates in the birth of a mountain chain.

In some areas of the world today, plates just glide past each other rather than either moving towards or away from one another. This may suggest a fairly passive state of affairs but these Conservative Plate margins do manifest their own problems. Occasionally, somewhere along their plane of contact, the two bypassing plates may become jammed. Elsewhere, movement continues and this results in enormous stresses being built up in the rocks adjacent to the jammed area. The strain progressively accumulates and, eventually, the resistance of the rocks to the motion will be overcome and they will move violently and suddenly against each other.[8]

The people of San Francisco well know the consequences of such sudden motion. They live in the knowledge that some day the San Andreas fault must compensate for its years of inactivity; the longer they wait, the more catastrophic will be the earthquake produced.[9]

The overall picture points to zones of high activity along the plate margins. The birth, or *orogenesis*, of mountain chains, regions of high intensity earthquakes, and nearly all volcanoes are related to interactions at the plate margins.

It is at least symbolic that the UFO sighting that gave rise to the term 'flying saucer' in 1947 was near Mount Rainier in America's Washington state, a region with a history of earthquakes and, as the spectacular recent events at Mount St Helens have shown, volcanic activity.

As we are going to use parts of the British Isles as 'laboratories' for studying UFOs, we must consider where they fit into this dynamic scenario of tectonic creation and obliteration. Nor is this choice of locations merely convenience—there is good geological sense in selecting British geology for such an experiment. As Niger Calder puts it:

> As it happens, Britain is the most fascinating place on Earth, geologically speaking. Within it are compressed . . . a great variety of features and rocks of different ages that, elsewhere, are usually spread monotonously across hundreds or thousands of miles. Lest this seem like prejudice let me quote from a Japanese book '. . . England has a great geological advantage for, amazingly enough, strata of every geologic period from the Pre-Cambrian to the Quaternary are to be found on this small island . . .'[10]

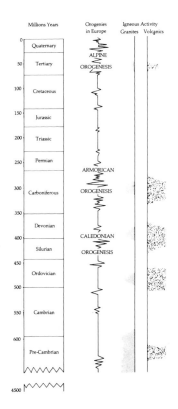

3   Geological Time Chart. The 4,500 million years of the Earth's history is illustrated. Specific times when mountain building episodes injected intrusive and volcanic rocks into the crust are depicted. (*P. McCartney*)

What threatens San Francisco will not happen to London or Manchester. Britain is not near any modern active margins. However, this was not so in the distant past. The heavily faulted, intruded and metamorphosed British Isles confirm that there was once a great deal of tectonic activity affecting them.

Figure 3 is a geological time clock. Sometime during the Pre-Cambrian, at least once and most likely on several occasions, large areas of the north and west of Scotland, together with Northern Ireland, were subjected to intense metamorphism, deformation and faulting during episodes of mountain building – orogenies. Many igneous rocks, both intrusive and extrusive (volcanic) in origin, were emplaced at this time. Weathering and erosion has made sure that the evidence of these ancient events are at hand by exposing large tracts of these Pre-Cambrian rocks.

We have evidence that these effects influenced a far wider area of the British land mass. Here and there, in isolation, small outcrops or inliers of Pre-Cambrian material hints at what might lie below. Anglesey and the Malverns possess highly metamorphosed Pre-Cambrian rocks; Charnwood and the Wrekin possess extrusive igneous rocks indicating particularly active regions of vulcanism. Charnwood in Leicestershire and the Long Mynd of Shropshire display ancient sedimentary deposits, but elsewhere younger rock cover has obscured what may be considerable areas of Pre-Cambrian basement.[1]

A long period of comparative calm followed, interspersed with sporadic volcanic activity, until the advent of the Caledonian orogeny which culminated at the end of the Silurian and the beginning of the Devonian periods some 400 million years ago. No mountains conceived during this orogeny are still with us, but the surface of the Earth does not always conceal its past readily, for many rocks formed prior to the orogeny are heavily scarred with intense faulting and folding. The Highlands of Scotland experienced faulting and folding of their rocks, which has been superimposed on past structures leaving them highly contorted—the sum of several mountain building episodes.

The Southern Uplands of Scotland, the Lake District, North Wales and parts of Pembrokeshire (Dyfed) also exhibit a complex geology resulting from the catastrophies. Central Wales was also faulted and folded but this was not accompanied by metamorphism of the rocks expected in zones of high tectonic

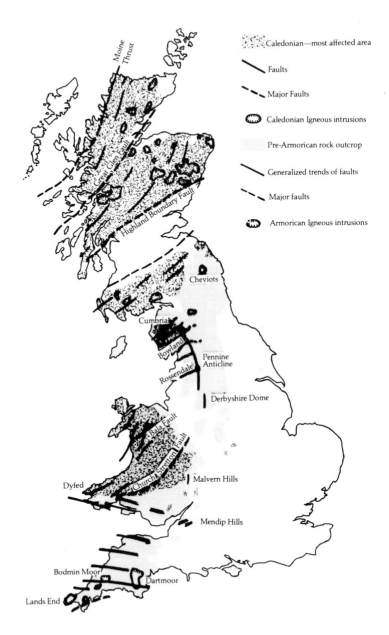

Legend:

- Caledonian—most affected area
- Faults
- Major Faults
- Caledonian Igneous intrusions
- Pre-Armorican rock outcrop
- Generalized trends of faults
- Major faults
- Armorican Igneous intrusions

Labels on map: Moine Thrust, Great Glen Fault, Highland Boundary Fault, Cheviots, Cumbria, Bowland, Pennine Anticline, Rossendale, Derbyshire Dome, Bala Fault, Church Stretton Fault, Dyfed, Malvern Hills, Mendip Hills, Bodmin Moor, Dartmoor, Lands End

4   Caledonian and Armorican Structures. The areas of Great Britain most heavily influenced by faulting, folding and igneous activity are illustrated. (*P. McCartney*)

activity;[12] it escaped the brunt of the decimation, a fact which will prove important in UFO correlations to come. The very deep-seated Church Stretton fault signifies the south and eastern limits of the Caledonian influence, as shown in Figure 4.

The deep-seated faults, such as the Moine Thrust, Great Glen fault, Highland Boundary fault and Southern Uplands fault, are noteworthy results of this period![13]

The granites of the Lake District (Cumbria), Cheviots, the Southern Uplands and many of the Highland intrusions were injected into the crust taking their toll on the surrounding country rocks![14]

Land to the south and east had, as yet, avoided the large-scale effects of an orogeny; the rocks showed little disturbance apart from some gentle folding and small-scale faulting.

After a long interval in which both arid and swampy conditions prevailed over much of the British area, another orogeny took place. The Armorican orogeny reached Britain towards the end of the Carboniferous period.

This time, it was the south and western areas of Britain that felt the strongest influences of the plate movement. All pre-existing rocks in the south-west peninsula were highly folded and some important faults were also produced. Pembrokeshire, particularly the western coastal regions, was highly contorted[28, 16] and this is manifested in the tight folding of the rocks and the numerous faults in the region. This is another noteworthy point when the UFO incidence in this area is dealt with in Chapter 7.

To the north, the effects were less intense but nevertheless worth mentioning. The Pennine anticline and the Derbyshire Dome were created. The Malverns and parts of Lancashire and Cumbria were folded and faulted. In the latter stages of the orogeny, the massive igneous intrusions of Devon and Cornwall were emplaced. Extensive mineralization also accompanied the Armorican orogeny, with rich mineral veins being produced in south-west England and in parts of the Carboniferous limestone to the north. Figure 4 outlines most of the important Armorican structures and the areas they influenced.

The Armorican orogeny subsided some 250 million years ago. Since that time the British area has been far removed from any active plate margin. However, such are the magnitudes of the earth movements around the plates that the Alpine orogeny, responsible for the building of the Alps in the comparitively recent Oligocene epoch, brought some areas of Britain under its influence. Rocks in Wiltshire, Devon and Dorset were faulted and folded during the late Cretaceous period, and the later and major movements during the orogeny imposed folding in the Isle of Wight and created the Weald, the Hampshire and London Basins.[18] It must be stressed that the effects of the Alpine orogeny in these areas are considerably less severe than the havoc that the Pre-Cambrian, Caledonian and Armorican events wreaked on the rocks of the north and west of the country. No metamorphism or igneous activity is evident in the British area stemming from Alpine movements. It must be mentioned that a very different set of events occurred in western Scotland during the time of the Alpine activity. Vast lava plateaux and swarms of small intrusions (dykes) were to cover large areas, adding further complexity to the region.

In summary, a broad definition can be made between the outcrops of Pre- and Post-Armorican times. A glance at a national geological map of the British Isles clearly reflects the intricate complexity or rock formations of Pre-Armorican age. The broad, uncomplicated outcrops of the younger rocks emphasizes their more simple tectonic structure.

The following table illustrates a scale of earthquake intensity with the resulting damage expected if such shock waves were to pass through the crustal rocks.

Of particular interest are the less intense earthquakes, of prime importance in the context of this book. They are very common occurrences but go unnoticed by all but the most sensitive of people and animals. How are they caused? Faults are evidence of ancient earthquakes and, on rare occasions, old faults do yawn. Although they may be the products of severe earth dislocations many hundreds of millions of years ago, *movement can still occur along them*. Seemingly, our planet takes that long, or longer, to reach a state of equilibrium in any given region. From time to time, minor adjustments need to be made; small displacements cause a sudden dissipation of energy along a fault plane and a minor tremor is often the end result. This is not surprising. It is difficult to imagine the magnitude of the energy exchanges that occur during earthquake activity. Not all this energy is released at once. Some must be bottled up, occasionally escaping and revealing itself in later small earth movements or in some other way.

MODIFIED MERCALLI INTENSITY SCALE

I Not felt. Marginal and long term effects of large earthquakes.

II Felt by persons at rest, on upper floors, or favourably placed.

III Felt indoors. Hanging objects swing. Vibration like passing of large trucks. May not be recognized as an earthquake.

IV Hanging objects swing. Vibration like passing of heavy trucks, or sensation like a jolt, like a heavy ball striking the walls. Standing motor cars rock. Windows, dishes, doors rattle. Glasses clink. Crockery clashes.

V Felt outdoors; direction estimated. Sleepers wakened. Liquids disturbed, some spilled. Small unstable objects displaced or upset. Doors swing, close, open. Pictures move. Pendulum clocks, stop, start, change rate.

VI Felt by all. Many frightened and run outdoors. Persons walk unsteadily. Windows, dishes, glassware broken. Books off shelves, pictures off walls, furniture overturned. Weak plaster and masonry cracked. Small bells ring. Trees shake visibly or are heard to rustle.

VII Difficult to stand. Noticed by drivers of motor cars. Hanging objects quiver. Furniture broken. Damage to masonry, including cracks. Weak chimneys broken at roof line. Fall of plaster, loose bricks and stones. Waves on ponds, water turbid with mud. Large bells ring.

VIII Steering of motor cars affected. Partial collapse of walls. Twisting and fall of chimneys, factory stacks. Frame houses moved on foundations if not bolted down, loose panel walls thrown out. Branches broken from trees. Changes in flow and temperature of springs and wells. Cracks on wet ground and steep slopes.

IX General panic. Much masonry heavily damaged. General damage to foundations. Serious damage to reservoirs. Underground pipes broken. Conspicuous cracks in ground. In alluviated areas sand and mud ejected, earthquake fountains, sand craters.

X Most masonry and foundations destroyed. Serious damage to dams and embankments. Large landslides. Water thrown on banks of canals, rivers etc. Rails bent slightly.

XI Rails bent greatly. Underground pipelines completely out of service.

XII Damage nearly total. Large rock masses displaced. Lines of sight and level distorted. Objects thrown into the air.

Records of the distribution of such minor earthquakes in the British Isles show how many of the earthquakes flock round major faults and other complex tectonic features. This is not to say that this will always be the case. Remember, the geologist can only examine rock 'exposures' and identify them with any precision. Even sophisticated seismic methods have their limitations in the detail they can recover from deep-seated formations. The great earthquake at Colchester in 1884 must be related to movement along a fault somewhere—but where is it? East Anglia and Essex have few mapped major surface faults. *They must lie deep below the more recent sedimentary cover.*[19] Out of the reach of the critical eyes of the geologist, and probably of Pre-Cambrian age, lie rocks of great complexity, likely to be riddled with faults, some of which are still searching for ultimate stability. This factor accounts for otherwise spurious distributions of earthquakes in superficially tectonically straightforward areas such as south-east England.

So active plate margins lead to large-scale alterations in the geology of the surrounding areas. Another important aspect of plate movement is mineral enrichment.

Many authors have noticed a high positive correlation between metallic mineral ore deposits and the sites of former plate margins.[20, 21] The word 'enrichment' is important because, of course, minerals are everywhere; all rocks are composed of mineral aggregates.

The involvement of plate margins in mineral enrichment is complex and beyond the scope of this present work, but some important basic mechanisms can be outlined. In one such mechanism, igneous intrusions play an important role. As they rise and begin to solidify from molten magma, hot gases and fluids are expelled and percolate into the surrounding rock. This process, known as contact metasomatism, alters the composition of the country rock and often establishes rich mineral veins. Typically, the metallic sulphide ores of copper, lead and zinc are emplaced by granitic intrusions in this fashion.

Hydrothermal solutions also produce concentrates of metallic ore minerals in the vicinity of intrusions. The hot magmatic fluids released from the rising magma force a path along cracks in the surrounding rocks and solidify to provide rich ore veins.[22] Faulted rocks are ideal zones of weakness and contribute significantly to the end result.

The mineral distribution map of England and Wales is shown

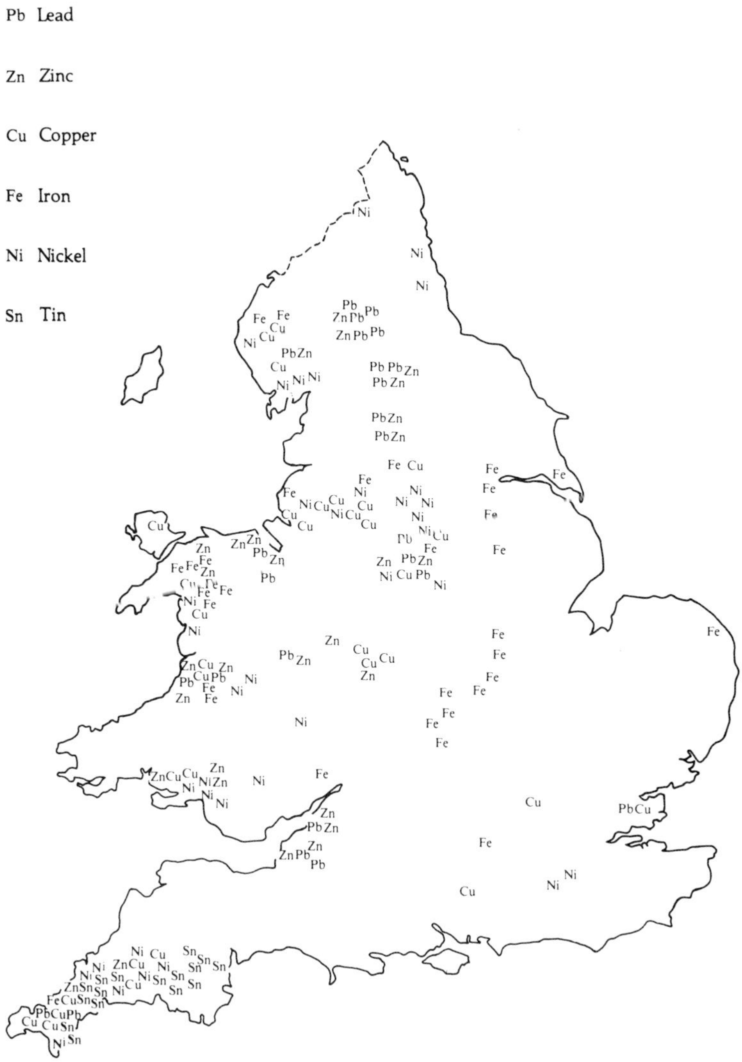

Pb Lead

Zn Zinc

Cu Copper

Fe Iron

Ni Nickel

Sn Tin

Mineral Distribution, England and Wales. The localities of the highest concentrations of metallic ore distribution are depicted by means of the chemical symbols of the metals concerned. (*P. McCartney*) in Figure 5. It has been carefully compiled using the computer-based distributions of the *Wolfson Geochemical Atlas of England and Wales*.[23] The chemical symbols of the metals involved are placed on the map presented here where the highest concentrations of their ores are found.

The mineral distributions closely mimic the overall patterns of faulting, intrusive and volcanic activity and the similarity is not one of chance. The only major anomaly to appear is that of iron mineral distribution. This occurs because we have been scrupulous to include all high intensities of iron minerals in England and Wales. In fact, the broad band from Hull to Gloucester is related to an *entirely different geology*. Some iron minerals are distinctly sedimentary in origin and are formed by relatively sedate mechanisms unassociated with plate movement. For this reason *they must be regarded as a separate entity*, unrelated to the tectonic activity responsible for the patterns of metallic ore distribution so relevant in the context of this study.

Minerals and rocks contain natural magnetism because the Earth behaves as if it were one giant magnet. The origin of the Earth's magnetic field is thought to lie deep in its interior, set up by electric currents which are able to produce a magnetic field in fluid bodies.[24] It is not the existence of the electric currents that is of prime importance, nor is a complex treatise on how they form paramount. The real centre of the issue is how they are perpetuated.

Seismic surveys have established that much of the core of the Earth is a molten body consisting of a highly conducting alloy or iron and probably nickel; an ideal medium through which an electric current may pass. To prolong its passage, geophysicists have adopted (and considerably modified[25]) Faraday's simple dynamo model based on the theory that mechanical motion can be converted into an electrical current. His laboratory model consisted of a copper disc on a spindle. The disc was spun over a bar magnet and the motion of the conductor, the copper disc, through the magnetic field of the magnet produced a small current. No such induced current, however, could be maintained for long since it was soon dissipated by the resistance of the copper conductor.

The Earth's magnetic field is self-perpetuating so the simple model just described does not seem to be applicable. However, an adaptation of the model has been shown to be consistent with

known data if applied to a conductor (the Earth) of global proportions. The electric current set up by moving conducting
fields in the core of the Earth would be virtually self-
perpetuating.

Movement of the fluids within the core is a necessary pre-
requisite of such a model and evidence does suggest that this is so
since the Earth's magnetic field is constantly changing in time
and place. Magnetic maps used in navigation must be updated at
regular intervals.[26]

The rocks themselves produce variations in global patterns of
the Earth's magnetic field due to the variation in the intensity of
the magnetism possessed by the different minerals in the
structure of the rock.

When a rock is 'born' it inherits magnetism from the Earth's
field. Later, in an ever-changing fashion, the rock also
experiences an induced magnetism provided by the magnetic
field of the present day. The resulting polarity of the rock must
be calculated by considering both factors together but it usually
means that the rock body will possess a polarity of a different
orientation to that of the global pattern.[27]

Rocks with a high proportion of magnetic minerals, primarily
those of iron, will have a higher magnetic susceptibility to those
with few magnetic minerals. Igneous and metamorphic rocks,
found in areas where tectonic activity has been, or still is, important, tend to generally exhibit higher magnetic suscept-
ibilities than those of most sedimentary rocks;[28] ironstones are
the notable exceptions.

Airborne methods can map an area 'magnetically'. The resulting maps reflect the local anomalies superimposed on the Earth's
field by the mineral and rock formations of the area. *The complexity of a magnetic anomaly map is very often indicative of the
geological complexity of the area.* For instance, mountain
building episodes induced by plate movements tend to
congregate many different rock types and metallic mineral veins
in a comparatively small area. The contours of the anomaly
map will consequently be closely spaced together. Over areas of
relative calm or geological uniformity, the map will appear
simple.

Figure 6 shows the magnetic anomaly map of Wales, and is
adapted from the official Geological Survey of 1965. Anglesey,
the Barmouth area and Pembrokeshire were heavily scarred and
decimated during the orogenic events of the past. Their

6   Aeromagnetic Map of Wales. The complexity of the rock formations
    in Wales is mirrored by the closeness of the contouring in the magnetic
    anomalies found in the region. (*After the O.S. Aeromagnetic Survey*)

geological complexity is mirrored in the extraordinary anomaly patterns found on the magnetic map. Central Wales, away from the focal points of past activity, has a more straightforward geological and magnetic history. The border regions around the Church Stretton fault enhance the situation further, the anomaly contours closely paralleling the more complex geology of the region.

It will be seen in further maps that the magnetic anomaly regions of Wales exactly correspond to the areas of peak UFO incidence in that country. This perfect correlation is not so complete for England, however, so the evidence suggests that while a disturbed magnetic environment seems to play some part in UFO manifestation it can only be a secondary factor. There must be more vital characteristics of fault regions as far as UFO appearance is concerned.

We have established that a dynamo model of the Earth predicts that electric currents flow deep in its bowels. This is indeed true, but near its surface the solid rocks are poor electrical conductors. But there are exceptions. Rocks containing high concentrations of metallic sulphide minerals, or those containing ionized groundwater may display considerable conducting properties. We may have here an underlying mechanism to explain the effectiveness of dowsing in geological surveys (see Chapter 6).

High metallic mineral concentrations produce complex magnetic and electrical anomalies. Since these, in turn, can be attributed to geological events around tectonic plate margins we must consider plate movement as the prime, overriding 'sign' in the Earth.

6.

The Prehistoric Enigma

I am the maker of music
And the reader of the heavens
I am the worker of magic
And the fearer of storms

Ralph McTell, *First and Last Man*

Cosmic and geological forces leave effects and marks on our planet on a vast scale, but signs in the earth on a human scale are also to be found. These are the awesome stone and earth structures left in landscapes all over the world by ancient peoples. To confront these mounds, standing stones and stone circles is like landing on another planet and finding the remnants of a long lost, alien culture. In effect, that is precisely the position we are in when trying to interpret the motivations and understanding of prehistoric peoples.

Not only do we have very little knowledge about the earliest people who roamed the Earth, we are also becoming increasingly estranged from the natural life of the planet itself—the key stimulus to those ancient societies. We are urban spacemen stumbling around on a planet that is more strange to us than we dare admit.

Amongst the very oldest of these prehistoric monuments are the earthen and megalithic (large stone) sites of western and northern Europe. Here can be found gigantic and sophisticated structures older than the pyramids of Egypt.

As already noted, because it has boundaries drawn by Nature, a wide range of geology, a workable population-to-area ratio, good archives and is well-mapped, we are using Britain— or, rather, parts of it—as a convenient laboratory for aspects of our study of UFOs. With regard to the number, variety and age of prehistoric monuments, the British Isles also lend themselves as a convenient 'test area' for the investigation of possible links between UFOs and ancient sacred sites.

It is an over-simplistic pattern to divide prehistory up into Neolithic, Bronze Age and Iron Age periods, but it does suffice as a general framework in which to arrange our understanding of what went on in prehistoric Britain. So, for convenience, we can envisage the Neolithic period as stretching from approximately 4000 B.C. to around 2000 B.C. This is followed by a Neolithic-Bronze Age 'overlap' period of a few hundred years. The Bronze Age proper can perhaps be considered as starting around the middle of the second millenium B.C. By 800 B.C. to 700 B.C. we enter a period that is generally termed the 'Iron Age'. We can consider this ending with the Roman invasion of A.D. 43.

Before the Neolithic (New Stone) age there were the nomadic Mesolithic and Palaeolithic peoples. Our view of these is very obscure indeed. The Mesolithic peoples emerge like shadows in the wake of the last Ice Age. That they were materially primitive cannot be doubted, but whether that was because of an innate crudeness or a simple lack of resources and social structure is open to question. Certainly the sophistication of their cave paintings, their stone tools and possible bone calendars suggests that they may have been the decimated remnants of a former culture of some achievement that did their best to cope with the results of a massive global catastrophe. If the polar ice sheets moved down on Europe and North America tomorrow, how well would we fare?

Whatever the case, it was not until the Neolithic period that people began to settle, farm, and monumentalize their sacred sites in the British landscape. The 'Bronze' and 'Iron' ages seem to have been induced by the influence of other peoples coming into the British Isles.

Henges, megalithic barrows, long barrows and cursuses are amongst the structures belonging to the Neolithic period. Long barrows are earthen mounds which sometimes contained interments and sometimes did not. Moreover, there is some excavational evidence that the mounds covered open sites marked out by wooden poles that had been in use for centuries before. Long barrows were not simply graves.

Possibly associated with the long barrows were the cursus structures: these are great earthen avenues of ditches, usually running in straight lengths, or in connected straight segments, across country beginning nowhere and going nowhere. They simply start and stop. There is no mystery about their construction, but their purpose is unknown. The longest so far discovered is in Dorset and that runs for about six miles. The ravages of weather and time have meant that most of these features are now only visible from the air as crop marks.

Henges are large circular areas defined by ditches and banks of earth. Most of them were composed only of earth with probable wooden superstructures, but a few of the more famous ones, such as Avebury and Stonehenge, also had large stones added to the overall concept.

These henges were major undertakings, especially for the non-mechanical societies of the Neolithic period. It has been claimed, for example, that Avebury, in Wiltshire, must have taken something like five hundred years to construct. Not only is there the deep ditch and the inner settings of megaliths; there are also two stone avenues approaching the site and surrounding features such as Silbury Hill, which were probably part of the overall concept. Silbury on its own is an engineering feat: at 130 feet in height it is the largest man-made mound in Europe. Originally thought to have been a Bronze Age burial mound, recent research has confirmed that it belongs to the Neolithic period and that it almost certainly never contained a burial. All that excavators have found is a mysteriously empty chamber deep within the artificial hill.

Several hundred stones were deployed at Avebury, each of them weighing anything up to fifty tons or more. Attempts at re-erecting fallen stones at the site this century have shown just how difficult it is to handle such huge megaliths. The Neolithic megalith builders must have used substantial wooden sleds to bring the stones in off the surrounding downlands. Aubrey Burl[1] has suggested that ropes to cope with such stones were probably made from rawhide thongs plaited into hawsers 15cm thick. For one stone, Burl estimates, the hides of a hundred head of cattle would have been required to make the necessary rawhide ropes.

This phenomenal effort must have gone on for centuries, the plan of the undertaking passed from generation to generation by word of mouth (for the Neolithic peoples were, of course, pre-literate) for a period longer than our own much-vaunted Industrial Age. And yet traditional prehistorians picture the

Neolithic period as peopled by crude barbarians, arranged in feudal tribes, suffering from all manner of diseases; crippled, murderous, under-fed.

Sites like Avebury show that this cannot be the whole picture even if it is partially correct. Avebury was not constructed by crippled members of a fragmented culture, and that, really, is all there is to it. There had to be physically strong, intelligent people and sufficient social stability to have guaranteed the generations-long continuity of concept. Sooner or later the orthodox prehistorians are going to have to think again—and perhaps a little harder.

The most famous henge of all, Stonehenge, some miles to the south of Avebury, was commenced in the Neolithic period but had alterations and additions made to it over several centuries so that the latest phases of its construction were still being undertaken well into the Bronze Age. A significant feature of Stonehenge is the presence of the bluestones (the smaller stones at the site). These tell us that the megalith builders did not monumentalize their sacred sites by heaping up whatever dirt and rocks were to hand, like a child constructing a sandcastle on the beach. On the contrary, there are many sites where great stones were brought considerable distances to be erected at specific locations. Nowhere is this more true than at Stonehenge. The bluestones are believed to have been brought from Preseli in South Wales (the nearest source of the stone). A land-and-water journey of two hundred miles or more. This tells us that the *material* that went into the constructions was important to the builders. At Stonehenge, even the 'local' gargantuan sarsen stones, comprising the later trilithon uprights and lintel features that we usually associate with the site, were brought from distances further than twenty miles away on the surrounding plain. The centuries-long evolution of Stonehenge tells us clearly, too, that *place* was important to prehistoric consciousness.

Again, henges are not fully understood. The consensus of current opinion is that they were ceremonial centres. Even this might not be completely accurate. Euan McKie, pointing out that at least some of the henges supported wooden structures, has suggested that the henges may have housed the 'universities' of early Bronze Age astronomer-priests.[2] C. A. Newham and, later, Gerald Hawkins[3] put forward evidence that Stonehenge could have been used for precise astronomical observations, an idea studied at the beginning of this century by one of the fathers of astro-archaeology, Sir Norman Lockyer.

It is possible that the henges were more secular than sacred in nature. But, as will be suggested, it may not be possible to separate secular and religious, or scientific and magical, functions in these early societies.

Chambered barrows also belong to the Neolithic period. These are long earthen structures that are distinguishable from the simple earthen long barrows by containing stone-lined chambers and passages. They are faced at their entrances with megaliths. A famous example is the West Kennet chambered barrow near Avebury. Although sometimes referred to as tombs, these structures were certainly 'open' for much of their working lives. While interments were undoubtedly made in many of these types of site, one set of bones seem to have been moved aside to make way for another, and so on. There is some excavational evidence, apparently, that activities of some sort were carried out in front of these chambered mounds. They seem to have been temples in which sepulchral activities only played a part. In some of these sites only odd scraps of bone, and animal bones at that, have been found, which perhaps should caution us that it is unwise to claim that sepulchral activity was involved *at all* in the primary conception of such sites. It may have been a later function applied to such sites, or the deposit of bones may have had a magical rather than a sepulchral significance.

Dolmen structures—upright stones supporting a capstone —are believed to be the denuded central chambers of megalithic barrows, though this view is not shared by everyone.

The construction of stone circles clearly began in the Neolithic period, but the majority of them are believed to have been erected in the Neolithic-Bronze Age 'overlap' period. They range from several feet to a few hundred feet in diameter; the majority are truly circular but many are elliptical or of various egg-shaped groundplans. In some circles there is a clear indication that the deliberate usage of stone height was sought for various effects, and in even fewer instances there seems to have been a deliberate effort to erect stones so that a perfectly horizontal surface was produced. Most circles are assembled from unworked stones but there are exceptions to this. The functions behind these stone circles is, as ever, unknown. Even their age is uncertain, being derived from carbon-dating of circumstantial material found at such sites (which may not necessarily be contemporary) and from astronomical dating based on the assumption that many such sites were used for astronomical observations. True stone circles have a largely different distribution in Britain to the henges and the circles that sometimes occur within henges should perhaps be thought of as fulfilling some other purpose to that of the 'simple' circle.

There are thousands of extant standing stones, or monoliths, ranging in size from the largest British example—the Rudstone monolith at over twenty-five feet—to examples only a few feet in height. In some cases such megaliths were dragged distances of some miles before being erected, again hinting that certain places had specific qualities sought by the builders. Again, standing stones were put up in the Neolithic period but many of those now surviving are considered to have been erected during the Bronze Age.

Long rows of stones, usually small ones, occur mainly— though not exclusively—on Dartmoor. No one seems able to even hazard a guess at the function of these, though a generalized astronomical purpose has been suspected, and they are usually dated to the Bronze Age as well.

Round barrows—tumuli—are more confidently ascribed to the Bronze Age, and are usually considered as burial structures. They are earthen monuments of a round plan but having a variety of profiles, though even here the function of such features has to be naggingly uncertain, because some tumuli in Cornwall seem not to have covered burials and to have been constructed from non-local clays.

Stone mounds, cairns constructed from heaped-up boulders, also seem to belong to a similar period and to have been associated with interment. Such features are found particularly on moorland and mountainous terrain where it can be seen that they also possessed sighting functions—often on moorland it is noticeable that they are set at the extreme limits of perception one from another, and in hill country they are often conspicuously placed on 'false crests' rendering them clearly visible from valleys.

Many hills in Britain bear evidence of prehistoric activity— minimal traces as at Windmill Hill overlooking Avebury, to the grand ditches on Maiden Castle in Dorset. The more evident earthworks on such hills usually date from the Iron Age and such features are often labelled as 'hillforts' or 'British camps'. While there can be no doubt that some of these hilltops were further fortified and were used as sanctuaries in times of battle, there is also evidence that many of these features were never occupied. There are even examples of 'hillforts' occurring not on hills but on low ground which was militarily unsound! So their complete function is still not fully understood and their convenient usage as forts in a few instances may not necessarily relate to their primary purpose. What is clear is that some hills that have undoubted Iron Age earthworks around them also bear traces of much earlier usage. Maiden Castle has evidence not only of Iron Age usage but also contains the more subtle, eroded remains of earthworks stretching back at least two millenia earlier. Again, at the Trundle, an Iron Age fort overlooking Goodwood racecourse in Sussex, there are nearly obscured Neolithic earthworks. Windmill Hill was a gathering point for people for the best part of a thousand years before even Neolithic Avebury was constructed. As Evan Hadingham puts it: 'Men and women were gathering on prominent hilltops in southern England as far back as 4200 B.C.'.[1] We may justifiably ask why. And even more importantly, why should particular hilltops have been favoured over thousands of years in some cases? The importance of place, the concept of the *genius loci*, presents itself again. What was it that made a place sacred?

Different structures probably had different purposes—and the functions of even similar types of monument may have differed to some extent—but the old stones especially convey the most esoteric mood. Here, at these remains, we sense that some spiritual, shamanistic, non-secular function was performed. We find ourselves attempting to plumb the depths of our racial, cellular memories. Yet archaeology tells us little of real substance more than the information already given in these few pages; it holds some of the answers to the prehistoric enigma, but by no means all of them.

There are alternative researchers into remote antiquity. They can be grouped together under a single multi-disciplinary umbrella, although some of the researchers, perhaps, would not like to think of their contribution being related to certain other ones. Nowadays, this dynamic arena of research, thought and speculation tends to be termed 'Earth Mysteries' or 'Geomancy'.

One of these groups of alternative researchers into the mysteries of the past consists of the dowsers. Popularly known as 'water-divining' or 'water-witching', dowsing is a method of finding many other things besides water: missing objects, murder victims, oil and other minerals are all equally dowsable. In fact, probably the first Western description and illustration of dowsing—in Agricola's *De Re Metallica* of 1556—relates to the use of dowsing in geological surveys for mining purposes. Dowsing consists of the practitioner seeking his chosen requirement by means of a pendulum or one of the forms of dowsing rod, be it forked twig or a pair of cannibalized wire coathangers! The dowser keeps a physical or mental 'sample' of the sought-for item before him, and when the target is reached the dowsing instrument responds in a certain way in the dowser's hands telling him he is over the correct spot. In fact, the dowsing instrument is believed to act simply as an amplifier of subtle muscular responses within the dowser's own body. Very good dowsers are able to divine simply with their hands. Experiments have shown that some dowsers can be rendered insensitive by having parts of their body shielded by metal plates[5].

Dowsing appears to be a general term covering a range of little-known human sensitivities. While on-site dowsing for water and minerals seems to be based on the body's ability to respond to surprisingly minute electromagnetic cues in the physical environment, it is also possible to dowse from maps and photographs. This *remote dowsing* suggests that the dowsing ability can draw on ESP faculties[6].

The late Guy Underwood discovered by dowsing that megalithic sites—and some earthen structures and even certain ancient churches—stood over what he called 'blind springs' (the apparent meeting of underground water courses). He discovered other dowsable patterns—water lines, aquastats and so on—that formed his 'geodetic system'[7]. Ancient sites seemed related to this system of subterranean features. Underwood noted that animals and insects tended to congregate over blind springs and he had no doubts that ancient peoples also had an affinity for such places. Other dowsers also discovered that underground water seemed particularly associated with the siting of ancient structures, Captain F. L. M. Boothby and Reginald A. Smith among them[8]. Underwood was in no doubt that 'water divining was part of prehistoric religions'.

But as British dowser Tom Graves makes clear[9], other dowsers were finding this connection with ancient sites and considerably more besides. Dowsers such as Bill Lewis, John Williams as well as Graves himself have, for many years now, been detecting *above-ground* energies at megalithic and other

7   Tracing mineral lodes with a diviner's rod (from Roessler, *Speculum metallurgicum politissimum*, 1700). The illustration shows miners locating veins of ore by the use of dowser's rods, whilst the limits of the lodes are pegged.

old sites. Standing stones, for example, seemed sheathed in a helix of some form of force, the spiral twists of which reverse at certain points in each lunation and which are very susceptible to changes in the electromagnetic environment. This helix of subtle power creates between five and seven 'nodes' of influence in a megalith; two below ground, possibly associated with Underwood's geodetic system, one at about ground level and the rest at different points up the stone. These nodes all have different effects noticeable to a dowser. The fourth and sixth nodes seem to be associated with 'overground' lines of force connecting a megalith with certain local stones and, in some cases, going off into the distance from a site. Graves states that these overground lines are analogous to masers or lasers, in that they seem to be carrier-beams for occasional powerful pulses of dowsable energy. No one is yet clear where in the electromagnetic spectrum such strange forces fit in. Some faint hearts are already taking the line of least resistance in their thinking and are postulating non-physical, 'astral', or whatever, forces. This is, I suppose, easier and more picturesque than the unglamorous grind of attempting to calibrate this dowsing response at ancient sites against physical detection methods so that other forms of measurement can be introduced.

Not only dowsers, but psychics too have stated, over the years, that prehistoric sites have mysterious forces operating around them. Psychometrists (sensitives who can pick up images and information from objects and locations) have repeatedly claimed that the stone circles were erected for the purpose of drawing down cosmic power and that they attract spirits or entities of various sorts.[10]

The ages-old testimony of folklore also suggests that there are peculiar properties about ancient sites. Faeries are said to inhabit the prehistoric mounds and earthworks; the barrows and stone circles are said to be enchanted; stories abound of people falling victim to other time-space realities at such places. The old stones were once people who were petrified for dancing or playing music on the sabbath,[11] or they rise out of the ground at midnight and revolve, dance or go down to a nearby stream to drink. Mysterious tunnels are said to run beneath some of the sites. Circles are bewitched, so the number of their stones cannot be counted. The stones have the power to heal; they can bring down lightning and storm. They bring ill-luck to desecrators. Treasure that cannot be found or removed exists beneath many sites.

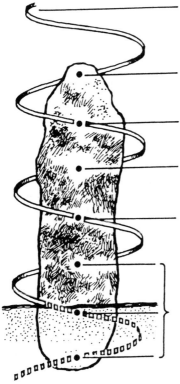

Energy collection/emission takes a spiral form which reverses direction, on a lunar cycle, on the 6th day after new and full moon. The energy may be 'tapped' or transmuted at various points on the stone.

Point 7: Acts directly on spine muscles of dowser, producing a violent electric-shock-like catatonic reaction.

Point 6: No direct action on dowser; but 'transmits' as long-distance straight-line overground communications.

Point 5: Acts directly on dowser's balance, thrusting dowser to left or right; direction of apparent thrust changes on the lunar cycle.

Point 4: No direct action on dowser; but transmits short-distance ('interval', stone-to-stone) straight-line overground communications.

Points 3 to 1: No direct action on dowser; but link up in some way—not as yet understood—with Underwood's patterns.

(as described by Tom Graves)

8   Identification of the energy nodes or points which some dowsers are able to detect on standing stones (*Ian Thomson after Tom Graves*)

Such legends are legion throughout Britain. Undoubtedly they are pictorial, allegorical storytelling and the fruits of superstition relating to sites that the peasantry through the ages must have held in awe and dread. Some megaliths are called 'hoarstones'—'hoar' is a Saxon word implying age, 'grey or hoary with age', so even as long ago as the Saxon period such stones were recognized as being ancient. But the question is— are there seeds of a real folk *memory* encapsulated within these colourful stories? The basic consistency of such traditions argues strongly that such is the case. I believe the peasantry, the old folk living close to the land, knew that the ancient sites had strange powers and properties.

It has been folk knowledge for centuries if not millenia that the midsummer Sun rises behind the Heel Stone at Stonehenge when viewed from the centre of the sarsen circle. The work this century of the astro-archaeologists (or archaeoastronomers) such as Lockyer, Newham, Hawkins and, particularly, Pro- fessor Alexander Thom, strongly suggests that at least that piece of folk knowledge was soundly based. Research into ancient astronomy strongly indicates that many other stone circles could have been used in prehistory for astronomical functions to produce not only general calendrical information suitable for an agricultural society, but also to provide far more sophisticated understanding of lunar motion(a complex study) leading to the ability to predict solar eclipses and other esoteric knowledge relating to cosmic behaviour.

It is really on the basis of Thom's work that astro-archaeology now stands as a serious contender for consideration as an acceptable science in its own right. Thom, an engineer, spent decades of his life surveying hundreds of stone circles around Britain. In most cases his were the first professional surveys carried out at such sites. His first book[12] in 1967 was like a 'well- packaged parcel bomb', as the distinguished prehistorian Professor R. J. C. Atkinson put it, in that it took a while for the complex evidence it contained to register fully with orthodox archaeologists. The implications of Thom's work are stunning and, if correct, it could mean the end of any notions that people late Neolithic and early Bronze Age societies with ignorant savages.

Thom's research indicates three basic findings: that stone circles were not just crude circular configurations of stones but were laid out to specific groundplans of some geometrical sophistication; that a basic unit of measurement was employed (Thom called it the 'Megalithic Yard'—2.72 feet), and that circles acted as backsights for distant foresights composed of natural and artificial features marking significant moments in the solar and lunar cycles. All these findings are statistical but the data base established by Thom and his co-workers is currently unsurpassed.

All his findings have come, or are about to come, under question by other researchers—there has been some quibbling about the absolute standardization of the Megalithic Yard everywhere in Britain, for example—but this is to be expected. His work has touched a few nerves. And there can be no doubt that aspects of Thom's findings are open to adjustment, correction and improvement; but the main thrust of his findings have shown that some unexpectedly sophisticated activities were going on four thousand years ago in Britain.

The stones at the Castlerigg circle in Cumbria, for example, may seem like a meaningless jumble until you watch an event such as the midwinter sunrise from the site. The first beam of golden light raying over the snowy mountains streaks across the

Midwinter sunrise, breaking across the Castlerigg Circle, Cumbria, on a line indicated by two low stones. (*Author's photo*)

circle, the two lowest stones forming a clear 'cleft' or alignment within the circle, precisely on the relevant orientation. As you walk round the circle, stopping on other alignments indicated in Thom's survey of the site, the stones and skyline features again resolve into clearly indicated lines of sight. The language of the stones is easy to decipher for those with eyes to see. The jumble has, until now, been in the minds of modern people, determined to establish their superior intelligence and progressive way of life by proving their ancestors to be more savage and more stupid than themselves. An unconscious self-interest has clouded some of modern archaeology's perception of pre-history. The ingrained belief in a linear evolution from savage to enlightened modern man done as much damage to the study of prehistory as the ETH has done to the study of UFOs.

Even more remarkable astronomical behaviour has recently come to light in the current research of Martin Brennan and his fellow researchers in Ireland![13] Brennan began his study of the exceptional Neolithic remains in Ireland by attempting to decipher the enigmatic carvings to be found on so many Irish megaliths: spirals, chevrons, lozenges, circles, petals, cup-and-ring markings and the like. These strange ciphers had befuddled many other researchers. The breakthrough came at Newgrange.

Standing at Newgrange one can have no doubt that the Neolithic megalith builders were a race apart—they were not ignorant savages. Newgrange is the greatest of all chambered barrows, in Meath's Boyne Valley in the company of two similar mounds, Knowth and Dowth, and lesser tumuli. Newgrange towers over the visitor; it is like a structure from some other world. In a sense, it is. There is no doubt, in the presence of such awesome megalithic majesty, that the oldest and wisest Neolithic peoples came from the west of the British Isles, wherever they may have come from before that.

Newgrange is a mound of alternating layers of stone and soil. This in turn was probably covered with quartz. Around the perimeter of the mound are slabs of decorated stones known as kerbstones. Surrounding the whole structure is a stone circle which probably pre-dates the mound itself. Entering the mound, it is necessary to go down a stone-lined passage some sixty-two feet in length. At the end of this is a twenty-foot high stone chamber with a corbelled ceiling; there are side-chambers off this. Everywhere are to be seen carvings—and these exist even where they cannot be seen without dismantling the structure! This suggests that the function of such incised glyphs was other than simple decoration. A few scraps of material that may indicate cremation interments have been found—but was so mighty a structure built just for that? Hardly. Above the entrance to the passage there has been discovered a 'light box' which admits a beam of light at sunrise on midwinter's day. This twenty-yard long laser-like beam of light moves down the passage until it hits the far end of the main chamber. Those fortunate individuals who have witnessed this event claim that the dark, dank interior of the chamber (the structure was more waterproof before reconstruction, apparently!) is then illuminated in a golden light; the stones take on the appearance of living gold. As the minutes pass, the solar beam gradually moves back out of the chamber, the full effect not to be re-enacted for another year. Archaeologists claim to have discovered this occurrence at Newgrange but Brennan has information which states that an old lady, acting as guide to the site, noticed it as long ago as 1919![14]

One of Britain's leading geomantic researchers, Nigel Pennick, points out that this astronomical function in passage mounds like Newgrange 'indicates that the barrows were in reality celestial observatories and that any burials, as in a modern cathedral, were by-products of the sanctity of the site, not primary motives for construction'.[15] In a letter to me, Brennan has put it more bluntly—'the only things buried at

Newgrange Entrance Stone.

Newgrange are the beliefs of the archaeologists'.

One of the kerbstones visually blocks the entrance to Newgrange. It contains the famous double-spiral motif. It also has a vertical groove exactly on the midwinter alignment. Brennan, like John Michell before him, wondered if this was the Neolithic glyph for alignment. He checked kerbstone 52, on the other side of the mound and thus also on the midwinter alignment: there was another clear, vertical groove. Subsequently, Brennan's research has revealed other carved vertical lines on other demonstrable astronomical alignments in monuments. He feels that lightbeams from the Moon and, just possibly, Venus, were also employed in the Neolithic chambers around Ireland.

Discovering what he believes to be a unit of measure employed by the builders of Newgrange and other Irish monuments, Brennan has found that some of the stone carvings, with the addition of gnomons of the appropriate length, could have been employed as sundials and moondials of an advanced nature. The 'laser beam effect' seems to have been a more accurate method of marking the course of Sun and Moon.

Some miles away from the Boyne Valley, at Cairn T on the Loughcrew mountains, Brennan and his colleagues have witnessed the entrance of sunbeams at the equinoxes. At the vital moment the penetrating beam of light halts on a petalled symbol before starting its journey out of the mound. Is the Sun here pointing out its own symbol? Are the actions of the Sun and Moon the software that decodes the stone carvings?

In Ireland, and particularly in the Boyne Valley, it is difficult to avoid the feeling that some of the structures are parts of a Neolithic museum, with items like alignments clearly marked and with the instruments of the Neolithic science still functioning. The notations of that science, the carvings, are clearly displayed. They encode the measurements, the computers and the understanding of the Neolithic astronomer-shamans. The colossal, monumental structuring of the mounds and stones invites the suspicion that this 'museum' was built to last into an age when understanding would again flower. Why else were the mounds designed to function over vast periods of time—why else was the Newgrange light-box made sufficiently wide to accommodate the subtle changes in the position of the midwinter rising sun for several millenia? The Irish megaliths are time-capsules of ancient knowledge.

If astro-archaeology is almost accepted as a valid study and the work of dowsers and psychics totally dismissed by orthodoxy, the ley theory hangs in a limbo in between. In 1921, Alfred Watkins, a prominent Herefordshire business man and public figure, then in his sixty-sixth year, noted that certain ancient sites in his county seemed to fall into alignments across the landscape. The more he studied this pattern, the more fieldwork he undertook on it, the more questions he asked, the stronger the evidence became in supporting his initial observation.

Prehistoric sites, and certain later features such as pre-Reformation churches on evolved locations, formed the markers in this network of alignments. Watkins called these lines 'leys' for what he felt to be good etymological reasons. He considered that they were the remnants of traders' routes laid down in the Neolithic period, hence the title of his main book on the subject, *The Old Straight Track*, first published in 1925.

The idea of surveyed alignments across the countryside in the prehistoric period was an anathema to establishment archaeologists, who reacted with some venom to Watkins' work. That was to be expected in the 1920s, but the poses struck then have lasted more with stubborness than validity up to the present time. It was only in 1981 that a leading archaeologist was prepared to discuss the whole theory in public in a reasoned way.[16] The most comprehensive and up-to-date account of the whole subject of leys is given in *The Ley Hunter's Companion*.[17] It is sufficient to indicate here that the modern research into leys increasingly confirms their actuality. Every year, from British research, from studies of alignments in Ireland, from comparative material such as the old straight tracks of Peru and Bolivia, the ley theory grows in stature.

The link between leys and UFOs was forged by Tony Wedd picking up on Aimé Michel's work on orthotenies, as mentioned in Chapter 1. Michel's orthotenies have apparently been dismissed by ufologists after a brief love affair, but the notion of ancient sites and the alignments between them being linked with the incidence of UFO activity was indelibly made. Ideas that leys were lines of telluric force were put forward; power lines, veins of energy, utilized by ancient people and visiting spacecraft. It was crazy, magical, marvellous stuff. In the great revival of the ley theory in the 1960s these ideas, well-seasoned with the visionary ambience created by the widespread use of hallucinogenic substances, created a fresh vision, a previously un-thought-of possibility. It made fertile ground for the infamous and erroneous 'ancient astronaut' school of thought to take root. The link between the remote past and UFOs had been made.

It is my feeling that a genuine racial or cellular memory had burst through under the prevailing extraordinary conditions, and even if the details produced were largely imaginary, the gut reaction was correct. And the hunch is still being worked on, as this book alone testifies. The idea was probably correct for all the wrong reasons.

As I indicated in Chapter 1, this approach to the baffling problem of the UFO mystery seemed to me to be the most fruitful. But after being fortunate enough to have been able to take part in extensive and leading research into leys I have to say that there is precious little evidence to associate them with UFOs.[18] However, the association of certain types of prehistoric site with UFO incidence is another matter, and one that Part 3 of the present work will investigate to some extent.

The keen new ley hunters of the 1960s felt they had discovered nationwide systems of leys, but more recent and careful research has shown that there is no topographical evidence for such a belief.

It is becoming clear, though, that two types of *local* ley systems exist. The most pronounced of these is the 'holy hill' pattern.[19] This was brought to the attention of British re-searchers by the work of Nigel Pennick, Prudence Jones and Michael Behrend in translating and publishing the work of pre-World War Two German researchers into geomancy.[20] One of these, Dr Josef Heinsch, a regional planner, noted a pattern of alignments involving ancient churches and certain hilltops in Germany, Britain and elsewhere. Work by Tony Morrison[21] on old straight tracks in the Andes has shown that straight lines radiated out from, or converge onto, hilltops venerated by local indians. Interestingly, another of the German researchers referred to German landscape lines as *hielige linien*—holy lines. Pennick has pointed out that 'the omphalos/holy mountain/four directions represented by road layouts . . . is found from Japan to South America via the Middle East and Europe'.[22] Ian Thomson and I picked up the pattern in Britain while research-ing *The Ley Hunter's Companion* quite inadvertently. Only after publication did we see what we had uncovered: famous holy hills such as those marked by chalk figures at Wilmington, Cerne Abbas and Uffington all displayed well-indicated alignments through prehistoric earthworks on their summits from old ecclesiastical structures, presumably marking evolved pagan shrine sites, at their bases. Other holy hills, such as St. Catherine's Hill at Winchester, or Dinedor Hill at Hereford, also display the same attraction for alignments. Most of them are of very similar orientations.

The other pattern is related to stone circles. This is not so clearly defined but this is probably because insufficient research has been carried out on it so far. What has been found is that some stone circles have short alignments—of only a few miles in length—coming into their circumferences. These lines are very precise as they are marked invariably by standing stones only. John Michell was the first to give a good example of this type of line.[23] Another is that presented by mathematician Bob Forrest.[24]

Both these patterns may give a clue as to a possible function of leys, a clue I will pick up briefly and speculatively in Chapter 8. It can be said that these patterns are the only ones supported by strong evidence to relate to leys; and though leys may well have dowsable characteristics—they may be synonymous with the overground lines mentioned earlier—it is important to state here that there is no clear evidence that leys themselves are channels of terrestrial energy. The idea may be correct, but it is *only* an idea at present. It may be that the alignments are simply the involuntary products of the location of the places of power—marked by the sites themselves.

There seems to be a worldwide blank in human memory regarding ancient linear features. We do not know why the leys, the Andean lines, the stone rows or cursuses were built. The only hint is that straight features in the landscape facilitate the passage of spirits—the ancient Chinese *Feng Shui* geomancers said it, the Bolivian indians claim it and the Irish talk of faery paths. We need to know more about the nature of these 'spirits' flitting through the landscape. Leys are a mystery at the heart of a mystery: it is that which makes their study so important.

We have already seen that the prehistoric sites themselves have a record of being special places of power. This was further confirmed in the late 1970s by Francis Hitching when he was researching his book and film *Earth Magic*.[25] The Welsh master dowser Bill Lewis had shown Hitching a stone that possessed the helical sheath of energy detectable by dowsing. Hitching was

Bill Lewis, one of Britain's leading dowsers, using angle rods to dowse a burial within the Rollright Circle. (*Author's photo*)

persuaded by Lewis to bring in a physicist to see if any instrumentally measurable effects could be noted. At Hitching's instigation, Dr Eduardo Balanovski visited the megalith in question, near Crickhowell in Wales, armed with a gaussmeter —an instrument for detecting magnetic field strength. Anomalies were found around the stone that were much greater than would normally have been expected. Balanovski felt the positioning of the stone was not accidental. 'The people who put it there,' he said, 'knew about its power, even if they didn't know about electromagnetism.' Further work at the stone by Balanovski and Professor John Taylor confirmed the anomalies; moreover, Lewis had marked in chalk the dowsable nodes on the megalith and most of these showed a marked deflection on the gaussmeter's dial compared to elsewhere on the stone.

So the situation had become compounded: not only did folk-lore, the psychics and dowsers claim strange properties at pre-historic sites, but preliminary scientific results endorsed the idea. The time seemed ripe for a closer look at the whole issue of anomalous energies at ancient sacred sites.

In November 1977 *The Ley Hunter* magazine called a meeting of around twenty scientists, dowsers, electronic technicians and other experts to investigate the feasibility of setting up a project designed to study over a period of years the nature of the curious forces apparently present at some prehistoric sites. It was

Sig. Lonegren of the American Society of Dowsers, testing 'the fifth node' on a Rollright stone. (*Author's photo*)

decided to run a programme of physical monitoring concurrent with a psychic archaeological schedule using dowsers, sensitives and biofeedback methods where possible. It was hoped that by the end of the project there would be some correlations between results recorded by both approaches. Dr G. V. Robins was to co-ordinate the physical monitoring and John Steele the psychic effort. My role was overall co-ordination.

Being a typically British, shoe-string affair, it was not until October 1978 that the first on-site, practical work got under way. The programme was called 'The Dragon Project' in reference to the ancient Chinese geomantic practice of using the dragon symbol for terrestrial currents. The Rollright Stones about twenty miles north-west of Oxford became the Project's field headquarters. The stones were suitable as a test site for a number of reasons, including the fact that the stones comprise a megalithic complex of circle, dolmen and monolith with the circle being privately owned. The site has a set of legends attached to it second to none. At Rollright, the stories relate, the stones can move, they are people—a king and his men—turned to stone, the stones cannot be counted, and so on.

To begin with, one-day visits to the stones were carried out by various researchers, but when funds allowed this gave way to occasional round-the-clock monitoring of the site. Slowly and extremely painfully data began to be collected on apparent ambient effects taking place in the vicinity of the megaliths. Some of these results were checked at certain other megalithic sites as well as at non-megalithic locations as a control.

This is not the place to attempt a full account of the programme's findings; but as the emerging, embryonic results of the investigation to date may have a bearing on the UFO problem, a general reference to certain findings is called for.

It is easy to find literature today dramatically claiming that megaliths possess energies and weird forces. So they might; but such speculation comes cheap and easy. The *real* front-line research involves more sweat than glory, more grind than results. What findings there are have been hard won.

One effect that *seems* to occur around the stones, at certain times of the year only and most consistently around dawn, is the production of ultrasound. This is sound beyond the normal range of hearing, like that produced by a dog whistle. There was no predicted reason why such an obscure phenomenon should occur; we only monitored for it because of anecdotal inform-

Dr G. V. Robins with one of the Dragon Project's ultrasonic detectors at the Rollright Circle. (*Author's photo*)

ation passed on to us from a zoologist who had inadvertently noticed that an ancient site gave off ultrasound one dawn when he was studying bat behaviour with an electronic detector.[26] The presence and behaviour of apparent ultrasonic emissions at the Rollright Stones were discovered and manually recorded by Dr Robins. The effect has been noted too at other megalithic sites, to a lesser extent near natural stone outcrops and not at all at concrete features also monitored at dawn.

Rollright is in the depths of the countryside—where could the ultrasonic effect be coming from? It is possible that geological movement in fault lines can produce ultrasonic emissions (Chapter 3), and such movement is most likely to occur at dawn (Chapter 4). There is a surface fault close to Rollright (less than a mile away). This could be of significance in the siting of stone circles. But Robins' orthodox though advanced work with energy states of stone has led to another possibility—and it is only that at the moment. Robins' hypothesis, based on data currently to hand, is that microwave radiation from the sun at dawn could possibly energize the stones, causing populations of trapped electrons within them to vibrate. This is how Robins has put it:

There are many figures of speech which invoke the intractable nature of stone, and popularly, these are borne out by the physical appearance of the stone. A look at the structure of the stone at a deeper level, however, reveals a totally different picture. I have described elsewhere the so-called 'defect' structure of stone which exists as an incomplete silicate lattice. This lattice, however, is not empty. Among other things it contains a shifting population of trapped electrons, split from the lattice by ionizing radiation (either from radioactive elements in the lattice, from surrounding soil or from cosmic rays) that are trapped at imperfections in the lattice or in microcrystalline cavities.

These electrons form an equilibrium population in that they are continually being formed and trapped while others are escaping from their lattice traps and migrating through the stone. At any given time, therefore, a stone will contain a small but definite drifting potential and in a standing stone, it is reasonable to expect this current to drift to earth. This electron population prompted us to consider that the role of stone in any manifestation of earth energy might be in producing electrical phenomena, but we still had to consider how the electrons might be energized to provide more than this minute background 'noise'. In other words, the electrons could be thought of as potential current carriers but their capacity could be enhanced by their absorption of suitable electromagnetic energy. We are considering here almost a semiconductor effect in that if sufficient electrons can be energized they will be freed from their lattice traps and create a large current, and it may seem unfamiliar to consider stone in the same way as our modern transistors and integrated circuits.

The electromagnetic energizing of the electrons can only occur within narrowly defined parameters. If the energy is too great, the electron will transfer it to the lattice, if too small it will not be absorbed. The radiation which satisfied all criteria is microwave radiation in that electrons can absorb it undergoing 'spin-flip' —that is, change of spin . . .

In looking for a natural, low-level microwave source we first considered the Sun. The Sun emits electromagnetic radiation through most of the spectrum, and the Earth's atmosphere blocks most of it, except for two important 'windows': the optical window, which allows through visible light, and the radio window, which allows wavelengths of about 1cm to 30cm through. The microwave region of interest is just at the edge of this optical window, and it might be postulated that at sunrise, when the disc is just clearing the horizon, this microwave region will be maximized in that the shorter wavelength visible and infrared radiation are only just clearing the horizon whereas the longer wavelength radiowaves are ineffective (it might be noted that the red colour of the rising and setting sun is explicable in terms of the maximization of the long wavelengths when the sun is at the horizon). We were led to expect, therefore, that a microwave energizing effect might be expected at the time of sunrise, and we determined to carry out a monitoring programme at dawn.

Robins goes on to postulate that some of the energy produced by vibration of the electrons in their lattice traps could possibly be transduced through the lattice structure of the stone into pressure waves such as ultrasound. According to this view, the ultrasonics would be a side-effect of an electromagnetic process occurring within the megaliths. Robins continues:

> We are tempted to view the circle, with its relation to menhir and dolmen, as a three dimensional dielectric antenna whose orientation allows maximum energy transduction at the time around the equinoxes. Such an interpretation raises some interesting questions concerning the form and function of stone circles and their place within the leyline hypothesis . . . Thom-type geometries and alignments seem too sophisticated and profuse to be accounted for by the calendrical or ritual explanations, and the subtle geometries of many sites are often unnecessary for their astronomical purpose. Moreover, *a major objection to the simple calendrical use of stone circles is that weather conditions and ground cover could well have made precise sightings difficult in ancient times.* These three objections may be overcome by our observations in that if the site geometry is the major determinant of energy levels and exchanges, then the dimensions of the circle and its total astronomical alignment, together with its exact placing in the landscape, are all essential elements in the energy transduction process. Furthermore, since the atmosphere is transparent to the energizing microwaves, cloud cover and horizon haze are unimportant factors, and this has been amply borne out by monitoring in all weather conditions.
>
> The implication of this viewpoint is a large one: if the calendrical and ritual purposes are subsumed within this energy transduction process, then it seems that ancient man must have had an awareness —*at whatever level*—of the energy exchange system involved and sought to manipulate it, although for what ends we are not sure. Two possibilities that have emerged are the healing effect associated with weak electric fields, and the enhanced grain germination rates achieved with some ultrasonic frequencies, but this analysis of uses has barely begun.

This last point could mean that there is a grain of truth in the legend linking certain megaliths with healing and fecundity. It

Equipment used on the Dragon Project for Kirlian sound scanning of megalithic energy fields; at the base of one of the stones in the Rollright Circle. (*Author's photo*)

has fairly recently been found, for instance, that *low* levels of carefully applied electromagnetic stimulation can speed up the healing process in humans.[28]

Robins is at pains to point out that all this is, as yet, hypothetical. But an effect has been noted and early attempts at putting it in a conceptual framework must be made. The results so far obtained by the Project in this area are too rudimentary to be placed before sceptical scientists outside of the Project; work is going on at the time of this writing in the development of the instrumentation used to a very high level so that further findings can conclusively be shown to be free of any spurious effects. While this work is going on, though, two entirely different types of ultrasonic detection device have been used at the stones. One of these is used as part of a very recent system designed to scan *living systems*. This has just begun to show changes in megalithic energy fields at dawn. The other device has also responded to what appear to be genuine, though anomalous, ultrasonic signals. But the ultrasound effect is only one out of others that the Dragon Project has noted at Rollright and other sites.

Recent work combining artificial energizing of megaliths with

Roy Cooper, local co-ordinator of the Dragon Project, at the Rollright
Stones with a geiger counter. (*Author's photo*)

geiger counter monitoring at Rollright has apparently confirmed an exo-electron presence around such stones. This result
is particularly fascinating in that certain areas in and around the
site have yielded above-average geiger counts. This was at first
thought to indicate small deposits of radioactive minerals
beneath the general area of the megaliths. This fitted in well with
what is known about different kinds of ancient sacred sites elsewhere in the world. John Steele has pointed out that native holy
sites in North America, Australia and elsewhere have been
found to be located above uranium deposits—this is at the root

of the land rights controversy in Australia, for example.[29] But it currently appears more likely that an *ionization effect* is being recorded by the geiger counters. This is particularly likely to be so as recent monitoring has shown *variations* in geiger response at peak locations.

The stones at Rollright have been photographed with infra-red film on several occasions; at dawn and at other times. Frames exposed at dawn on three occasions revealed a hazy glow appearance around the monolith near the circle, known as the King Stone. The films have been professionally examined and no mundane explanations have so far been confirmed. The effect captured on the film *may* in some way relate to an aspect of the exo-electron activity that seems to be present around the stones when energized.

It is not easy to get these results: the stones can be photo-

An anomalous effect captured on infra-red film at the Kingstone, Rollright, at one dawn in April 1979. The sun is rising off-picture to the left. A hazy glow seems to be capping the top of the stone, and stretching up into the sky. This infra-red effect has been caught on two other occasions also at dawn. (*Author's photo*)

graphed several dozen times with no unusual results for every
one 'aura' effect captured on a frame. The only successes so far
have been precisely at dawn; photographs taken in exactly the
same conditions only at other times of the day have revealed
nothing unusual. I recall telephoning the dowser Bill Lewis
about the first infra-red success we obtained. I had only got as
far as mentioning that we had apparently captured a glow-effect
around the King Stone when he cut in: 'Does it go off the top of
the stone at an angle?' I replied in the affirmative. 'I've been
dowsing that effect for the past twenty years,' Lewis muttered
matter-of-factly.

There has been, and continues to be, other types of physical
monitoring taking place as part of the Project, and other startling discoveries are being made, but it will be some time before
we can definitely confirm or reject such indications. Absolute
proof of the apparent results being obtained is likely to be forever beyond the resources of the Project. There is so much
testing and re-testing required, and an ever increasing requirement of equipment of improving sophistication, that time and
finance within the Project must become exhausted. The Dragon

The author detecting a localized area of radio anomaly in a ruined Irish
cairn. (*Photo: John Steele*)

Project must be more realistically seen as a pilot programme producing the best research to date within its area of investigation. It can only produce indications. It will be for others with better resources to follow up these early leads. The Dragon Project will have been the first such enterprise, but I hope it will not be the last.

But while we cannot claim total certainty about the results currently to hand, it has to be said that it is looking increasingly likely that the stones at Rollright (and therefore, presumably, at other megalithic sites) are acting in some way as energy stores— some form of natural capacitor system seems to be involved. This system receives its input of energy perhaps from the sun, as Robins suggests. But the ultrasonic effect, for example, behaves in ways that suggest that such a simple connection can be only part of the answer. As we will learn shortly, stone circles tend to be closely related to geological faults, so another input of energy may be from the seismo-electrical fields associated with such geological dislocations. The megalithic capacitor system would seem to have its own methods of discharging, perhaps causing ionization effects when it does do.

It also seems that human beings can sometimes discharge the stored electricity that has built up in the stones: Earth Mysteries literature is full of accounts of people touching megaliths and receiving tingle or shock sensations. There is even a Tingle Stone in Gloucestershire. David Hollingsworth, a volunteer warden at Rollright, told us that some time ago he had touched the southernmost stone of the circle early one morning and had received a shock like static electricity. He was quite relieved to learn he was not alone in having such experiences. Jack Roberts, a co-worker,with Martin Brennan in Ireland, told me how three years earlier he had touched the lintel stone separating the entrance from the light box at Newgrange around midday on one occasion and had received a static-like shock which travelled up his arm. He gingerly touched the lintel again but there was no effect—the stone had discharged. The late T. C. Lethbridge reported how he obtained a similar sensation when he was dowse-dating the Merry Maidens stone circle in Cornwall:

> As soon as the pendulum started to swing, a strange thing happened. The hand resting on the stone received a strong tingling sensation like a mild electric shock and the pendulum itself shot out until it was circling nearly horizontally to the ground. The stone

itself, which must have weighed over a ton, felt as if it were rocking and almost dancing about. This was quite alarming. . . .[30]

The sort of impression people receive by this discharge mechanism in stone might have given rise over the years to stories about megaliths dancing and moving.

There are many more accounts of this sort. Presumably, any stone will produce this effect to a greater or lesser extent when the circumstances are right. The suspicion at the moment is that the placing of the megaliths at places of power—at places where an optimum confluence of cosmic factors, subterranean water and geological conditions exists—helps to maximize the energy storage and transduction effects occurring naturally in stone. It is also possible, as Robins suggests, that the groundplan geometry noted by Professor Thom may also have an enhancing effect. The apparent early prehistoric obsession with astronomical observations also begins to make sense within such a framework.

No one is suggesting that the late Neolithic and early Bronze Age megalith builders went around in white lab coats with detection equipment when setting up their circles. Rather, it is postulated that these early peoples would have had a natural sensitivity to the world around them that has been lost or obscured by the cruder and less natural conditions surrounding us in our industrial world. There is no reason to doubt that a sensitivity of the sort we call dowsing today was employed by the megalith builders. A *New Scientist* article[31] refers to Russian geologists who now experiment with dowsing—they call it the Bio-Physical Method (BPM)—in the location of mineral deposits such as copper, lead and tin. They have found the method to be at least as accurate as traditional geological methods of measurement. The article states:

> Mineral veins and flowing ground water are both associated with geological discontinuities such as faults, fracture and shear zones, prominent joint planes, old stream channels, solution cavities in limestone, lava tubes in volcanic rocks and so on. These discontinuities cause small geophysical perturbations, in magnetic field strength for instance, that could be responsible for the dowsing reaction.

Stone circles, it will be shown, occur in just such geological areas. If this form of detection can be achieved now, why not in the past?

Moreover, it is highly likely that the sensitivity to such electromagnetic cues was greater in Neolithic and Bronze Age people than is the case today. Just how sensitive human response can become is indicated by the occasional occurrence of children who have been brought up in almost totally primary conditions, uninfluenced by modern urban environments. Usually, such children have become lost and are thought to have died but are subsequently discovered surviving like animals in the wild. In other instances, they are brought up in conditions that deprive them of the normal range of sensory input—the mysterious 'Child of Nuremburg' is an example. In May 1828 this youth turned up on the outskirts of the city with a note in his hand. It gave his name as Kaspar Hauser. When the child was taught to speak, read and write, it was possible to learn from him that he had been brought up in a closed, small cell in which he had no knowledge of night or day. When he woke he would find food and water. Occasionally, when he drank this water it would have a strange taste that would send him to sleep. On coming round he would find himself in fresh clothing. He never saw who was looking after him. On the day of his release he was propelled on foot to the edge of Nuremburg. When he found he was suffering terribly from blisters because he was so unused to walking.

His investigators found him exhibiting exceptional responses —he would retch if coffee, beer or a strong drink was even in the same room as he was, for instance. John Michell has described how sensitive this child's faculties were:

> He was sensitive to electricity. A magnet held towards him affected him peculiarly, the north pole in a different way to the south; he became an excellent rider partly through the attraction his feet had for the iron of the stirrups; a thunderstorm—he had never heard thunder in his cell—caused him violent shuddering and pain. He was also able to distinguish between different metals by passing his hand over them even when they were covered by a cloth. Professor Daumer conducted several such experiments with him using gold, silver, brass and steel. Always he could detect their presence and tell one from the other.[32]

Ultimately, the foundling of Nuremburg was to some extent 'normalized' and met an untimely and mysterious death at the hands of an unknown assailant.

There is clear evidence in cases like this that human sensitivities can achieve levels that seem almost supernatural to those of us in the modern world who have to rely on technological wizadry to overcome our descreasing natural abilities.

It is not difficult to assume that the ancient megalith builders would have been able to detect the electromagnetic fields surrounding ore deposits, fault lines and the megaliths themselves. Theirs would have been a natural science based on careful observation and a high level of sensitivity to minute physical cues. As Balanovski said, they may not have understood the powers they were dealing with in terms of electromagnetism as we do today, but they could have been aware of the occurrence of such energetic effects.

It is even conceivable that the groundplan geometry of the stone circles was not originally drawn on the ground, but was simply a *result* of the stones being placed in optimum relationships to enhance the effects being sought by the builders. Perhaps it was only after many years of observing how certain patterns kept recurring that groundplan geometry became formalized. In the same way, the marvellous geometry of snowflakes is not prepared on a drawing board; it is the end result of the way certain substances have to be structured under certain

Neolithic Stone Ball, showing carving of geometry.

conditions. All Nature is a slow motion geometrical event.

We do know the ancients had an excellent grasp of geometric principles in Nature. In the nineteenth century curious, carved stone balls began to be discovered in Neolithic structures in eastern Scotland as well as in the Orkneys and the Isle of Skye. The great geometer Keith Critchlow has written:

> When archaeologists were confronted in the second half of the last century with beautiful and precise solid geometrical figures . . . they were either reluctant to recognize their sophisticated symmetry or lacked the perceptual ability to fully appreciate it. It seems they simply didn't believe that the archaic inhabitants of Britain were capable of making or even conceiving such sophisticated mathematical forms.[33]

Critchlow reminds us that each of these carved objects, made from granite with the use of only stone implements, would have taken months and exceptional skill to produce. There can be no doubt that they were of great value to their makers or certain other members of the community. These solids are unambiguously three-dimensional geometric statements. They are not crude figurines or the like, nor can the catch-all term 'ritual object' dismiss them as we are not speculating on their use but observing the fact of the knowledge of their makers preserved in the artefacts' forms. Detailed and expert analysis by Critchlow has demonstrated the extreme sophistication of these objects. All the so-called 'Platonic solids' were carved in stone in Britain at least a millenium before Plato!

There can be no doubt that there were people in the megalith building cultures who were intelligent, highly observant, skilled manually and mentally and very sensitive to subtle forces, whatever else may have been present in those societies.

The work geologist Paul McCartney has been doing within the context of the Dragon Project has shown the larger scale geological factors associated with the siting of stone circles. If such sites are placed at points of natural power, we would expect from a geological point of view, from what has been presented in Chapter 5, that megaliths will relate to those parts of the landscape bearing evidence of major tectonic upheavals where the forces of the Earth are in greater flux than in less affected areas. Essentially, this means circles could be predicted to correlate specifically with fault lines or igneous intrusions, which are the hubs of areas of exceptional tectonic stress.

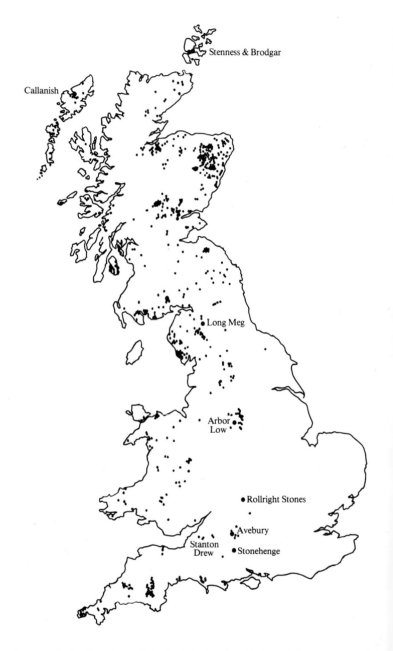

9   Stone Circles in Great Britain. Notice the high concentration in the
     north and west of the country, and their total absence in the south-east.

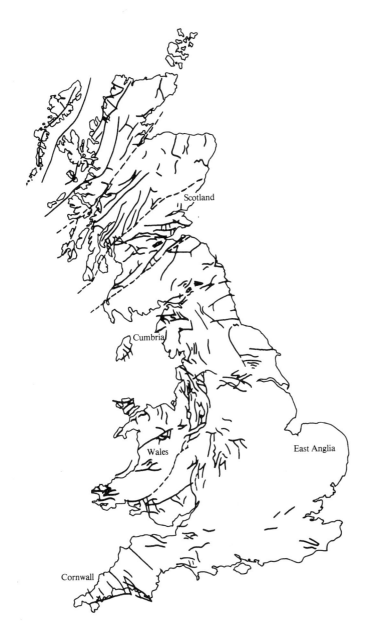

Geological Faults in Great Britain. All the major faulting systems are
illustrated. Minor localized faulting, which would unnecessarily
complicate the pattern, is omitted. (*P. McCartney*)

As long ago as 1969 John Michell was associating sacred sites with geological faulting,[34] but more by intuitive observation that anything else; the lie of the land surrounding most stone circles gives the secret away. McCartney's work has now been able to confirm this earlier suspicion. From the work he has currently done on stone circle distribution in England and Wales, McCartney is satisfied that *every stone circle in those two countries is within a mile of a surface fault or lies on an associated intrusion.*

Even in areas one would not initially associate with faulting, like that around the Rollright Stones, the pattern holds. About three-quarters of a mile away from the circle runs a local surface feature called the 'Rollright Fault'. That is the sort of pattern that is repeated throughout the country.

To obtain a clearer, and thus more generalized, picture of the association of main stone circle distribution with geologically faulted areas it is best to determine the extent of pre-Armorican rock outcrops, as these will contain the greatest number of surface faults. Elsewhere in the country these rocks have been overlaid by more recent sedimentary cover, or else they do not

Callanish Circle. (*Photo: John Glover*). Magnetic anomaly zones are recorded in the general area of this structure, and in 1981 a meteorite landed in its vicinity.

occur at all. It has already been pointed out in the previous chapter that such areas of geological stress tend to produce zones of mineral enrichment. If these three patterns in England and Wales are juxtaposed, as in Figure 12, the correlations need no further amplification.

We can take details out of this overall pattern to demonstrate that the pattern holds at al scales. Figure 13, for example, shows the relationship between stone circles and fault lines in the Outer Hebrides, off Scotland's western coast. The pattern of stone circle, fault and intrusion distribution in Cumbria tally with precision, too.

In south-west England megaliths tend to cluster on the great intrusions of Dartmoor, Bodmin Moor, and so on. This pattern is clearly evident in Figure 11; it is a pattern found also at Carnac in France, as will be shown.

In England and Wales, some 36 per cent of the land mass has outcrops of pre-Armorican rocks, the other 64 per cent having outcrops of the tectonically simpler post-Armorican sediments. The relationship suspected between stone circle distribution and

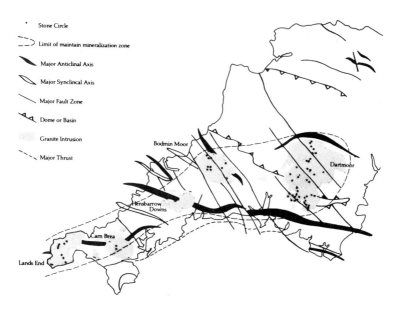

Circles and Intrusions in South-West England. All the major tectonic influences in the south-west peninsular are indicated. All the stone circles in the area fall within those tectonic boundaries.

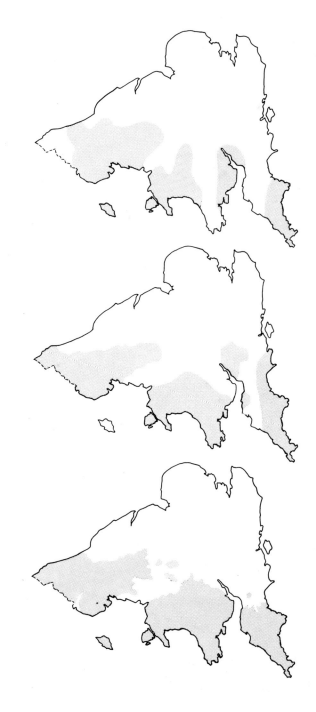

12   (a) Pre-Armorican Structure; (b) Stone Circles; (c) Mineralization zones. Maps (a) and (c) linking the tectonic influence on pre-Armorican outcrops and its associated mineralization are mimicked by the human factor of the stone circle distribution map (b). An emphatic correlation exists between the lithosphere (the Earth) in (a) and (c) and the biosphere (in this case the megalith builders) in (b). (*P. McCartney*)

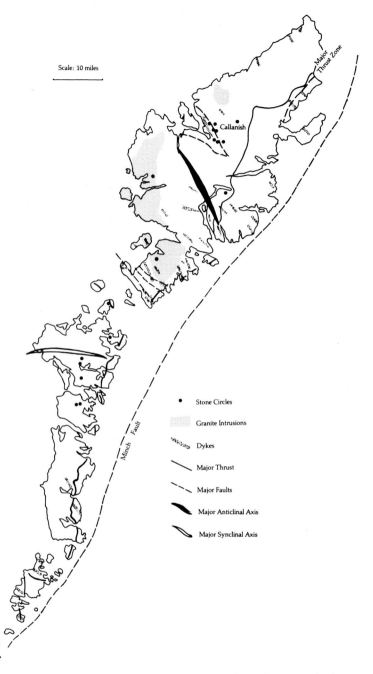

Faulting and Stone Circles in the Outer Hebrides. The major faulting systems in the Hebrides and the close correlation with the stone circle distribution is shown. Notice the localized faulting adjacent to the Callanish group of circles. (*P. McCartney*)

geology can be verified by use of the Chi (χ) squared test:

$$\chi^2 = \frac{(O - E)^2}{E}$$

O = observed number of circles
E = expected number of circles assuming a random distribution

Total number of circles in England and Wales = 286

	Post-Armorican	Pre-Armorican
O	51	235
E	183	103

$$\chi^2 \quad \frac{(51 - 183)^2}{183} + \frac{(235 - 103)^2}{235}$$

$$= 169.35$$

With 1 degree of freedom χ^2 0.995 = 7.88
The number 169.35 is of course dramatically higher than this,
Therefore probability of relationship > 99.5%

It can be seen that stone circle distribution presents a statistical certainty of almost 100 per cent against randomness. It may satisfy some archaeological minds to assume such apparent deliberate placing of circles was because of availability of stone. More thoughtful researchers naturally realize such simplistic notions are for the kindergarten. There are enough examples to show that the ancients did *not* necessarily site their structures within easy reach of the stones they wanted—the bluestones of Stonehenge spring immediately to mind, and the siting of Stonehenge was not particularly convenient for the source of the sarsen stones either. If availability of stone was the main siting criterion, why choose a site miles away from a source to erect the Rudston monolith, or the Devil's Arrows, or Long Meg? The list could be a long one. And this is not to mention the problems to such a simplistic explanation presented by the presence of stone circles on offshore islands. There simply cannot be any doubt that the *place* was paramount to the megalith builders. It so happened that the requirements for their places occurred in heavily faulted or intruded areas. And *that* is the clue not to be missed.

Stone circles have provided the main type of megalithic sacred site to be studied in this way because their distribution pattern is comprehensively available through archaeological and cartographic sources. The pattern holds good for Scotland too. Only in the eastern, Aberdeenshire, area of Scotland do we find intensive circle building that is not closely related to faulting or intrusions—though there is a looser association with intrusions even here. This is exceptionally interesting because the group of circles in this region have a peculiar characteristic— many of them are *recumbent* circles (they have a stone or stones apparently deliberately laid down on rather than inserted into the ground). The archaeologist Euan MacKie has called the Aberdeenshire megalith builders 'certainly a group apart'.[35] In the light of the geological associations being noted here it is difficult not to assume that circle design differed in this region because it presented a slightly different tectonic environment than that associated with other circle sitings. This interesting case indicates that much might be discovered by applying the geological approach being pioneered here. It is hoped that McCartney's Dragon Project work will show up more inform- ative correlations.

Scotland, of course, possesses the huge, ancient Great Glen fault. Naturally, we are by now not surprised to learn that megalithic sites abound in the region of the feature. Around the north-eastern end of the fault there are over fifty chambered cairns, including the famous Clava barrows. Most megaliths congregate around each end of the fault, but it is interesting to note that over the last few years archaeologists have come to think that the waters of Loch Ness, occupying most of the fault, cover long-submerged stone circles.

McCartney and I have not done work of this sort outside Britain as yet, but it is instructive to learn that a French researcher, Pierre Méreaux-Tanguy, has undertaken similar research at the great megalithic centre around Carnac in Brittany.[36] This region is populated with thousands of megaliths, most of which are arranged in long rows. Méreaux has noted that the megaliths are situated in a granitic zone rich in quartz and magnetite. In other words, they are on an intrusion, like the stones on Dartmoor, for example. Because the intrusion is thrust through the Earth's crust at this point it has naturally produced folded and faulted rocks around its perimeter. The ranite platform is an area of relatively stable magnetic fields within an otherwise disturbed magnetic environment occasioned by the tectonic disturbance of the surrounding rocks (Chapter 5). The faulting attracts earth tremors: Méreaux observes that the region of south Morbihan, adjacent to the megalithic groupings, is more prone to tectonic disturbance than even the volcanic Auvergne. Because the quartz-bearing granite intrusion containing the megaliths is next to this seismically active area, Méreaux reasonably assumes that the stones must be surrounded by piezo-electrical fields when such activity is taking place. This would also be true for many of the British circles. Méreaux has observed gravity anomalies in and around the region, or so he has claimed.

Remarkably, eight of the Carnac alignments define the actual boundaries between the stable and disturbed zones of magnetism, and the rows of Le Menec, Kermario, Kerlescan and Petit Menec are practically on the interfaces between the zones of

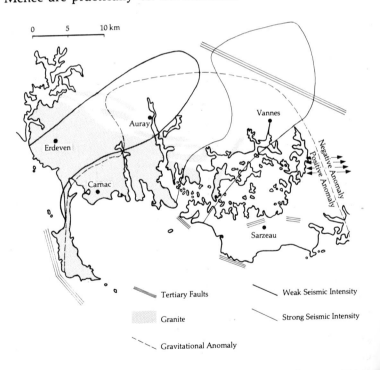

14   The Carnac area in Brittany. This diagram shows the megalithic groupings at Carnac in relation to tectonic features and certai‑ geophysical anomalies.

positive and negative gravity anomalies, the high and low areas of seismic activity as well as the stable and disturbed magnetic regions.

So the apparent tendency for the megalith builders to site their structures in the immediate environment of intruded or faulted regions can be found in the one area outside of Britain where the relevant tests have been made. It is a strong pattern indeed.

To the distribution of stone circles in Britain we have added other megalithic monuments for which we happen to have data to hand. This is by no means a complete picture of total megalithic distribution in Britain, but must provide some general indications. On the basis of this, we have found no substantial differences between the distribution of monoliths, chambered mounds and dolmens and that of the circles. It is again instructive to learn that the Aberdeenshire circles have no chambered cairns associated with them. Henges, however, show a predominantly negative correlation with regard to the patterns being discussed here. Henges seem to be a different type of animal to the stone circles and other megalithic sites.

There is an interesting correlation between stone circle distribution and thunderstorm days in Britain (Figure 15). Virtually all the stone circles fall in areas that habitually have relatively *low* thunderstorm activity. This may seem just an irrelevant novelty of a pattern but it does fit in with trends to be mentioned in the next section.

Professor Thom was puzzled as to why megaliths that seemed designed for detailed astronomical use were often clustered together. Why duplicate effort? (This factor is also a problem for the lazy minds that glide over stone circle functions as being 'ritual'.) One of Thom's theories—and he does not speculate very often—is that the complex observations possible at such sites may have been used for detailed knowledge of tidal behaviour in addition to calendrical uses. I suggest that the marked relationship between certain geological features and stone circles indicates a further use. It was shown in Chapter 4 how the Sun and Moon can act on the Earth's geology, adding to the mechanisms causing seismic movement: and if these bodies affect actual earthquakes, then their influence on more subtle earth movements must be far more pronounced and complex. I think the ancients needed a detailed knowledge of lunar and solar motion to determine their effects on the tides not only of the sea but also of the planet's crust itself and, probably, on

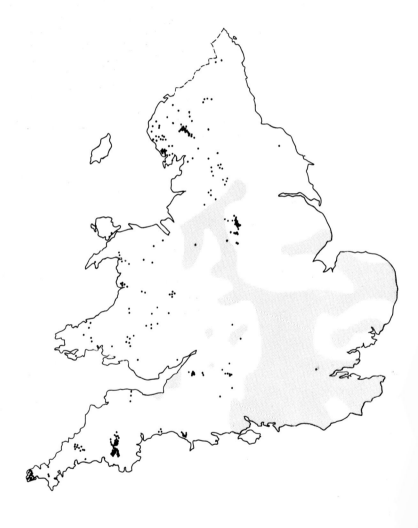

High Thunderstorm Frequency

15   Circles and Thunderstorms, England and Wales. Is it just an extraordinary coincidence that virtually all stone circles are situated in relatively low thunderstorm areas?

certain functions of the human mind. The astronomy that went on in ancient times in the wild regions of our landscape was part of a broader concern, a concern that may have involved a co-ordination of geological and biological aspects. A geopsychic magic—was that the drive behind the ancients' natural science?

★　　★　　★　　★

The Earth is surrounded by an ocean of forces which impinge upon many of its structures, processes and lifeforms. The great body of our planet heaves, shudders and sighs in response to the influences bearing on it from within and without.

The Earth and its cosmic environment set the stage. A long, long time ago, human beings came onto that stage. They were far more sensitive to the planet and the subtle forces operating within it than we are today. They had an obsession with astronomical events, a predeliction for certain types of geology, and they knew their geometry. These clues speak volumes.

The importance of *human* signs in the earth is that they tell us of certain responses to their environment made by people physically and mentally more sensitive than ourselves. As such, they act like signposts in the landscape. They tell us that here, or there, on that moor, by this mountain, was something special. The megaliths key us in as human beings to the vast impersonal processes of Nature.

If UFOs are natural phenomena, if they have haunted our planet through countless ages, then the remarkable peoples of the late Neolithic and early Bronze Ages in Britain, and their counterparts at the same and different periods around the world, would have known of them.

If such natural phenomena were useful to their societies then, like human beings at all times and in all places, they would have made use of them. The force we call electricity, which Nature turns into lightning and we harness to power television sets, washing machines and computers, is an example of human beings natural opportunism. In the same way the ancients would have studied the phenomena we refer to as UFOs. They would have *identified* them. They would have studied their behaviour, their haunts and the laws relating to the appearance of such events. Gradually, they would learn how to ensnare the phenomenon and to draw it to them for their own purposes.

Some of the signs these people left may relate to this process.

By reading those signs, by learning all we can about the megalithic structures, we may be taught what the ancients knew
about UFOs.

The hunt for the lair of the UFO has led us to ground.

PART THREE:
Towards a Synthesis

7.
UFOs As Earth Phenomena

The earth speaks softly
To the mountain
Which trembles
And lights the sky

Japanese haiku

In 1972 Andrew York and I commenced a study of a particular
English county in which we sought to study correlations, if any,
between the distribution of old stones, meteorological and
seismic phenomena, the incidence of UFOs, alleged paranormal
events and geological features of the landscape. The study was
to take us, on and off, over three years and even then, by its very
nature, the investigation was anything but complete. But as far
as I know, this was the first attempt at a multi-faceted investigation of this sort. We had no precedent to refer to and we
simply did not know what we would come up with.

The tract of land selected could have been anywhere in the
world. We chose an English county because we happen to be
English, English counties conveniently have centralized archives
stretching back many centuries as well as, usually, their own
newspaper, and the land area represented by an English county

is small enough to be adequately investigated in the field. We
chose the county of Leicestershire situated close to the centre of
the country. We were both Leicestershire men, Andrew York
was living in the county and I had easy access to it from London.
These were the arbitary factors that led to the selection of our
'laboratory'.

This is not the place to go into the full details of the study as
they would provide a book of their own. Some of our findings
have been published,[1, 2, 3] but a large part of the work has not. I
will present here only those aspects that relate to the main theme
of this current work.

In the north-west of the county is an area known as
Charnwood Forest: this region is higher than the surrounding
landscape but is not a forest. It was described in Domesday
simply as 'a waste'. Its wild landscape is punctuated by jagged
outcrops of rock and odd tree clumps. Here are some of the
oldest exposed rocks in Britain. Around Charnwood the landscape has been fractured and contains important local faults and
considerable secondary faulting.

Records of tremors and earthquakes either centred on Charnwood or its immediate environs go back centuries. The earliest
written record we came across related to an event in 1580 when
the steeple of Stoke Golding church, south of Charnwood, was
shaken down by a tremor. There have been larger and smaller
seismic events in the county down the years, with the largest
recorded earthquake occurring in 1957. It was of such severity
that although its epicentre was on Charnwood it affected eleven
other counties. It caused considerable material damage but no
loss of life. There were many accounts of people having seen
lights in the sky prior to the event.

Working from the records we were able to plot where the
worst effects of seismic incidents since 1580 were felt. We then
collected all the accounts we could of exceptional or abnormal
meteorological events. One of our earliest records dated from
1659 when Sir George Booth described a curious happening on 7
September of that year. It took place at Markfield, a village on
Charnwood named after a megalith that used to stand in an
adjacent field—the mark in the field. 'Extraordinary flashes of
lightning' broke from angry-looking clouds, accompanied by
'terrible' claps of thunder. This went on for about an hour. No
rain resulted but, instead, 'a most black and dreadful storm of
hail, and instead of hailstones there fell rattling down from the

air halberts, swords and daggers; which were found to be of the same nature as were the hailstones; and after a little while both the sight, and the fright the sight brought with it, did melt away at once'. The Markfield population was not spared for long, however, because it soon heard crackles and bangs as if muskets 'in repeated volleys, did discharge their cholerick errands'. Flying in the air were 'prodigious eruptions of fire' and these came so low as to destroy houses and kilns and uproot large trees. Eventually, this incredible geophysical display 'was seen by all to take its course up the hill, where it vanished away'. From the crackles in the atmosphere and the curious lightning and fiery discharges we can be sure that an exceptional atmospherical electrical event occurred at Markfield. As for the shaped ice, in forms meaningful to the people of the day, we can only speculate. Somehow or other, while in formation, some of the hailstones were obliged to follow a blueprint that must have come from the human mind.

As extraordinary as this incident clearly was, it was only one of many we collected. Over half a century later, for example, a vicar at Shepshed, also on Charnwood, was recording unusual 'aurorae' in the local skies. The first phenomenon of this kind was noted on 6 March 1715. It looked like 'a great house on fire at a distance'. More and more of them appeared as time went on. They usually took the form of 'spiral streams or columns' and displayed 'strong vibrations or dartings'. It might be thought that these were normal aurora effects until it is read in the vicar's diaries that they appeared in *all* parts of the heavens, in *every season* for a *nine year period*. Clearly, these were exceptional electromagnetic conditions manifesting in the skies around Charnwood.

The archives are peppered with accounts of odd 'meteors', of balls of lightning destroying churches, of fiery tempests and so on. We might have expected such a record from Leicestershire, named as it is after King Lear. Robert Graves links Lear with Llyr, Janus and ultimately with the oak, the tree of Zeus 'and all the other Thunder gods'. Thor in another guise.

What did surprise us was that on plotting the central zones of exceptional meteorological events, the areas primarily affected were in the west of the county, while the highest number of lightning strikes, normal thunderstorm activity, occurs in the east of the county. Normal and abnormal meteorological activity showed different distribution patterns.

Neither seismic nor meteorological events can realistically be considered point events; they tend to affect the local area. So having plotted the centres of reported seismic and meteorological events we designated an area around these zones to denote the main spheres of influence of such activities as far as could be deduced from the information available to us.

If this pattern is superimposed on a schematic sketch map of the faulting in the county a remarkable correlation can be seen (Figure 18). The seismic pattern would naturally relate; but we can see here clear evidence that *abnormal meteorological events also seem to relate to faulting.* As normal meteorological activity is greater in the east of the county it is difficult to avoid the suspicion that fault areas somehow interfere with the normal cycles of the atmosphere. It is as if frustrated meteorological processes are 'bottled up' or redirected until they explode in occasional displays of exceptional ferocity or manifestation. It could be the unusual electromagnetic fields and anomalies surrounding areas of tectonic disturbance and mineral deposits that affect the atmospheric processes, perhaps through the catalyzing effects of solar and lunar influence. At all events, it would

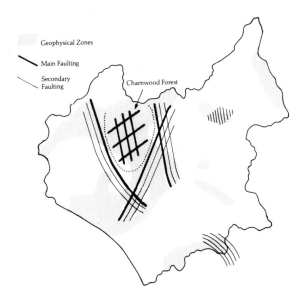

Geophysical Zones

Main Faulting

Secondary
Faulting

Charnwood Forest

16   A schematic map of main geological faulting in Leicestershire, with areas showing the main incidence of exceptional geophysical activity.

be irresponsible not to suspect a link between meteorology and geology, however 'heretical' such an idea might be.

Our investigation led us to make studies of many aspects of the county. Most ghost cases fell within the boundaries of the geophysically active zones, though the pattern was not absolutely clear cut. We collected UFO accounts for the period 1953-1974 as recorded in the files of *The Leicester Mercury*, to which we added one other case, of a humanoid sighting in the 1920s, reported in *Flying Saucer Review*. We logged only well-witnessed events that possessed really curious characteristics putting them beyond normal meteorological explanations. Incidents such as a light seen near Loughborough in north-west Leicestershire in 1967, which was 'swerving' in the sky and emitting a 'deep noise' while changing colour; a triangular formation of lights witnessed by an ex-R.A.F. man over Leicester in 1968; a white object like a ball emitting a siren-like sound witnessed by many people in Leicester in 1970; the ball of light the size of 'a double-decker bus' that 'buzzed' a woman in a car one night in 1971 near Croft Hill, south-west of Leicester, and so on. Odd-shaped lights, phenomena that stand still or perform manoeuvres in the sky, aerial events that are repeated over short periods of time: all part of the familiar pageant of UFO activities.

We went to considerable lengths to avoid plotting a UFO more than once where several reports were apparently describing the same incident, and we were as careful as possible to locate each sighting as accurately as we could on the Leicestershire map, taking into account what direction the witness or witnesses were looking in rather than the location of the witnesses themselves, as well as the estimated proximity of each UFO. We ended up with over 130 UFOs plotted on our map. As these were set against the 862 square mile land area of the county, I think it is probably true to say that not many studies have bettered this event-to-area ratio.

The compilation of this data soon revealed 'window areas' within Leicestershire. One of the primary such areas is that around Croft Hill. This is an isolated, symmetrical hill with a long history (it has provided the setting for meetings of the early Christian church in Britain, for open air courts and for traditional fairs). Our research uncovered evidence that was strong if circumstantial, suggesting that the place is the *mesomphalos* of Britain, the central sacred site, the holy hill at the fulcrum of

Exposed fault on the lowest slopes of Croft Hill, Leicestershire. (*Author's photo*)

Britain's magical landscape. Comprised of granite and syenite (a fact which has put it under risk of quarrying in the past), Croft Hill has therefore a large element of quartz in its composition. There is at least one minor, local fault in the base of the hill, part of which has been uncovered by erosion to reveal a great slab of rock, so regular as to look artificial, protruding from the lower slopes. Near the foot of the hill is an ancient church dedicated to St. Michael—a dedication often associated with locations of geomantic significance.[5]

We drew a ten-mile radius circle around Croft Hill and found that well over 50 per cent of the UFO sightings we had recorded fell within that circle. More significantly, almost 25 per cent fell within a five-mile radius circle. Indeed, there have been reports of aerial lights coming down right by the hill, but no ground traces have been discovered.

There are other 'windows' in the county—four or five other areas where the chances of witnessing a UFO event in the county seem to be greater than elsewhere.

Figure 17 shows the relationship between the peak UFO distribution we recorded and the key areas of exceptional geophysical activity which, in turn, correlate with the most important fault-

Peak UFO Incidence

Geophysical Zones

Map of Leicestershire showing peak incidence of reported UFO activity superimposed upon the zones of exceptional geophysical activity.

ing in the county. It provides a correlation that cannot be ignored.

It is particularly interesting to separate out the exceptional meteorological events and correlate them with the UFO distribution (Figure 18): not only is the distribution profoundly similar, so is the *clustering*. As with all visual correlations, it is important to note the *blank* areas common to both patterns. The implications of this would seem to be that *the influences causing exceptional meteorological manifestations must at least be partially shared by the atmospheric phenomena we refer to as UFOs.*

These, then, were some of the patterns Andrew York and I discovered during our Leicestershire study. For a variety of reasons we were not able to take them further or to prolong the study after the mid-1970s. But the investigation provided a microcosmic analysis that I was anxious to extend to a larger scale. In the case of this book, that means England and Wales.

It is not, of course, possible to study a larger area in the same depth as a smaller one, unless one has unlimited resources of finance, time and personnel. Hence the value of the microcosmic

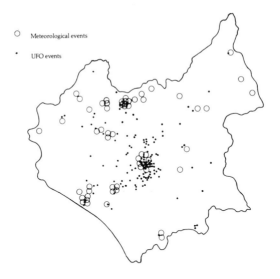

18   Map of Leicestershire showing reported UFO sightings (small dots),
      related to locations of recorded meteorological abnormality (circles).

study; small is beautiful in the case of UFO research as it is in
other spheres. Nevertheless, it is an interesting exercise to see
whether or not the same patterns can be extended to apply to a
larger canvas.

   The source primarily used for the nationwide set of UFO
reports was the British UFO Research Association (BUFORA).[6]
While I did not have the resources to log all the data available, it
was possible to take a representative sample. I asked BUFORA's
national investigations co-ordinator, Lawrence Dale, if he
would supply me with some UFO reports plotted geographic-
ally. He very kindly sent me two maps depicting the distribution
of reported UFO sightings for the years 1977 and 1978. The
choice of years was Mr Dale's. With the co-operation of
BUFORA's research director, Tony Pace, my wife and I were
able to spend two days sorting through BUFORA UFO reports
in the Newchapel Observatory in Staffordshire. The limited
length of time our schedule allowed us meant we could not enjoy
a leisurely perusal of all the material available at the observatory: the situation forced us to take a random sample of the
thousands of reports to hand. We simply worked our way
through as many as possible in no preferred order (except for

omitting reports for 1977 and 1978). We used the BUFORA investigators' evaluations on the reports as a general filter, rejecting all those thought by their investigators or other commentators on the sheets to be explicable in terms of misperception, hoax, meterorology, etc. Operating this way, we obtained samples from the years 1954 to 1979 excluding 1956, 1958, 1962, 1967 and, of course, the two years for which we already had been given the reports.

So McCartney and I had complete sets of reports for two years, plus a random sample of good or probable sightings for another eighteen years. To complete the range of this deliberately varied input (so no procedural biases would be likely to become dominant) we sought coherant reports of 'flap' zones in England and Wales that provided specific information on locations of UFO appearances. We had no control over where these would be, of course, and felt they would give the overall data some extra value in indicating peak incidence areas. Flap or wave zones are those where a distinct wave of UFO events are reported in a limited area and over a limited period of time—usually a period of a few months to a year or so. These waves of sightings usually involve small geographical locations, but there are also waves which can be interpreted on a larger scale covering whole countries or regions of the Earth. As our limits were defined by England and Wales we were naturally seeking the smaller species of wave phenomenon. It proved to be difficult quest. Only three coherently chronicled wave zones came to our attention—the Barmouth area of Wales, the Pembrokeshire (or Dyfed as it now is) area of Wales and the Warminster area in Wiltshire. We obtained the Barmouth material from the excellent research in Kevin and Sue McClure's study of the late 1904 to 1905 wave in their *Stars, And Rumours of Stars,*[7] and the Dyfed material from *The Dyfed Enigma*[8] by Randell Jones Pugh and the late F. W. Holiday, and from the *Journal Of Transient Aerial Phenomena.*[9] Warminster was more of a problem: there seemed to have been a genuine wave of UFO activity in 1965/66, but so much had been written about it, and so many investigators and interested onlookers drawn to the area while events were still being reported as occurring, that we were worried that we would be plotting an *artefact* caused by a concentration of reports rather than a genuine wave phenomenon. If you place from a handful to several dozen skywatchers every night for a few years on any hilltop anywhere the incidence of UFO reports will increase for that region. As the mid-1960s was covered by our random sample we felt it best to leave Warminster out as a specific flap zone and to see whether it would surface in its own right as an area of higher than average UFO incidence.

I had data on 130-odd UFO cases in Leicestershire, of course, but, again, to have put these on our overall map would have caused a false concentration of reported UFO sightings in the region—it would be an artefact because the list of Leicestershire sightings had resulted from a specific study of that county alone covering sightings reported over a nineteen-year period.

The Dyfed wave occurred in 1977. When we plotted the 1977 BUFORA material we deleted all Dyfed data to avoid any risk of duplication.

The final map appears in Figure 19. It represents a selection of all types of reported UFO event except the so-called abduction cases. It draws its data from a mix of random sampling, from complete annual sets of reports and from studies detailing events in apparent flap zones known to the compilers. Apart from cataloguing *all* known English and Welsh reports for the period it is difficult to imagine a more *representative*—as opposed to exhaustive—picture of UFO activity in the two countries. Altogether, there are in excess of eight hundred reported UFO events plotted. Against the land area for England and Wales of 58,392 square miles we feel this compares well in terms of event-to-area ratio with many other studies. (The Persinger-Lafrenière study referred to in Chapter 3, for instance, involved less than 1300 UFO sightings over a total area for the USA of 3,775,602 square miles.)

The distribution of UFO plots follows population *distribution* to some extent. Here we are faced with the perrenial problem in such studies—the 'confounding involvement of population' as Persinger and Lafrenière put it. *Phemomena are only known about if someone sees them.* Fault lines remain present until studied; stone circles do not wander about the country. Transient events can only be plotted if recorded. In the Leicestershire material there is a notable increase of sightings in the Leicester area, for example. Is this because of the greater population there, or because of some other factor—like the fact that the city is wedged between two local fault lines? I suspect it is a little of both; a genuine increase in incidence exaggerated by population factors. In other parts of Leicestershire, to continue the example, there are pockets of reported UFO incidence, and

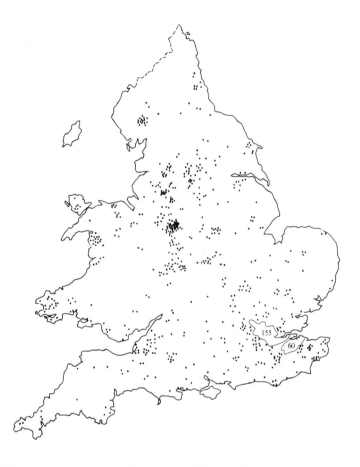

UFO Sightings sample for England and Wales. The collected reported sightings for the years mentioned in the text of UFOs in the region are depicted on this map. No correction for distortion due to population density is made.

vice versa, which do not bear a relationship with population density. The England and Wales material in Figure 19 likewise shows a relationship with population *density* in the London area but a density trend is not particularly marked elsewhere. Although it will be seen that a tremor epicentre has been recorded near London, the region contains nearly eight million people and this factor is undoubtedly distorting the true picture of UFO incidence.

It was obvious that our map needed to be filtered in some way to correct the distorting effect of population as far as possible. New investigations bring forth new problems which call for fresh solutions. Different researchers will seek different ways of ameliorating problems of research.

We sought to correct the population bias, to attempt at least to arrive at an indicative picture of what UFO incidence in England and Wales would really be if the population was evenly distributed over the land mass with each pair of eyes having an equal opportunity of observing a UFO. The fact is that in reality in the Greater London area and adjacent north Kent there are perhaps eight million pairs of eyes potentially available to observe a UFO event compared with possibly a few thousand, or a few hundred or less, in other parts. It was necessary, therefore, to *weight* the value of each sighting against population, so the overall trend could be more readily discerned.

In a sparsely populated area, between 0-50 persons per km^2 are available to experience a UFO event. A single sighting in such an area must be more significant than a single report received from a densely populated urban district. Much of London, for example, has well over 5000 persons per km^2. The weighted UFO map (Figure 21) has taken this into account. The final point distribution is, we feel, an effective attempt to show how many sightings could be expected if the population density of England and Wales was homogeneously distributed. If indeed we have erred, it is on the side of caution rather than optimism. In addition, to prevent some areas being swamped with dots, we decided to smooth the final map by discounting isolated sightings in highly populated districts. This is not an attempt to falsify the pattern. Quite the contrary, were we to give credit to every separate sighting and weight it accordingly, the 'window' areas would be even more accentuated—other regions, too, would certainly be enhanced.

Vallee and others have noted the rural tendencies of UFO incidence. Some researchers have rather curiously interpreted this in terms of people in the country being more likely to notice something in the sky than city inhabitants. I do not think this view seriously considers the incredibly increased chance of UFO observation in urban areas compared to country regions. If at midnight a great ball of light flew low over Snowdonia, the remote and rugged mountain region of north-west Wales, for example, would it really be more likely to be seen than if it flew low over Oxford Street or Birmingham's Bull Ring centre? I do not believe it. In fact, I recall an incident a few years ago when some hoaxer sent a fiery balloon aloft over Marble Arch in London. This must be one of the busiest urban locations in the world, yet there were dozens of reports of people seeing the aerial light and minor traffic accidents were precipitated because of drivers catching sight of it. There may be some validity in assuming that urban observers have their view of the sky curtailed to some extent in cities like New York with towering skyscrapers, but this situation does not pertain to British cities on the whole. And even in the country there are odd buildings,

Unexplained reports of UFO landings in France in 1954, dotted lines indicate areas with the population density of above 60 per sq. km. (*Jacques Vallee*)

trees, hills and mountains affecting views of the sky. There can
be no doubt that many UFO events must occur in rural and
remote areas without being observed and thus are not reported.

It is moreover far more likely that a light seen in rural skies
will prove to be a genuine anomaly than would be the case over
a city, where aircraft stacking for landing at nearby airports,
streetlight reflections on clouds, and so on, are more likely to be
misperceived by observers. The increase number of UFO reports
in urban districts are almost certainly artificially inflated by
misperception, thus exaggerating the already enormous
population density bias.

Jacques Vallee found that reported UFO sightings tended to
be distributed in a negative correlation with population density.
He compared all the unexplained landings in the 1954 French
wave with areas showing a population density above 60 per km^2
(Figure 20).

In any geographical assessment of UFO patterns, where an
understanding of genuine incidence is being attempted, it is an
absolutely crucial priority to at least blunt the sharp edge of the
population bias. No sensible interpretations can be made
without doing this. It is one thing to cover a map with dots,
another to arrive at a meaningful, informative picture. The
pattern has to be enhanced, like the raw visual data beamed
back to Earth from space probes, or like the latent image on an
exposed sheet of photographic paper.

In our case, this enhancement process involved us in superimposing our point distribution data, as shown in Figure 19, on
to a population map prepared by Her Majesty's Stationery
Office based on the 1971 census information. This information
is distributed in many forms, but the map we used was ideal for
our purposes as it depicts both population distribution and
density in one kilometre squares, each square having a colour
denoting the population for that tiny area. None of the UFO
events could be claimed to have been plotted with an accuracy
greater than 1km^2 (except for certain of the Dyfed and
Barmouth cases, which were precisely locatable), so the two sets
of data were suitably matched. Precise superimposition allowed
us to give each dot on the UFO map a value against the population map. The result can be seen in Figure 21. The largest dots
represent the highest intensities of UFO incidence (scaling down
through the range of dot sizes until we operated a cut-off point
to render the enhanced pattern as indicative as possible) that

would be expected from the UFO data used given homogeneity of population distribution.

This method has accurately shown up the wave zones of Barmouth and Dyfed. Indeed, Warminster has presented itself too. Moreover, a peak incidence area in Cumbria appeared that we did not expect. We were later able to confirm that there had been a Cumbrian UFO flap. Also, there is a display of activity in Anglesey apparent on the map, and it is a fact that there was a flurry of UFO events there too.

If this population-corrected UFO map is compared with a main faulting and earthquake epicentre map for England and Wales (Figure 22) then a *remarkable* correlation can be noted. It is surely impossible to look at these two maps and not conclude that a seismic connection with UFO incidence is highly probable. Wales in particular shows an almost one-for-one match. From the north part of Dyfed and sweeping up across the middle of Wales there are matching blank areas on both maps (and Chapter 5 tells us why this might have been expected). An east-west line from the Bristol channel shows a lack of activity on both maps. There is a blank fringe on both maps around the southern and western borders of the Wash, yet to the north-west a little pocket of both epicentre and UFO activity can be seen. The Staffordshire region is notable for both earthquake and UFO activity.

The largest earthquake known in historical times in Britain was the one at Colchester towards the end of the last century. Yet we have no record of UFO activity there on our map. This is the price that has to be paid for a randomized, representative presentation of data. There has been, in fact, a UFO wave around Mersea Island[11] coincident with the Colchester earthquake epicentre.

I am a little surprised that, after correction, UFO activity in the Manchester to Leeds area has not shown up more significantly, as there has been considerable tremor activity there. Again, this is probably a result of our random scan of years for the UFO data—we may have missed out those containing particular UFO incidence. I am sure members of the Northern UFO Network can confirm that there has been a respectable amount of UFO activity in the region.

It was sobering for us to learn when compiling the corrected map that, given an equal chance of being sighted, there would be eight times as many UFO sightings in the Warminster area alone

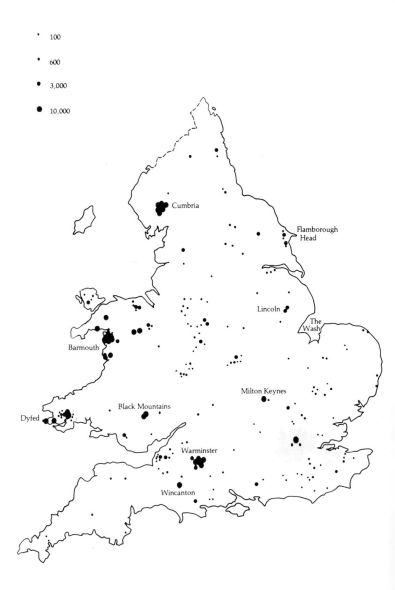

Scale legend:

· 100
· 600
● 3,000
● 10,000

Map labels:
Cumbria
Flamborough Head
Lincoln
The Wash
Barmouth
Milton Keynes
Black Mountains
Dyfed
Warminster
Wincanton

21   Population Corrected UFO sightings for England and Wales. The 1971 census map provided the detailed information which allowed the corrections due to population bias to be made. The above map is the result, revealing striking 'window' areas.

3m

3-4m

4-5m

5-6m

Fault Lines

Church
Stretton
Fault

Lizard-Start
Point Thrust

Earthquake Epicentres, England and Wales.

compared to the *whole* of East Anglia. And this ratio is even greater for Cumbria and parts of Wales.

But even though this processing of the data is a step in the right direction, it is still far from perfect. Though one tries to combat the distorting influence of population, other factors come into play. A major influence on our data is the fact that much of it comes from BUFORA sources. It is not only the distribution of population that affects the material, it is also the distribution of BUFORA researchers. Not only that, but the activity level of each investigator has to be considered: some are constantly out and about following up reports and sending in their findings, while others are, shall we say, more relaxed about it all. As there is a greater chance of someone wanting to be a BUFORA investigator in areas of denser population, the distribution of investigators will to some extent reflect population trends.

There is at least one anomalously high and one anomalously low incidence area on the map. The large dot to the north-west of London covers the area around Milton Keynes. There happens to be an excellent, active investigator there called Ken Phillips. As a result, the high reading for the Milton Keynes area is to some extent an artefact created by Ken's activities! I think it is probably also true to say that a substantial percentage of his reports are concerned with 'psychic' UFO case histories which I have already indicated are to be treated with some caution in terms of genuine UFO activity. At the other end of the scale, Lawrence Dale informed me that there is not a high level of investigative work going on in Cornwall so the apparent lower UFO incidence in that region as displayed on our map must be partially due to this factor—though the county has still registered as active to some extent, despite this.

Although London does display some slight seismic history to make one expect an increased incidence of UFO activity, it is certain that the massive concentration of population there has caused an exaggeration that still has not been fully ironed out by our correction procedures.

All these anomalies actually work *against* the UFO-tectonic correlation, yet the pattern still comes through strongly. If the correction procedures could be perfected, and the data base increased, I have little doubt that the correlation would be staggeringly convincing. It is remarkable enough in the pilot attempt presented here. The connection is, quite simply, there.

It may seem surprising that there is any earthquake activity in East Anglia as there are virtually no surface faults. The faults *are* there to some extent but are deep down beneath overlying sedimentary cover as explained in Chapter 5. If this was not the case, it would be difficult to explain the appearance of UFOs over East Anglia in tectonically related terms. In Britain it is in fact difficult to readily identify earthquakes with a particular fault. Some are associated with old fold areas, and the patterns underlying British earthquake distribution are by no means clear.[12] *This emphasizes the importance of relating UFO incidence to epicentre information rather than simply to faults*—it is the earth *movement* that is significant.

The research carried out by my co-workers and myself indicates that in England and Wales UFOs tend towards rural areas; they can occur in zones of peak incidence—'windows'—and are related to tectonic activity. All these findings are in line with results obtained by other workers in other parts of the world. It is the *tectonic correlation* which is crucial.

Persinger and Lafrenière state, as we have seen, that 'the data consistently point towards seismic-relate sources' in their North American studies. F. Lagarde,[13] studying material obtained in the 1954 French wave and referring to sightings of UFOs near the ground, found in an initial survey that 37 per cent occurred on or in the immediate vicinity of faults, and that 80 per cent of the sighting localities were associated with faults. For those who think it is easy to correlate UFO patterns with any factor, it is important to note that Lagarde tested this correlation by comparing communes with faults in the same areas: only 3.6 per cent of these fell on faults or 10.8 per cent if margins of 2½km were allowed for the faults. Later research showed a 40 per cent correlation between UFO incidence and fault lines. As Lagarde says: 'UFO sightings occur by preference on geological faults'. He pointed out that more detailed geological information than that used in his research would certainly enhance the correlation. Legarde was aware that seismic movement related in some areas to non-visible faults, covered by more recent sediments. We have been able to show in this book the value of correlating UFOs with recorded tremor epicentres; had Lagarde done that, there can be little doubt that his correlation would have been even more significant.

Lagarde goes on to state that 'It seems as though faults, as such, are not merely the external aspect of an irregularity in the

Earth's crust, but are also the scenes of delicate phenomena—
piezo-electrical, or electrical, or magnetic, and at times perhaps
of gravimetric variation or discontinuity'. Lagarde carried out
his research in the late 1960s, so his insight was far-reaching. The
French are always amongst the first to detect significant patterns
in UFO research.

Research by Lopez and Ares[14] on the Spanish UFO wave of
1968-69 also shows a large percentage of UFOs being sighted
over locations which are apparently on or near fault lines. They
have noted a trend towards magnetic anomaly areas too.

Our own Leicestershire studies powerfully support the idea of
a UFO-fault association. The work of the Michigan Anomaly
Bureau is beginning to at least suggest a similar correlation for
that state,[15] and only weeks before the completion of this book
The Sunday Times ran an item headlined 'Mother Earth's Flying
Saucers' in which it is reported that North American researchers
had been studying the major UFO event which occurred in New
Zealand near Wellington in December 1978:

> The Wellington UFO might have remained a mystery, but for an
> intriguing encounter between psychologists and physicists which
> has now produced the first workable general explanation of UFOs.
> The mystery lights in New Zealand can be explained not as visitors
> from outer galaxies, but as products of a mysterious process on
> Earth which physicists are just beginning to observe and
> understand.
>
> Psychologists at Laurentian University in Canada who were
> studying odd and unpredictable phenomena began searching for
> links between such events. Their computer studies showed a statis-
> tically significant correlation between unidentified flying objects
> and minor earthquakes. In their hunt for an explanation, the
> psychologists contacted the U.S. Bureau of Mines in Denver,
> Colorado, where Dr. Brian Brady was studying rockbursts. He had
> simulated in the laboratory the strains that break rock apart.
>
> When quartz-bearing rock broke up, he noticed balls of light—
> short lived, but as intense as lightning. The luminescence from a
> single crack under a laboratory glass would last only for micro-
> seconds, but in that time it might streak away, hover and then move
> again following the energy source in the rock break. What Brady
> was watching could have been tiny UFOs . . . Where rock cracks 'it
> has to prepare itself', he says. Laws of thermodynamics are
> suspended. Matter implodes instead of exploding, and enough
> energy forms to dissolve the usual bonds between ions and
> electrons. The implosion forms a hole in the rock followed by
> shocks and strains and a growing failure along a fault line. The

minor version is a cracking fragment of quartz—but the full-scale version is an earthquake . . .

Brady has indeed shown that seismic activity can indeed produce the energy for mystery lights.

Brady explains that when rock cracks electromagnetic fields are created and these could act like 'magnetic bottles' to contain and give shape to the light. The energy in its 'bottle' could move and grow along the line of a fracture, perhaps spinning as it goes creating the domed 'flying saucer' shape. The author of the article, Michael Pye, continues: 'The theory is plausible, and it is more than conjecture: physicists have seen the light caused by rock breaks, and they know that electromagnetic fields do form on the surface of earthquake areas. Spectacular UFO sightings are reported from California, which is split by the San Andreas Fault.'[16] The Laurentian psychologists mentioned in the article are presumably Persinger and Lafrenière. The fault that Brady feels caused the New Zealand UFOs is the huge Alpine Fault.

England, Wales, France, Spain, North America, New Zealand, a 'test' English county, a 'test' American state: wherever the pattern is checked out, the correlation is found.

The production of earth lights: these unexplained atmospheric lights were produced in a laboratory of the U.S. Bureau of Mines by Dr Brian Brady, by subjecting a piece of granite to 32,000 lbs per sq. in. pressure. This experiment proves that there is a link between geological factors and photon-producing atmospheric phenomena. (*Photo: Dr Brian Brady*)

Some ufologists might not like it (I imagine sceptics will like it even less), but there is a pattern associated with UFO incidence that simply will not go away. That pattern is the tectonic connection. It is the most persistent, widespread and testable clue the UFO enigma has ever given us. It can no longer be ignored.

Using our English and Welsh data, we will explore that clue a little deeper. It will prove instructive to make a quick tour of the four 'window areas' or wave zones that have shown up in Figure 21.

The Dyfed material relates to the 1977 UFO wave there, though UFOs—including 'landings'—have been conspicuous over the area over the last two decades. LITS were seen in the 1977 wave, UFOs landed on and emerged from the ground, and humanoids were seen. These generally took the form of tall, silver, robotic-looking entities which sometimes appeared to be solid while at other times they were witnessed just fading away. All sections of the community witnessed aspects of the wave. One of the main centres of UFO activity was the Broadhaven area, on the coast at St Brides Bay, overlooking the tiny group

Stack Rocks, St Bride's Bay, Dyfed. Scene of numerous UFO events during the 1977 wave, it lies on faulting in the region of the major Church Stretton fault. (*Author's photo*)

of rocks known as Stack Rocks. On this, lights were seen to rise and descend, and even disappear *into* the rocks. (This gave rise to all sorts of weird and wonderful misinterpretations to do with 'space bases'.) The whole area has been orogenically affected, having felt the brunt of both the Caledonian and Armorican episodes of mountain building (Chapter 5). Geological maps mark part of one of Britain's most major faults precisely in this location—the Church Stretton Fault. The region teems with faulting and is a well-known study area for geological students. So complex is the faulting that the Ordnance Survey cartographers seem to have given up on the geological map of the St. Brides Bay area, writing simply 'many faults'. If one wanted a classic UFO-tectonic connection, it is surely here.

Figure 23 shows how the individual sightings related to the faulting. We have circled a point at Ripperston Farm. This is because UFO researcher Hilary Evans has shown that the reports of UFOs, humanoids and poltergeists emanating from there during the wave may be open to suspicion.[17] The map shows those UFO reports for which we had precise data and which occurred in areas of the county for which we were able to

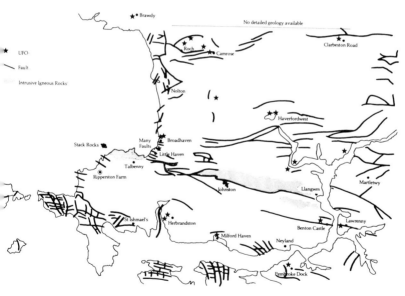

UFO Sightings correlated with geological faulting. Detailed geological maps were used in the compilation of this data. Virtually all UFOs reported fall in the close vicinity of the surface faulting.

obtain full geological information. These correlations must be amongst the most exact and detailed ever produced.

As classic as the Dyfed material is in terms of UFO-tectonics, it can be matched by the Barmouth area wave. The events here seem to have started just before Christmas 1904 and to have continued to July 1905, with the greatest number of sightings apparently occurring during January and February. Again, there was a history of unusual phenomena in the region, with reports dating from the seventeenth and eighteenth centuries. As at Dyfed, there were many witnesses of all types, from vicars to journalists. One of the earliest lights was seen at Towyn, close to where the proto-entity described in Case 34 (Chapter 2) was encountered. Here the western end of the great Bala Fault occurs, another one of Britain's most deeply-rooted surface faults. Three events were reported here, with at least fifteen others stretching along the coast road between Barmouth and Harlech. The lights were usually seen on the inland side of the road, on the slopes of the hills. The whole area is faulted and is dominated by the immediate presence of the Bala Fault. It has not been possible to depict the precise UFO-to-fault relationship for this zone because the plate for the large-scale geological map of the region was destroyed in the last war, and a special print of the map could not be obtained sufficiently swiftly for the schedule for this research. But there are clearly no problems in relating the UFO incidence here to major tectonic features.

The areas around the villages of Egryn, Tal-y-bont, Dyffryn, Llanfair and the town of Harlech seem to have been the main focal points of UFO activity. Phenomena was also witnessed during the wave further north at Pwllheli, and further inland along the Bala Fault at Dolgellau and, much further still, the area around Cefn-Mawr near Ruabon. The phenomena mainly took the form of lights of all colours, usually globular though sometimes in columnar form. They occasionally displayed vibrating and flame-like qualities. On one occasion an aurora appeared, followed by the manifestation of an individual, star-like light, and on another, as we know, a light appeared in the form of an anthropomorphic figure.

Apparently simultaneous with the onset of this wave of atmospheric phenomena a religious revival took place in the district, centred on a remarkable woman called Mary Jones. There seems to have been an understandable attempt to associate Mary Jones with the lights by some observers—a sort of

UFOs AS EARTH PHENOMENA   193

outward sign of her inward grace. Jones herself felt that the lights were accompanying her mission, though she had little to say about them or their nature. Indeed, she did not associate them particularly with herself. It was reported that if a light hovered over a particular house, then in most cases the occupant would end up at Mary Jones' chapel at Egryn seeking conversion. This reaction did not always occur, though, and while Egryn and its immediate area was undoubtedly a focal point for the phenomena, there are many instances recorded when the lights appeared far from the woman's presence. There was a Revivalist mood abroad in the whole of Wales at the time, and it might be a fruitful line of inquiry for other researchers to follow to see if a correlation between tectonic factors and religious upheavals of various sorts could be determined on a worldwide basis. It is possible that the changing electromagnetic field in a seismic stress area could affect mental patterns in some of the inhabitants of such areas at the time periods of geological stress were taking place. It is noteworthy that there had been a substantial earthquake along the Bala Fault in 1903, so we may reasonably suspect that energy was still being dissipated around the fault by small movements amongst the fractures or by some other means.

All this is not to say that Mary Jones was not an inspiring and remarkable woman, nor to necessarily dismiss the notion that the lights, when manifesting near her, may have been attracted to her personal energy fields, her 'L-fields', which must have been considerable. But the reports make it clear that what was happening in reality was that a wave of light phenomena was taking place at the same time as Mary Jones was carrying out her mission. Exceptional electromagnetic elements accompanying tectonic events may have triggered mental processes producing the contagious religious zeal she was experiencing, but the link with the lights seems otherwise fortuitous when it occurred. Naturally, mysterious lights occurring along with such social events were viewed by many as being paranormal or as messages from heaven, rather than electromagnetic effects being expressed through human processes and geophysical mechanisms simultaneously. Human beings have always wanted the mysteries in their midst to be the work of other intelligent agencies, as we see today with the ETH and ultraterrestrials.

Perhaps at Egryn and its environs we saw what happens to human beings when a holy site becomes 'active'. Perhaps this

A dolmen at Dyffren in the centre of the area affected by the 1904-5 wave.

precise confluence of mechanisms was what the ancients were seeking with their obsessive study of cosmic motion and unerring location of sites near tectonically unstable features. Clearly the Egryn area had been considered sacred for millenia, judging by the megalithic remains to be found there (as is the case in Dyfed, too).

It is as awkward as it is remarkable to record that just seventy years after the Egryn lights wave there were many reports of a strange sea creature, the 'Barmouth Monster', being seen off precisely the same stretch of coast![18] It is also perhaps worth recalling that the Loch Ness monster is similarly associated with an intense area of faulting—the loch lying directly on the Great Glen Fault.

A glance at the aeromagnetic map in Figure 6, Chapter 5, will show that the two wave areas of Wales, Dyfed and the Barmouth region, are also zones of complex magnetic anomalies. This would be expected in regions where there are equally complex geological features and a high incidence of varied mineralization, as is the case in both these districts.

The most northerly 'window' on our map is in Cumbria. Apart from being informed that there was a spate of UFO activity in this region, I am unacquainted with the details of UFO events which took place in this unexpected high incidence area. But Chapter 6 mentions the highly faulted and intruded nature of the area and, incidentally, the high number of megalithic remains to be found there.

Finally, the most famous 'window' of them all—Warminster.

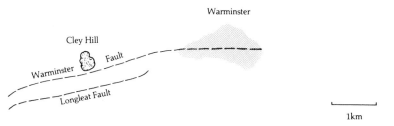

Warminster Faults. Only two small localized faults are known in this tectonically passive region, but they are at the centre of the mass of UFO sightings reported around Cley Hill and Warminster. There are no other recorded faults in the vicinity. (*P. McCartney*)

At first glance we thought that this would be where the UFO-tectonic pattern would break down. The general area is not noted for faulting. But a study of the geological map covering that part of Wiltshire showed just how strong the correlation is (Figure 24).

Even on Post-Armorican outcrops (Cley Hill is chalk) localized faults are found in an otherwise stable area. *No other faults are to be found on the 1:63360 geological sheet anywhere near the boundaries of the sketch map.* Two isolated faults, the Warminster and Longleat Faults, stand at the heart of this dense 'UFO country'. Cley Hill, one of the key 'ufocals' in the area, stands adjacent to the Warminster Fault which runs on into Warminster itself which is immediately beneath the main sky-watching location of Cradle Hill. There are many prehistoric remains in the area, though mainly ones of the earthen types. Megaliths are scarce. The area does not have notable magnetic anomaly complexes. Perhaps these last two facts are not unrelated.

If UFOs are Earth phenomena, if they result in the atmosphere as a result of electromagnetic events or 'discharges' emanating from seismic activity, then it is to be expected that there will be eyewitnesses who will have seen the appearance of UFOs from the ground or within the atmosphere close to earth. This is in fact the case. We *know* where UFOs come from—it has been witnessed. The information has been available all along yet, incredibly, no one seems to have picked up on it. The ETH flies in the face of data already at hand.

Here are a few random accounts of odd lights apparently emerging from the ground.

Two women witnessed a remarkable display of lights on the Dorset coast in 1876. It was a dull but sultry day in August when the women were walking on cliffs near Weymouth. Their route took them past a place where the Upper Greensand in the region is faulted against the Kimmeridge Clay. Over the crest of a hill they saw numerous globes of light, the size of billiard balls, moving independently and vertically up and down, from a few inches above the ground to the height of two or three feet. The balls were 'all aglow' and eluded the grasp like soap bubbles. They had a soft irridescence displaying 'charming colours'. There was no sound and the numbers of light-globes varied. The women watched the display for about an hour, when a 'vague and increasing apprehension' persuaded them to return home.[19]

A similar phenomenon was witnessed a few years before by a woman at Remenham. It was a very cold day in January, with snow on the ground. The room in which the witness was sitting suddenly 'flushed with rose colour'. She looked out of the window and saw a group of coloured bubbles of light rising into the air from a level space of snow. These 'bubbles' began moving up and down within a limited area. This lasted about two minutes until the lights seemed to be carried away by a current of wind. Another group of globes arose from the same spot and the display was repeated. An additional witness also saw the second display.[20]

On 10 November 1940, a man was working at the end of his garden in Coventry. The weather was normal with no sign of thunder. Suddenly, the witness found himself in the centre 'of intense blackness'. He looked down and saw at his feet a ball of pale green light about two feet across. He said that it seemed to be made of 'a mass of writhing strings of light'—a description we have become used to in this book, and an example of coherency of account that scientists would do well to take note of. The sphere rose up into the air, just missing trees and houses. It landed about a quarter of a mile away and seemed to explode, causing damage to a nearby building.[21]

An occurrence of an extraordinary discharge of light from the ground was witnessed by meteorologists in Tucson, Arizona, in March 1964. The region was experiencing a snowstorm—an unusual event. The observers were in an eighty-foot high observation room and began to witness short flashes of 'lightning' at random places around the town. These flashes had a number of unusual features: they did not display the usual lightning 'flicker', their light was less intense than that of normal lightning and they did not cast sharp shadows, nor was thunder heard at any time and no correlation between the flashes and static noise on the radio could be found. The observers were able to discern that the flashes originated 'from points at or very close to the ground'. All non-meteorological explanations, such as car headlights, were considered but had to be dismissed[22]

A UFO wave area would seem a likely hunting ground for accounts of atmospheric phenomena emerging from or closely associated with the ground—and so it proves.

Returning to the Barmouth flap of 1904-5 we can obtain a few telling cases. Local reporter Beriah G. Evans, in the company of four other people, was walking along the road towards Egryn:

> Having left the fields and proceeded some distance along the main road, all five walking abreast, I suddenly saw three brilliant rays of dazzling white light stride across the road from mountain to sea, throwing the stone wall into relief . . . there was not a living soul near, nor a house from which the light could have come.
>
> Another short half-mile, and a blood-red light, apparently within a foot of the ground, appeared to me in the centre of the village street just before us. I said nothing until we reached the spot. The red light had disappeared as suddenly and mysteriously as it had come—and there was absolutely nothing which could conceivably account for its having been there a moment before.

A correspondent from the *Daily Mail* was sent to investigate the Egryn mystery. He too saw the lights:

> Suddenly at 8.20 p.m. I saw what appeared to be a ball of fire above the roof of the Egryn chapel. It came from nowhere, and sprang into existence instantaneously. It had a steady, intense yellow brilliance and did not move.
>
> Not sure whether or not I was deceiving myself, I called to a man 100 yards down the road, and asked him if he could see anything. He came running to me excitedly, and said 'Yes, yes, above the chapel. The great light.' He was a countryman, and was trembling with emotion.

We watched the light together. It seemed to me to be at twice the height of the chapel, say fifty feet, and it stood out with electric vividness against the encircling hills behind. Suddenly, it disappeared, having lasted a minute and a half.

The reporter saw more lights a short while later. There were two of them and they flashed up to about 125 feet above the ground. They were flickering 'like a defective arc-lamp'. This flickering went on 'while one could count ten'. Then they became steady. Both went out within seconds of one another.

The lights were reported far inland in the region around Cefn Mawr, and three local clergymen conducted a 'skywatch' in the region to see if they could confirm the reports coming from the populace. They were the Revs. Huw Parry, A. Lloyd-Hughes and Thomas Jones. Parry reported:

We posted ourselves on the north end of the Pontcysyllte (Aqueduct) at 11.30 p.m., and watched continuously for over an hour over the valley of the Dee, and particularly over some fields near Argoed Farm. Twice I distinctly noticed a large ball of fire rise from the earth and suddenly burst luridly.

Egryn Chapel, near Barmouth Wales. This was at the centre of one of the regions most intensively affected by strange luminous phenomena during the 1904-5 wave. (*Author's photo*)

Hughes reported that the lights resembled electricity. Some rose *from the earth* and were definitely not sheet lightning.

In response to a questionnaire from the Society for Physical Research (SPR), Mary Jones herself had some interesting observations to make on the appearance of the lights: '. . . like two lamps and tongues of fire all around them going out in one place, and lighting again in another place far-off sometimes; other times a quick flash and going out immediately, and when the light goes out a vapour of smoke comes in its place . . ..'

In an account dated January 1905 to the SPR, a Mr J.J. of Dyffren wrote:

> The first form in which it appeared to me was that of a pillar of clear fire quite perpendicular. It was about two feet wide, and about three yards in height. Suddenly another small fire began by its side some two yards distant from the first pillar, and increased rapidly until it assumed the same size and form as the other two pillars. So there were three pillars of the same size and form. And as I gazed upon them I saw two arms of fire extending upwards from the top of each of the pillars. The three pillars and their arms assumed exactly the same shape and remained so for about a minute or two. As I looked towards the sky I saw smoke ascending from the pillars, and immediately they began to disappear. Their disappearance was equally swift with their growth. It was a gradual disappearance; the fire became small and went out . . . it was a very wonderful fire.

These columns were witnessed about half a mile from Egryn. Also in a report to the SPR a Mr L.M. wrote:

> March 25th, 1905 . . . my wife and myself . . . happened to reach Llanfair about 9.15 p.m. It was a rather damp evening. In nearing the chapel . . . we saw balls of light, deep red, ascending from one side of the chapel, the side which is in a field. There was nothing in this field to cause the phenomenon.

The husband and wife were to see more balls of light some time later, after 11.00 p.m.:

> Immediately there appeared ascending from a field high into the sky, three balls of light, deep red. Two of these appeared to split up, while the middle one remained unchanged. Then we left for home, having been watching these last phenomena for a quarter of an hour.

Llanfair Chapel, near Harlech, Wales. During the 1904-5 wave deep
red balls of light were seen emerging from the field in the foreground.
(*Author's photo*)

A Rev. E.E. encountered a columnar phenomenon one May
evening in 1905:

> It appeared to us in the form of a column of fire about two feet wide
> and several feet high, quite distinct, and of the tint of a fiery vapour.
> After looking at the column for a second or two, then some bright
> balls of fire appeared in the column near its base, the column would
> disappear, but in a moment would appear again in the same form, in
> the very same spot, and then the balls would appear in the column,
> and the balls burst and disappear upwards in the same way. This we
> distinctly saw six times.

There are several other reports of this type concerning sightings
in the Barmouth wave. Of course, there were also many reports
of the lights flying high and wide. But what we have here is
minutely observed phenomena occurring close to the ground
and apparently issuing from it or forming close to it. It is
ludicrous to suggest that the lights seen high in the sky were one
thing, and these ground-associated phenomena something else.
Clearly, some of these illuminated discharges formed events
close to the earth which then 'escaped' and flew off—or rose in
the air and were moved along by some internal process. The

higher and brighter they got the more likely it would be that greater numbers of people would see them.

UFOs form on or close to the ground. Their lifespan is variable: they can falter and go out, or they can build up an inner coherency and rise up in the atmosphere. Their normal lifespan seems to be anything from several seconds to about a quarter of an hour. On rare occasions, however, reports from around the world describe UFO events that can last into hours. Reports indicate that these light phenomena have a curious plasticity and can, on occasion, divide up into smaller, shape-shifting elements.

Consider these excellent accounts of a forming UFO, also from the Barmouth wave; there were several witnesses to this event which occurred in July 1905:

> Firstly, there appeared in the heavens a very large and bright ball of fire. It was of a much more brilliant lustre than an ordinary star—very much the colour of a piece of iron white-heated. It had two brilliant arms which protruded towards the earth. Between these arms there appeared a further light or lights resembling a cluster of stars, which seemed to be quivering with varying brightness. This was its form when I saw it, but others who had seen it before had noticed it *growing from smaller dimensions*. It lasted for ten minutes or more. (My emphasis.)

We then read the account of one of the earlier witnesses:

> The manner in which it appeared to me was, firstly, a ball of misty light in the heavens about seven or eight inches in diameter. It was very misty when it appeared first to me, then it got very much brighter, and as its brilliancy became indescribable, the ball grew very much larger and forming an oval shape, it quivered and glittered very much. Then there appeared to be two great long streaks of misty light coming from the ball . . . [which] . . . almost reached the earth.

We have here the description of the birth of a UFO. A discharge taking on form within the atmosphere, becoming visible by ionization or some other photon-emitting process. It builds up, becomes stronger, becomes coherent, taking on a structure —in this case the ubiquitous oval form—and begins to move through the air. To sight a UFO at all is a rare event; to be present to see one forming is even more remarkable. What is particularly interesting in this account is the reference to the streamers reaching from the ball of light down towards the ground. As the

sphere grew more visible, is it not possible that the strengthening
ionization process, or whatever process was involved, began to
disclose part of the discharge path emanating from the ground,
like iron filings dispersed on a card above a magnet disclose the
lines of magnetic force? Is this the origin of the UFOs that are
sometimes reported casting a 'searchlight beam' onto the
ground? As ever, it is the *assumption* that UFOs are inhabited
vehicles that colour the observation of aspects of the UFO phenomenon. The beams are surely *part of the phenomenon leading
not from the UFO to the ground, but leading up to it from the
Earth.* The beams are attenuated umbilical discharge streamers
from ground to UFO—the place where the discharge effect
localizes and becomes concentrated. It is usually at this local-
ization that the photon-emitting part of the event begins to
reveal the phenomenon, though occasionally just the beam is
seen.

Gordon Creighton reported similar phenomena in the Pereiro
region of Brazil.[23] He remarks that the area was prone to regular
earth tremors and that there had been literally hundreds of
quakes and tremors since 1918. Since March 1968 there had been
many reports of UFOs coming from the region; at the same time
tremors were occurring almost daily. Tremendous detonations
were being heard, and 'immense' bluish-green fiery balls were
being seen 'flying in all directions overhead'. They sometimes
hovered in one spot, at other times they moved up and down in
the sky or travelled in straight paths through the heavens.
Conical forms were reported, and the luminosity of the
phenomena was reported as 'blinding'. The UFOs carried
'brilliant lights, like searchlights, which are directed downwards'. The UFOs were appearing every night and were frequently seen to land, though generally in inaccessible spots. By
August 1968 the reports were emphasizing that the lights always
proceded tremors by a few hours: *'the balls of fire seem to know
where and when the [earth]quakes are coming'.*

Barry Gooding, editor of *UFO INFO Exchange Library*, has
conducted five years' research into sightings at Warminster.
Because there has been a lot of interest in the area it has attracted
more than its fair share of 'UFO-spotters'. As a result there is a
particular concentration of reports generated in the locale.
Gooding has come to the opinion that about 70 per cent of such
sightings are the result of over-eager skywatchers misperceiving
satellites, aircraft, flares from nearby Army ranges and natural

phenomena such as meteorites. Nearly all the rest relate to a
curious phenomenon he calls the 'Amber Gambler'—a spheroid
of light that dances around the Warminster skies. It has been
spotted clearly near Cley Hill, Cradle Hill and in locations a mile
or so to the north of the town. Gooding obtained an eyewitness
account of one of these 'Amber Gamblers' being formed:

> I was standing on the hill when I observed a candle-light effect on the
> ground; this light then merged into a beam which beamed upwards.
> On looking up I saw an amber ball which hovered for a few minutes
> then shot off at a fantastic speed and disappeared.[4]

The hill the witness was standing on was Cley Hill which stands,
as we have seen, right by the Warminster Fault. It is difficult to
imagine a more specific description of UFO-formation. We have
the clear observation of the 'beam' discharging upwards to the
forming sphere. It is easy to understand why Gooding is coming
to think of UFOs as a natural phenomenon, as 'a new energy
source'.

Fault-girdled Cley Hill, topped by a prehistoric earthwork, has
displayed much phenomena in its immediate vicinity over the
years. I remember Arthur Shuttlewood, the local journalist who

Earthworked Cley Hill, near Warminster, Wiltshire. The hill is a centre
for UFO activity and stands immediately adjacent to a surface fault.
(*Author's photo*)

has chronicled Warminster UFO events for several years, telling me that he considered the hill to be one of the 'gateways' in the Warminster district from which UFOs issued.

Gooding has informed me that the farmer at Cley Hill Farm, just to the north-west of Cley Hill itself, saw an object the size of 'a full moon' coming from the *side* of the hill in the early hours of the morning. The spheroid then moved off in a north-westerly direction. One evening in the summer of 1977 John Rowston was one of four 'skywatchers' on Cley Hill:

> I remember we hadn't been there long when an orange light was seen moving towards our vantage point from somewhere in the direction of Chapmanslade [a village to the NNW of Cley Hill] . . . after a short while, no more than half a minute, this light seemed to fade away . . . We were now at a point some two hundred yards from the base of the hill and hadn't been there many minutes when whitish, ghost-like images were seen moving at extremely high speed *into the right-hand side* of Cley. These images appeared to be in pairs, one above the other, three sets in all, looking somewhat pear-shaped . . . the next thing we saw resembled a Rugby football. This just hung in the air a couple of seconds or so, then like the others *disappeared into the hill* at terrific speed. This light appeared more condensed than the previous ones were, looking more solid and not so ghostly . . . A few minutes had passed by the time the girls had joined us and we had walked further to the right of the hill. I would imagine that probably fifteen to twenty minutes in all [had passed] when from some place half way up the right side of Cley Hill a ghost-like image appeared . . . this time moving away from the hill. This one was much larger and appeared to be spinning but this aspect may have been a trick of the light or something. [My emphases.][25]

Here we have accounts of UFOs, in different stages of manifestation, both emerging from the hill and returning to it— earthing themselves. On the bases of these reports we can see that the Cley Hill 'ufocal' does not attract the UFOs from outer space: *it produces them itself*. Cley Hill, a 'holy hill', is a generating and earthing point for the phenomena we call flying saucers or UFOs. The process must be closely akin to the 'mountain-top discharges' described earlier (page 97).

Accounts of UFO-genesis are rare, as might be expected, but, like the following account, they do exist. In October 1977, just after midday, a police constable's wife saw an unusual aerial phenomenon from the kitchen window of her Anglesey home. It looked like a 'long, thin red-coloured flame in the sky'. It appeared to be vibrating but not moving in any direction. The husband takes up the story:

At first my wife thought it was an aircraft on fire, but within seconds the 'flame' appeared to form a circle and a domed figure appeared. This figure then started going backwards and forwards. There was no mistaking the shape and things such as portholes could be seen quite plainly.

At this time I arrived home by car and my wife was running into the garage . . . I rushed into the kitchen and there was no mistaking this object was in the sky. I can only describe its colour as that of the setting sun. As regards size, I should say it was about double the size of the sun as we see it . . . the object seemed to go backward and fade away.[26]

We have all been so obsessed with seeking an extraterrestrial, paranormal or psychological source for UFOs that such accounts simply have not been recognized for what they tell us. Another example of this appears graphically in Randles and Warrington's *UFOS—A British Viewpoint.*[27] Towards the end of their book, in a chapter called 'Subjectivity— the Key to the Mystery', they give the following account:

A better defined report comes from Bridgend, South Wales, in the mid-1960s and tells of a sighting by a man and a wife from their back garden. Hearing a noise like a distant jet they saw a white patch of sparkling mist appear low on the horizon, where nothing but a building site stood. A reddish light then materialized by the side of the mist, joined up with it and then started to blink. The mist then began to glow and pulsate, dividing into two sections. These sections began to spin round and around. The smaller of the two now moved on top of the larger one, giving the overall impression of an object looking like a squashed bowler hat. Lights of many colours now came on the bottom of the object which now *began to solidify into a metallic looking disc shape* with a dome on top broken only by a reddish glow underneath.

After this object spun round for a few minutes the noise similar to a jet plane began again. Once again the object became mist-like in appearance and the blinking lights reappeared. Then suddenly the whole thing disappeared. [My emphasis.]

This is a superb description of the formation of a UFO from a ground emanation, with the increasing coherence of the form so that it even took on the appearance of a metallic object (possibly occasioned by discontinuity refraction as suggested by Stuart Campbell—see Chapter 3). But it is clear that UFOs are essentially very unstable phenomena and for every one that does become generated into a sufficiently coherent form to become self-mobile there must be many that collapse or disperse their energy in some way. That is what seems to have happened in this instance. The authors at this point actually remark: 'Was this an instance of a UFO phenomenon actually being created and then returning to the state from which it came?'. Unfortunately, they made this remark in the context of musing over whether or not witnesses somehow created the UFO forms themselves by some psychokinetic process; hence the more obvious import of the account was not visible to them. The very next sentence takes their book onto another topic completely.

Now that this material relating to UFO-formation has been consciously identified, perhaps a collection of such reports could give us an insight into the processes that go into the making of a UFO. Some of those processes have already been outlined in this chapter.

Even the apparently 'solid' UFOs, when manifesting first of all as fireball types of phenomena, or when degenerating into such appearances before flying off, are just aspects of an evolving transient atmospheric event. Even when viewed close up, the solid type of UFO often has ghostly or insubstantial characteristics, as instanced in Case 22 (Chapter 2). Or, again, apparent metallic UFOs can display alarmingly non-tangible aspects of themselves as noted in Cases 12 and 14. UFOs seem attracted to energy sources such as vehicles and power lines and, perhaps, the energy fields surrounding animals and human beings. This gives them a spurious appearance of intelligence, as has been noted in ball lightning behaviour. Also, like ball lightning, UFOs can on *very rare* occasions leave ground marks and burns. I suspect that UFOs are only distantly related to ball lightning, however, because, as Figure 25 shows, the higher UFO incidence takes place in zones of relatively low thunderstorm activity, on the whole, while ball lightning occurs most frequently in connection with normal thunderstorms. (F. Lagarde, though, has claimed that in France ball lightning is associated with fault regions.[28]) This is supported by a map—although based on a very small sample—published by Neil Charman in *New Scientist*,[29] which shows ball lightning frequenting areas of high thunderstorm incidence. Nevertheless, there may very well be some shared processes in the formation of both UFOs and ball lightning. The close relations of UFOs, of course, have to be the 'earthquake lights' type of phenomena.

As I explained when introducing the 'proto-entity' concept in Chapter 2, I suspect that UFO aeroforms and 'occupants' are

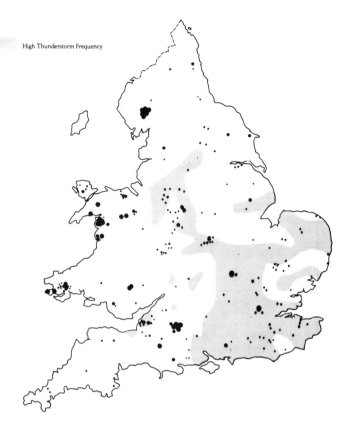

High Thunderstorm Frequency

UFO sightings and Thunderstorms in England and Wales. We have already seen how stone circles and low thunderstorm areas appear to be directly related (diagram 15). This relationship is further confirmed with high UFO incidence in the same areas.

formed out of the same substance or energy matrix as one another. One can evolve out of the other, they can appear side by side, or individually. The independent entity may be closely associated with the columnar discharge noted in the Barmouth wave. A smokey, gaseous or unknown condition of similar appearance is associated with such discharges, but at night it is the glowing part of the phenomenon that most captures the attention. Near New Buffalo, Michigan, several witnesses saw a 'misty, flowing figure' floating outside their home. One of the observers interpreted the glowing mass as being a 'ghost' or an 'angel'. The drawing of the elongated, upright 'blob', about five feet tall, made by one of the witnesses shows that the phenomenon had only the mildest anthropomorphic tendencies.[30]

In the north-west of Leicestershire are the ruins of Grace Dieu Priory and in the field alongside stands the remains of a monolith. In our research on the county Andrew York and I learned of a legend which stated that a 'White Lady' ghost could be seen in this field on rare occasions. It was supposed to be the ghost of one of the nuns belonging to the former priory. To our surprise we discovered that this was not merely a legend, but that it was also claimed that people nowadays had allegedly seen the spectre, even that a country bus which runs along a road down one side of the haunted field had, at night, stopped for a white figure only to find it was the ghost. It was our good fortune to learn of an eyewitness account of the phenomenon. According to this witness, on the bus one evening when one of these incidents occurred, the 'White Lady' was simply a softly glowing, misty column of light, not a figure at all, that floated off across the field.

In daylight, this type of event, or something very similar,

The remains of a standing stone in a field by the ruins of Grace Dieu Priory, Leicestershire, said to be haunted by a 'White Lady' ghost. (*Author's photo*)

seems to appear more as a dark column of gaseous or cloudy substance—a veritable vapour. A witness near Trowbridge in 1979 saw 'smoke' coming through a hedge as he was driving his van along the main road. 'Whatever it was, I don't want to see it again,' the witness remarked. 'Six foot of it came into the middle of the road. It stopped, and tilted on end. I thought I was going to hit it with the van.' The smokey column travelled ahead of the van, which was moving at about 35 m.p.h., for a short distance —then it 'just went into a gateway'.[31]

Such prosaic mysteries, if I can use such a paradoxical term, can become romanticized, as Ian Thomson and I discovered when researching *The Ley Hunter's Companion*. Ragged Stone Hill is at the southern end of the Malvern range which divides Worcestershire from Herefordshire. A legend attached to the hill says that the ghost of a monk can sometimes be seen wandering about on it. The story goes that this monk was given the wretched penance of having to climb up the hill on his hands and knees every morning. Eventually, the unfortunate man could take no more and while cursing everyone from the summit of the hill suffered a fit, collapsed and died. Fortunately, an eyewitness obtained a close look at this ghostly monk last century. He was walking on the hill when he saw 'a black columnar cloud which rose up from between the two peaks of the hill'. This phenomenon detached itself from its point of issue and began moving over the slopes of the hill. The witness decided to make himself scarce and reached the bottom of the hill in a very short space of time. Viewed from a distance (and most people keep their distance from such apparitions) such a man-sized column would easily pass as a cowled monk wandering uneasily around its haunt. Perhaps the slightly more developed anthropomorphic form witnessed by mountaineer Showell Styles in Snowdonia (Case 40) had its origin as a terrestrial emanation of this kind. The author Anthony Roberts has told me that one evening at twilight he thought he saw something moving near the ruined tower on Glastonbury Tor, one of the greatest holy hills of them all, in Somerset. Being at the bottom of the hill he took the pair of field glasses he was carrying and studied the cause of the movement. He was shocked to see two dark columns moving about. They were a good deal taller than a human being, and displayed a moving, gaseous structure.

While I am not for one moment attempting to explain away all types of ghost events, it is obvious that such columnar effects could, at a distance, be mistaken as ghostly figures, and must account for some ghost stories as well as some 'entity' reports.

The terrestrial discharge or emanation, then, initially emerges from the ground as a streamer—a potential 'searchlight beam', 'pillar of fire' or columnar phenomenon—and then, presumably depending on the vagaries of the ambient electromagnetic fields, either develops as one of the varieties of columnar shapes or localizes as a spheroid. At Barmouth we saw that spheres could form actually within the columnar forms and float upwards, often with the column disappearing. At a certain point in the whole process photon-emission occurs revealing the form of the discharge. Only a small percentage of such discharges last for any length of time, and even fewer develop sufficient stability to move away from the point of issue.

The underlying mechanism behind this curious phenomenon must be the force fields associated with seismic movement. When this movement is great we can expect the vast displays known as earthquake lights and mountain peak discharges. But the event of a major earthquake itself is likely to cause such lights to disappear as the potential energy being released in that form is suddenly disgorged in an orgasm of kinetic energy. The relatively milder seismic movements afterwards might again cause light forms to appear in the local atmosphere.

UFOs are most likely to appear in areas associated with faulting and tectonic disturbance but, as we have seen, such areas are not always apparent and a check of tremor epicentre activity in an apparently stable area will reveal the presence of overlaid faults. These types of areas also attract UFOs, or rather, they also produce them. Persinger and Lafrenière have pointed out (Chapter 3) that an actual earthquake is not necessary to produce their idea of a seismically-based atmospheric light phenomenon: the simple waxing and waning of tectonic stress would be sufficient to produce UFO phenomena. People on the surface above such areas need not be aware of the geological movements taking place beneath them.

UFOs, and some 'ghosts', result from a particular kind of terrestrial discharge event. The energy body produced has unique characteristics. The work of Brady et al may perhaps give us insights into the nature of this newly-discovered, but long observed, phenomenon.

The 'mundane' occurrence of this discharge phenomenon accounts for the bulk of all genuine UFO reports: it can appear as a disc or a sphere, it can fly, it has little mass and its direction can be quickly changed by the whim of surrounding electromagnetic fields and, possibly, air movements as well when the phenomenon reaches a certain degree of density. It can change colour and shape. It can 'land' (i.e. it can earth itself). It can be a 'landed object' (i.e. after forming it does not take off, or does so only after initial observation by a witness). The surface of this energy body can take on a dark aspect at times, sometimes producing a metallic appearance, perhaps through some refractive process, as suggested by Campbell, or perhaps for other reasons such as the formation of some kind of electrical 'sheen' effect. The phenomenon can be attracted to energy sources, thus giving the appearance of rudimentary intelligence or inquisitive behaviour. It can be surrounded by a static field of some kind and can cause certain forms of skin irritation in witnesses. It very occasionally can give off a sound, usually a whistling, whining sound or a buzzing like a swarm of bees. These are probably electrical sounds.

All these effects, and possibly more, can be accounted for by such a phenomenon. Some isolated natives in Melanesia, seeing an aircraft flying overhead think of it as coming from the other side of the sky, as a messenger from the gods. They create votive offerings in the shape of aircraft and airport paraphernalia to attract the heavenly messengers to the ground. It is sobering to realize that a similar response to UFOs may have informed our thinking on the subject for the last thirty years or so. Because we hardly ever see where a UFO comes from, we think it has to originate in the sky, since that is where such phenomena are frequently seen. When encountered on the ground, a UFO is assumed to have landed. Much of our thinking on UFOs has been little more than the intellectual equivalent of a cargo-plane cult. Brighter UFO natives are now substituting 'paranormal' for the other side of the sky, but it is still another form of the same cult. Like aircraft, UFOs are made on Earth, even though they can take off, fly, land and, occasionally, take off again.

It will be instructive to learn more about this intriguing form of terrestrial discharge or emanation, because though its 'normal' modes account for most genuine UFO appearances, the records show that on exceptional occasions the phenomenon can demonstrate an awesome extra quality. It is to that we must now turn.

8.

The Geopsychic Epiphany

*Epiphany, n. Manifestation . . . of a superhuman
being (from Gk. phaino, show).*

From a dictionary definition

Most UFOs are seen as shapeshifting blobs of light, often of an
essentially discoid form. Sometimes vaguely anthropomorphic
forms are observed, but there are occasions when the forms of
these things are seen to 'harden' and take on a very clear
appearance of a machine or an entity.

The terrestrial discharge phenomenon seems able, under
certain circumstances that are by no means clear, to act as a
carrier of imagery, its own substance accommodating the
image's form. The UFO itself is non-sentient but sometimes
seems able to support intelligent displays, like the television
screen representing images from signals transmitted electronic-
ally by human intelligence many miles away in the television
studio. Some medieval person coming into a modern home and
seeing someone speaking on the television might suppose that
there was a little man in the television set, whereas we know that
the instrument is merely a non-sentient intermediary between
the studio personnel and our minds. I think UFOs are an
analogous intermediary.

No theory attempting to explain UFOs can be complete unless
it takes into account what Jung called the phenomenon's
'psychic relatedness'; unless it goes some way to accounting for
the pageant of mythic imagery UFOs have always displayed.
*We must not confuse the exterior, objective nature of the UFO
'carrier' with the imagery it sometimes translates itself into.*

Persinger and Lafrenière think that the electromagnetic fields causing the objective event can trigger imagery in the witness' mind. There are problems with this notion. While not denying that electrical impulses can certainly instigate moods and mental imagery, to suppose this identifies itself in perfect synchronization with an exterior event is hard to accept. If the hallucinated UFO imagery starts behaving in different ways to the external phenomenon, what happens then? We presumably must have a negative hallucination cancelling the witness' perception of the objective phenomenon to allow the electrically stimulated positive hallucination to continue uninterrupted. A complex mechanism indeed.

My own Ravensbourne UFO experience, recounted in Chapter 1, convinces me that UFO forms are *modifications of the UFO material itself*. Non-witnesses may want to believe that the witness is not *really* seeing an objective UFO change its shape and is, rather, superimposing internal mental imagery on to a basic exterior form, *à la* Jung; but I have to disagree. As a witness, I am sorry to have to insist that it is the UFO that changes form, not the observer's perception of it. The objective existence of the UFO form is beyond doubt.

It is the UFO that changes. The UFO 'hardens' into the form that is finally identified as a spaceship, robot or little green man. The data clearly tell us that UFOs can shapeshift: *it is a prime characteristic of the phenomenon.* The body of data I have put under the 'proto-entity' label shows that entity forms assumed by UFOs can be incomplete or badly proportioned like a child's drawing. UFO 'machines' themselves sometimes seem to have trouble in maintaining 'solidity'. In all cases the coherence of such displays is transient and sooner or later the whole thing disperses its energy and suddenly goes out like a defective bulb or fades away like a mirage. Sometimes remnants of the discharge material is left in the atmosphere, as happened in the Ravensbourne event or the Hill family's sighting (Chapter 3), which slowly disperses on currents of air. This remnant material therefore seems to have some measure of density.

Dutch researcher Jan Heering has made a study of the 'solid light' characteristics apparent in some UFO events. Here are examples of five different events taken from witnesses' experiences quoted in an article by Heering:[1]

> My first impression was that the machine stood on the ground by means of legs or pillars. Then I realized they weren't legs but light beams.

I thought for a moment that it was a telescopic antenna coming out of the device; however, a few instants later, I realized that it was actually a beam of light . . . it came out with an exaggerated slowness, like the antenna of a snail.

Lower down something like a lampshade was hanging. It was shining with a strange purple light . . . the light was flowing and pulsating from the 'lampshade' like water from a fountain. Where the light hit the ground I could see a sparkling effect.

. . . a six-storey object . . . It gave off rainbow colours which appeared to pour off its edges like water in a fantastic display.

During a couple of seconds nothing happened; then, to our great consternation, out of this light, which was bewildering in its fixedness, came a white, threadlike light, zig-zag shaped with sharp angles, which slowly started falling vertically downward like a rope ladder being unrolled from a roof.

The impression of fluidity is strongly noted by witnesses of this apsect of the UFO phenomenon. UFO light can bend and curve, and tends not to light up surroundings. The beams of light are sometimes withdrawn into a spheroid *slowly* so the end of the light beam can be seen. One way to explain such odd appearance of light is to assume that the electromagnetic effect is present but invisible and only becomes discernible through some process of illumination which reveals it in stages. So in the case of the light beam, the 'end' is only the point where the photon-producing process ceases. Heering admits that ionization could be part of such a process but feels it does not answer all the characteristics of the phenomenon. However, UFO theorists need not feel embarrassed about being unable to come up with a slick explanation of the process causing photon-production, because light emission from events such as ball lightning still remains a mysterious mechanism from the point of view of scientists. We have not yet learned all the secrets of light. Heering observes that sometimes the light beams seem to be of the same substance as the UFOs—as, indeed, has been noted in this present work. The appearance of 'solid light' is sometimes accompanied by sounds—in one case a crackling noise was heard. 'How the light is produced and how the production mechanism can be kept confined to such a well-defined zone remains unexplained,' Herring writes, 'but there can be no question that "solid light" is an objective phenomenon. It will not succumb to psychological interpretations.' The objective nature of solid light phenomena is clear when one studies the large numbers of witnesses' experiences worldwide collected by Heering. Similarities of expression and description are remarkably consistent and there is no way such an unusual appearance could have been independently invented by scores of widely dispersed people.

Whatever the process, the localized, invisible UFO and its attendant discharge streamers take on appearance through some method of self-illumination. This process can go on until what appears to be a semi-solid form is created. In some cases this form—of very low mass—can become mobile and can divide itself, cell-like, and will almost invariably at this point change speed and colour. It is unstable, although at a certain phase of manifestation it seems to possess a 'solid light' plasticity that enables it to harden its shape into precise contours for fairly brief periods. The full nature of this phenomenon is as surely unknown as it is real and natural. We know that very slow lightnings and almost malleable discharges have been observed for decades around the world;[2] with the UFO we have the most perfect expression of this natural phenomenon.

So, UFOs are non-sentient, geophysically produced phenomena—transient pockets of energy or tenuous matter—produced anywhere under the right conditions (the full range of which we are currently ignorant) but particularly in areas of geological faulting or disturbance—which also tend to be areas of mineral enrichment and low thunderstorm activity. Their nature has been widely observed but not yet studied by science due to inherent defects in scientific outlook and organization—not necessarily the scientific method—as it exists today.

One of the most bizzare aspects of this observed but uninvestigated phenomenon is that it is highly sensitive and responsive to energetic effects produced by human mental processes. *This has to be the case, because UFO imagery has been shown to contain elements belonging to the human psyche: the imagery must therefore derive from human consciousness.* The UFO appearance, whether as space machine, entity or alien monster, is to some extent analogous to the image produced on photographic paper when a negative is projected onto it (see Case 29 for a precise parallel to this analogy). In other words, the material comprising the UFO form must be Jung's 'as yet unknown substrate possessing material and at the same time psychic qualities' or Vallee's 'natural phenomenon whose manifestations border on both the physical and the mental';

although I feel it is unnecessary to assume that UFO material is anything other than a very sensitive energy form. It is an un-investigated construct of material forces, and there is no need to involve unknown 'mental substances'.

The UFO can only respond to mental content if that inform-ation is somehow transmitted to it. The only way this can be done, presumably, is by the process we call 'psychokinesis' (PK) —the action of the mind-brain on external matter. There are those who cannot bring themselves to accept that such a process is possible despite the clear evidence in support of it provided by such impeccable and careful researchers as Professor John Hasted of Birkbeck College, London. The matter that comprises UFOs is, I suspect, the most responsive to mental cues that exists outside the human brain (everyone accepts—sometimes too glibly, perhaps—that the non-corporeal mind can manipulate the physical energy systems of the brain; the 'machine a ghost can use'). *The UFO is a profoundly sensitive energy form.* Practical magicians develop their PK expertise by concentrating on a candle flame, as this is matter in a particularly tenuous state susceptible to subtle influences. The UFO form is 'a very wonderful fire' as one witness in the Barmouth wave put it.

In discussing the concept with author and geomantic re-searcher Anthony Roberts, he came up with the idea of the UFO phenomenon, viewed in this way, as being a sort of 'planetary ectoplasm'. I feel this is—to some extent—a convenient way of thinking about it.

It seems likely that the remarkable genius Nikola Tesla (1856-1943) may have isolated an energy form similar to the nature of UFOs, if the following account is anything to go by:

> I was confident . . . that with properly designed machinery signals could be transmitted to any part of the globe, no matter what the distance, without the necessity of using such intermediate stations. I gained this conviction through the discovery of a singular electrical phenomenon, which I described early in 1892 . . . and which I have called a 'rotating brush'. This is a bundle of light which is formed, under certain conditions, in a vacuum-bulb, and which is of a sensitiveness to magnetic and electric influences bordering, so to speak, on the supernatural. This light-bundle is rapidly rotated by the earth's magnetism as many as twenty thousand times per second, the rotation in these parts being opposite to what it would be in the southern hemisphere, while in the region of the magnetic equator it should not rotate at all. In its most sensitive state, which is

difficult to attain, it is responsive to electric or magnetic influences to an incredible degree. The mere stiffening of the muscles of an arm and consequent slight electrical change in the body of an observer standing at some distance from it, will perceptibly affect it. When in this highly sensitive state it is capable of indicating the slightest magnetic and electric changes taking place in the earth. The observation of this wonderful phenomenon impressed me strongly[3]. . .

Tesla remarked on the difficulty in maintaining the phenomenon in its most sensitive state, and it is possible that he never managed to reproduce the full characteristics of the phenomenon in the way that Nature can. And it is unlikely that Tesla ever tested the phenomenon's potential response to PK!

There is a valuable hint in UFO reports of the Second World War that should alert us. Both Allied and German fliers were frequently 'buzzed' by spheres of light the Allies called 'foo fighters'. Each side thought the other had a secret weapon, for a while. What is important is to note that some airmen reported that the lights *seemed to be responding to their thought processes*[4].

The mental signals affecting some UFOs will, presumably, come from different levels of consciousness, and the intensity with which a UFO is likely to respond to such an input into its system will vary with a number of conditions—the proximity of the human 'transmitter(s)', the phase of development in the UFO, its level of plasticity and stability at that phase, the ambient electromagnetic conditions, the strength of the PK, and so on. It is worth noting that some UFO witnesses do seem to have a history of psychic experiences. Should one of these types be present at a UFO event it is likely that they will act as involuntary shamans and that the UFO form will be strongly affected, whereas a UFO appearing in the vicinity of someone with more stultified psychic and PK abilities may be less modified in form and perhaps unaffected altogether, proceeding serenely with its mindless, natural shapeshifting and discoid appearances. It is indeed possible that the electromagnetic fields associated with UFO production might in themselves enhance mental processes, causing the 'involuntary shamanism' of the witness. This may be precisely what happened at Barmouth, and why the 1967 UFO wave, at the peak of psychedelia, sported more than its fair share of exotic UFO forms—the mental 'signals' already being enhanced by psycho-sociological processes.

In a wave area, where the geophysical conditions temporarily exist for exceptional UFO production and the idea begins to spread throughout the community that either a heavenly, devilish or extra-terrestrial agency is at work, it would be expected that humanoids would begin to make their appearance —angels and saints, demons, robots and spacemen. We could see that process beginning to take place at Towyn (Case 34) during the Barmouth wave, as it certainly did at Dyfed where the wave lasted for a longer period. But these signals will not be consciously produced and projected by an individual. He or she will, at the simplest level, share the prevailing imagery of the culture they live in. In our case, that means a technological outlook. This was made clear to me many years ago when I was standing on Cradle Hill, Warminster, with the Buddhist teacher Sthavira Sangharakshita: he mentioned that aerial lights in the Himalayas tend to take on the appearance of Hindu and other deities known to the people.

Behind this subsurface level of shared imagery there are deeper realms. There are the archetypal images expressing functions of the collective unconscious, that separate entity about which we know nothing as Jung reminded us, which will be common to all humans though their appearance will sometimes be modified by racial symbolism and current cultural overlays. And we must remember that these images, from a source unknown to the conscious mind, is being reflected back to the normal waking consciousness of the witness who may then further filter and misinterpret what he or she is seeing.

I rather suspect—though I hardly dare put the concept into words as it is so strange to our way of thinking—that there may be another source of input into the UFO form: the Earth itself . . . or herself. If we can extend the idea of 'Gaia', in which the *whole* planet is seen as a single, self-monitoring organism, is it not possible to consider that the planet may dream? Images of this planetary dreaming would be likely to be seen by us as geometric and possibly zoomorphic and anthropomorphic forms—expressions of the functions of Nature. Perhaps this is where the images of 'elementals' and 'devas' come from.

But even assuming only human input into the ufological 'planetary ectoplasm' it is important to realize that the ensuing images will not necessarily relate to the personal interests of the witness. The resulting UFO display may appear quite accurately as 'other worldly' to the observer: in reality, a confrontation with the unknown and, to everyday consciousness, alien appearances. Aldous Huxley emphasized the autonomous nature of the unconscious in his essay *Heaven and Hell*:

> The typical mescalin or lysergic acid experience begins with perceptions of coloured, moving, living geometrical forms. In time, pure geometry becomes concrete, and the visionary perceives, not patterns, but patterned things, such as carpets, carvings, mosaics. These give place to vast and complicated buildings, in the midst of landscapes, which change continuously, passing from richness to more intensely coloured richness, from grandeur to deepening grandeur. Heroic figures, of the kind that Blake called 'The Seraphim', may make their appearance, alone or in multitudes. Fabulous animals move across the scene. Everything is novel and amazing. Almost never does the visionary see anything that reminds him of his own past. He is not remembering scenes, persons or objects, and he is not inventing them; he is looking on at a new creation.[6]

Huxley went on to quote Dr J. R. Smythies, who said that the contents of the deeper, visionary parts of the mind were 'the work of a highly differentiated mental compartment, without any apparent connexion, emotional or volitional, with the aims, interests, or feelings of the person concerned'. Jung, it has been noted, also stressed the independent nature of the deeper psyche. At one point in his life he experienced an aspect of his psyche which appears to have become quite externalized. It appeared to him as a winged figure he called Philemon:

> Philemon represented a force which was not myself. In my fantasies I held conversations with him, and he said things which I had not consciously thought. For I observed clearly that it was he who spoke, not I. He said I treated thoughts as if I generated them myself, but in his view thoughts were like animals in a forest . . . and [he] added, 'If you should see people in a room you would not think that you had made those people, or that you were responsible for them.' It was he who taught me psychic objectivity, the reality of the psyche. Through him the distinction was clarified between myself and the object of my thought. He confronted me in an objective manner, and I understood that there is something in me which can say things that I do not know and do not intend, things which may even be directed against me.[7]

So the content appearing through the UFO medium *can be superior to conscious human knowledge*. In such circumstances the UFO witness is confronting superior intelligence, and human

understanding can be enhanced by such contact. We can agree
with the film poster that 'We are not alone' but more accurately
put the alien presence in the context of *inner* rather than *outer*
space.

On the one hand the mysteries of the universe can be reflected
back to the stunned conscious mind of the witness, while on the
other—a far more common occurrence—all that is displayed are
elements from the common cultural ethos, usually in the comic-
strip media imagery that has now become the mental currency
for keeping our collective beliefs, fears and dreams alive. If the
UFO pageant today resembles nothing more than the incoherent
ravings of a fevered mind, then that is the true reflection of our
current collective mental situation.

For a brief period in the mid-1960s comic-strip cosmology was
surpassed by the effects of hundreds of thousands of western
minds plumbing deep recesses of their psyches with psychedelic
drugs. The changing awareness this began to bring about was
actually augmented by the media for a while, caught as it was by
surprise. (This did not last for long, however, and the media
reasserted its omnipotent crudeness by launching what is
probably the most vicious attack on expanding consciousness
for which we have any record.) Hence UFO forms took on more
archetypal images: there were flying crosses over Devon, aerial
Christs over Northampton in amongst the more mundane
fireballs and shapeshifters. I can have no doubt that the Ravensbourne event was an archetypal image being displayed on a geophysical 'screen' in real time-space. Primordial Man, the cross,
Adam Qadmon—interpret the archetype as you will—was able
to take on transient appearance over the fields of Bromley just as
long as the geophysical event, the UFO, could structure it. The
richness of the archetype was only to become apparent to me
years later when I was attending a seminar conducted by Keith
Critchlow. We were discussing how the fundamental geometry
of Nature can be echoed in artefactual forms. One such was the
door: Critchlow pointed out that the door is essentially a $\sqrt{5}$
proportional rectangle[8] because it has to accommodate the
human frame which grows to $\sqrt{5}$ proportional systems. My first
thought when I saw the fiery rectangle coming from the Bromley
direction was that it looked like a flaming door in the sky. That it
changed to a 'universal man' type of image is exceptionally significant and indicative of an archetypal sequence. *Such an event
can only have been orchestrated by the unconscious mind, and*

yet, there is the fact that it was also happening out there in exterior space.

With hindsight, I comprehend the glowing form at Ravensbourne as tenuously physical material, churning, receiving the mental cue when its configurations momentarily resembled that of a human figure in cross-like pose. The interference of the conscious mind was held in abeyance by the simple action of shock, and the deeper levels of consciousness were able to model the UFO form. Whether that mental signal came through the individual mind of myself or one of the other witnesses, or whether it was transmitted collectively through all our minds, it is impossible to tell.

It may be that there is some form of symbiosis between UFO phenomena and human beings: some reports do indicate that they sometimes show a tendency to 'home in' on people, even more effectively than ball lightning. It could be that they are attracted by the electric field surrounding human bodies—and perhaps subtler energies—or it may be a natural consequence of the Gaia principle.

Whether that is so or not, my own experiences and investigations leave me in no doubt that an interaction between a geophysical phenomenon and the human mind can, on rare occasions, take place: a geopsychic process, in which mind and external Nature meet. A perfect illustration of this process was provided by an experience undergone by Frank Earp of Nottinghamshire. He gave his account in *Northern Earth Mysteries* and because it is so valuable I will quote from it at some length:

> The incident I am about to relate is entirely true. It happened fourteen years ago, some time around October 1966, when I was fifteen years old and still at school. Although it happened half my lifetime ago, I'll remember it for the rest . . . I and a small group of school friends had, a year or two previously, formed what was then called (and probably still is) a 'Contact group'. I relate this information to set the scene as it were and to show that at the time our minds were very 'UFO oriented' . . . I and two friends, who I shall refer to as John and Barry, met together at John's house, as we often did. Within 120 yards . . . runs the course of the disused Nottingham Canal. John's road is a cul-de-sac, terminating in a short footpath which leads, between the end houses, to an old dirt track known as Woodyard lane. At right angles, the old canal crosses the lane about ten yards south of where this path emerges. The course of the canal continues as waste ground and allotments parallel with John's road, behind the houses.

On this particular fine evening we decided to walk along the tow path of the canal about half a mile westward to the site of Wollaton Colliery, for which the canal had served as transport. The mine was now disused . . . The exact time and day has escaped me but it must have been a weekend or half-term holiday for it was still quite light, perhaps about 4.00 p.m. Having walked to the spoil-heap on the north bank of the canal it was too light for our 'skywatch'. We spent our time in pursuits usual to boys of our age, like doing Tarzan acts from a rope tied to one of the large trees in the bank . . . We decided as the light was fading into dusk to make our way back. We had seen no one else . . . but this was not unusual . . . It was thought an ideal skywatch place and as we crossed over to the other bank and began our walk back there were frequent glances at the sky for that ever elusive glimpse.

As the dusk faded into the eerie twilight before the onset of darkness proper the ground mist started to rise from the bed of the now semi-dry canal . . . we had seen this on other occasions but for some reason this time it gave us an uneasy feeling. We quickened our pace. Looking back, we saw that the mist had gathered in a cloud some four feet above the swampy ground. To our amazement, a patch of this smoke-like vapour seemed to take on independent action and detached itself from the rest. It formed, as we watched, into a 'doughnut' shape (minus the hole) seen end on, and was about the size of a fairground bumper car. It seemed to glow with a strange, pale, lucid light. The now independent disc of mist moved slowly forward from the rest and then onto the towpath, about twenty yards behind us, then stopped. I made the suggestion to the others that what we were witnessing was the natural phenomenon of 'marsh gas' or 'Will o' the Wisp'. This, however, did nothing to ease our growing feelings of discontent. Inevitably, our fear overcame our curiosity and we thought it prudent to move off. We spoke a few words of uneasy conversation as we walked slowly on, but a glance over our shoulders disquieted us even more. The mini mist cloud, complete with its internal illumination, was slowly following us. It glided noiselessly two feet above the ground and its translucent form filled the towpath from the hawthorn hedge on one side to the canal bank on the other.

We stopped and it stopped; we moved and it moved. Each time it drew a little closer. We stopped again, knowing that this was not just a methane glow. It was now well clear of its parent cloud, which had not moved and, indeed, was out of sight around a slight bend in the course of the canal. A feeling of excitement grew in us as we thought of the prospects of witnessing—a UFO?

By now the evening light was failing fast and, as we watched the glow in the centre of the mist cloud, two milky white spheres began to materialize. They were about the size of a car's headlamps and just under the same distance apart. They did not shine like lights, but there was a strange luminosity about them. Could it be the longed-for sighting?

As we watched, to our horror and dismay, the whole thing, lights and all, advanced slowly towards us, stopped, and came on. Our pace quickened almost to a jog. Looking round, I saw that the 'thing' had too quickened its pace, but was keeping its distance . . . A little way in front, another old lane crossed the canal. At this crossing point there had once stood a hump-backed bridge . . . the bridge had long since been pulled down and the lane crossed on a long earth bank. I remember feeling that if we crossed this bank the 'thing' would not dare to follow. After all, we were half way back to John's house and civilization; reality would—we hoped—shortly take hold. We crossed the bank at a running pace. On the other side we stopped to catch our breath. The 'thing' too had stopped . . . it was poised, almost uncertainly, and then began again to move towards us at a steady speed. The three of us looked despairingly at one another and ran in panic.

As we reached the end of the stretch of canal where it crossed Woodyard Lane, we could see the reassuring glow of the street light that illuminates the little footpath leading to the houses . . . This put new strength into us and we slowed our headlong flight . . . It was now quite dark, but the self-lit cloud could still be seen following us; it too had slowed its pace. Now it was much, much nearer, a matter of feet, not yards. Words were exchanged and we decided once more to stop and turn. This we did. Our pursuer stopped twenty or so feet away. It was as if we were watching it watching us. Slowly, it edged its way forwards. John now suggested that we retreat once more and make our final stand just before the lane. The ground opened out there and we had only sixty yards or so to dash to the road. It was also decided that I should confront the object and attempt to speak to it. We felt there was some kind of intelligence behind it . . . Why I should be selected for this dubious honour I'll never know . . . The three of us blocked the towpath, myself in the centre. John stood on my left near the tall hawthorn hedge; Barry stood on my right near the concrete post of the fence that blocks the canal. The cloud was now only six feet in front of us. The two luminous spheres seemed to dance up and down as if on an invisible piece of elastic. The mist swirled round the spheres and about the path on either side. For a moment we stood and stared, hardly believing our eyes. This thing was real and a matter of feet away; not high in the sky or over some distant field.

A nudge from my companion snapped me back to the present. Hesitantly, I took half a step forward, but was at a loss what to say in such circumstances . . . my words trailed off as I was interrupted by Barry, who was frantically tapping my shoulder. 'Don't say anything,' he whispered, 'just start to walk backwards, and when I say "run", run!' . . . John was still staring intently at the lights in the cloud, as if mesmerized by the swaying motion. 'Look!' Barry pointed to my left as he spoke and grabbed my arm. I followed the direction he indicated, but my brain was hardly prepared for what met my eyes.

The hawthorn hedge to my left stood out like a black silhouette against the night sky; no detail was visible—only the black outline. There was something else there, however, blacker than the night around it. A figure stood, or rather appeared to be standing, over to my left slightly in front of the cloud. It was only four or five feet away from John, but he appeared not to notice it. His eyes were still fixed on the spheres.

As far as I could make out, the figure should have been about six feet tall, but it was not standing on solid ground. The path here has a shallow ditch between it and the hedge and it was here that the figure appeared. Its eye-level was about the same as my own (I was then just over six feet tall). The figure did not appear to be three-dimensional, but looked flat, rather like a cardboard cut-out. It gave the overall impression of being hairy all over. Its head was mounted directly on its shoulder. No facial or other details were visible as we were seeing it lit from the back by the cloud.

The shoulders were hunched up and its arms hung low by its side. The arms ended without hands almost like a single finger which curled inwards. In each of these curved 'hooks' it held what I can only describe as a glowing rod. Each was about eight to ten inches long and thicker than the average pencil. They glowed red as if with heat. Its legs were straight, but disappeared from the knee down, not like the tapering arms. They actually faded out; the mist swirled round where its feet should have been. If one imagined the missing part of its legs in proportion to the rest of the body it would have been hovering a few inches above the ground.

This sight was all I could stand. The cloud and its lights, yes, but this—no way. It appeared to be looking at me . . . although I could not see its eyes—indeed, I didn't know if it had any. I must say I remained long enough to take it all in. The whole thing, from Barry tugging my sleeve to my headlong flight back to John's house, seemed to last an eternity. Barry and I took our backward steps, but I didn't need his signal to run. As we fled over the open space to Woodyard Lane and the footpath I did not look back. I heard John's voice calling out 'I can still see the lights, lads . . . lads, what's going on?' then the sound of his feet following hard on our heels.

'Did you see it?' Barry asked as the three of us now entered the path and stopped for breath. It was clear that we had not been pursued further by either the 'thing' or the cloud.

'For goodness sake, don't say a word,' I replied. 'Wait until we're back at John's house and we all draw what we have seen and then compare them afterwards.'

Barry and I both drew the figure and all the details mentioned above. We all drew the cloud and strange spheres. John had not seen the figure although I swear that if he had stepped forward and stretched out his hand he would have touched it![9]

We have in this experience nearly all the elements we have grown used to in studying the formation of UFO imagery. Emission from the ground, vaporous appearance, light emission —even down to the poorly-constructed entity. And Frank is in no doubt that he and his friends witnessed an event that had an external reality. Like me, he is prepared to undergo any test designed to ascertain veracity of statement—subject to similar conditions.

There are a few additional points of interest. Frank told me that the mist, when it detached itself, had a vaguely spangled quality—a description that is often made. The area was noted for hauntings. This experience happened during a period when Frank experienced certain psychic events: perhaps we have here the preconditions for involuntary shamanism. We have been

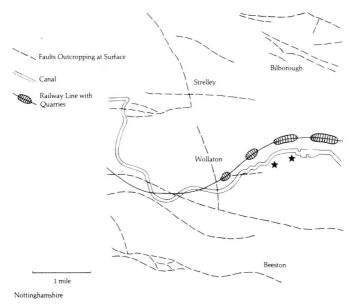

Nottinghamshire Faults. The amazing UFO experience of Frank Earp occurred in a highly faulted region to the west of Nottingham.

able to confirm that the immediate area of the incident is affected by faulting.

UFOs are terrestrial emanations and imagery can be formed within their substance. The geopsychic process does take place.

If this process is at work on our planet now, then it must have been in existence ever since conditions on Earth could produce UFO phenomena. Could the ancients have known of this geopsychic process?

I think the answer to that must be 'yes'—if we go back in time far enough. It is possible a natural science existed in the Neolithic period, the aim of which was the consummation of this interaction between the psyche and the 'planetary ectoplasm'. From the late Neolithic period onwards, perhaps, this knowledge began to fragment. The physical aspects of the process seem to have been lost first, while the mental preparation seems to have lingered in ever fragmenting form through priesthoods, sects, magical practices, secret brotherhoods and alchemy. With the onset of the industrial era these fragments were swept aside as occult rubbish, unwanted bits and pieces of a former system now discredited.

But the whole system did once exist, I am sure of that. In studying these occult groups and thinkers, one senses that something more complete, more awesome, so incredible as to be unspeakable, existed in remote antiquity.

Prehistory contains a great secret. Its magnitude cannot be overestimated. Part of the enigma has been tabulated in geometric and numerological language in the pyramids of Egypt and South America; in hundreds of stone circles; in the structure of pre-Reformation cathedrals; in the siting, proportions and decorations of ancient holy places, and in the writings of magicians and alchemists. This process of notation spans the world, the human race and vast periods of time. Perhaps nowhere but in the very oldest structures was there a full knowledge of the whole system expressed. In certain other cases such notation must have been by rote rather than understanding. The enigmatic information thus preserved hints at some profound knowledge and some remarkable human ability of the remote past. It is unquestionably a secret concerning something far greater than a mere system of symbolism or religious ideals. It involved the knowledge of a form of psychophysical mechanics that has left a blurred imprint on the racial memory.

The reasons for its decay could be many. Plague, feudalism,

invasion, natural catastrophy, the formation of elite groups . . . anything. We are talking about vast periods of time. In Britain, one senses that when social patterns changed during the Bronze Age there was a considerable loss of the old knowledge, a process that increased as society became cruder and more materialistic. The Iron Age Druids were at the end of a tattered line of knowledge—even though what they had must have been considerably superior to that known by occultists of the historic period.

We know that UFOs have their highest incidence in fault regions, areas of mineral enrichment and (relatively) low thunderstorm activity. It has been shown that the megalith builders displayed similar preferences. *This should alert us to the possibility that there may be some fundamental connection between these two patterns.*

We have already seen that three peak UFO zones in Britain— Dyfed, Barmouth and Cumbria—all fall in areas containing exceptional faulting and sitings of megalithic monuments. Warminster too was a major centre in prehistory, though its sites are more of the earthen variety. But here there are also differences about the geology: while faults are at the centre of the region the main area of the locale is geologically stable. At Warminster, one of the *hills* seems to be a centre of both UFO and former prehistoric activity. There is an echo of this in the prehistoric hills above Hereford and Winchester(where there was probably a stone circle on the site now occupied by the cathedral), both places with a history of exceptional UFO activity. Hereford, too, has suffered many tremors. Where there are abundant surface faults and other geological disturbance there are megalithic structures of various sorts; where there are more isolated faults there are holy hills. Glastonbury Tor is another example of a holy hill around which UFOs have been reported fairly frequently,[10] and it also has a history of earth-quakes—a church on its summit was destroyed by one several centuries ago. I have already mentioned Leicestershire's Croft Hill and China's UFO-mountain Wu T'ai Shan. There seems to be the basis of a pattern in all of this—though I do not pretend that it is anything other than embryonic at this stage.

In East Anglia we have far fewer prehistoric remains—and a far lower incidence of UFO activity. The seismic factors that give rise to what UFO events there are in the region are deep-seated, overlaid by considerable sedimentary deposits. Such

deeply embedded faults would be exceptionally difficult to
dowse—and it is probable that some form of divining akin to
dowsing was employed by the megalith builders—as modern
dowsers themselves are sure was the case. They would have
been seeking certain patterns of electromagnetic disturbance
occasioned by subterranean water, metallic ore concentrations
and surface faulting—just as the Russians are doing today. East
Anglia is notably lacking in some of these characteristics. This
combined with the high thunderstorm activity associated with
the region would have made East Anglia unsuitable for the
practices of the natural science being pursued by the ancients.
Whatever the circumstances, the observable fact remains that
the megalith builders required the proximity of *surface* faulting
and the electromagnetic conditions that accompany such
geology.

It is impossible to give a one-to-one correlation for stone
circles and UFOs, for a number of reasons. Megaliths are more
or less permanent; UFOs are transient. UFOs can and do occur
anywhere with a quake history but we have seen such places
would not necessarily been attractive for the practitioners of the
ancient knowledge. Whereas a distribution picture of old stones
can be built up without any reference to population trends,
UFOs are totally dependent on human observation. Even
though we have made our own preliminary attempt to offset the
interference of population patterns with UFO incidence it is not
possible to fully eradicate their effects and arrive at a full,
genuine picture of the *actual* distribution of UFO incidence. So
we are forced to compare a more or less complete set of data, the
location of the stones, with a forever partial data set, the UFOs.
In somewhere like London, of course, it is impossible to even
consider the correlation because we do not know what the prehistoric landscape there was like.

But even with all these difficulties it is abundantly clear that
*old stones and UFOs share the same siting characteristics and, in
key areas common to both patterns, exactly the same regions of
the landscape.* Holy hills may possibly relate to a secondary
pattern of geological features and the incidence of UFOs. It is a
common pattern that mutely suggests that the ancients were involved with some activity associated with the UFO
phenomenon.

When researching *The Ley Hunter's Companion* we found
that 37.5 per cent of the leys we were selecting showed some

evidence of UFO events occurring on them or in their immediate vicinity. It was impossible to determine whether this UFO incidence was associated with the alignments as such or with *the sites forming the alignments*. Because a ley is simply an implied line formed by the positioning of the sites it is very difficult to separate out which is the most significant aspect. It is best to simply state, I think, that ancient sites, and therefore leys, tend to occur particularly strongly in areas that attract considerable UFO activity. Although some people make wild claims about the relationship between UFOs and leys, I have not seen any hard evidence to make a more specific statement than that. But a 37.5 per cent correlation on what was, from a ufological point of view, a random sample of sites, seems a higher number than one might expect by chance.

Alignment characteristics of the deployment of some ancient sites was an underlying element in the ancient knowledge, but the exact function of such alignments remains obscure.

There are a few anecdotal fragments to support the association of ancient sites with unusual aerial phenomena. A particularly dramatic example occurred in January 1974. Exactly what took place is unclear to this day, but, basically, it seems a tremor was felt during the evening of 23 January. It was centred on Bwrdd Arthur (Arthur's Table), a mountain in the Berwyn range of northern mid-Wales. Seismic recording units in Scotland registered the event and said it was of 'unusually large magnitude'.[11] There were reports of an explosion being heard simultaneously with the tremor. It was heard over a radius of tens of miles. Before and after this event, curious fireballs were seen, both in the vicinity of Arthur's Table and nationwide. As far as I have been able to piece the fragments of information together, it seems that a white fireball was seen over the Isle of Man to the north, multi-coloured balls of light were seen over the Bristol Channel to the south, while I recall an astronomer speaking on the radio the next day talking of a blue fireball he had seen over East Anglia. This was speeding westwards towards Wales: he telephoned a colleague in Coventry who was able to confirm the westward course of the fireball. Inhabitants of Llandrillo, the village at the foot of Arthur's Table, reported seeing red disc-like lights encircling the mountain.[12]

An extraordinary sequence of events. It made leading news items that evening and the following day. The overall assumption seemed to be that a huge meteorite had impacted on

Arthur's Table; the seismographic evidence suggested it would
have been the biggest meteorite to have come down in Britain. A
police team was sent up the mountain to see if anyone had been
hurt. Such an event would, of course, have left an enormous
scar on the mountain, but subsequent detailed scientific investigation failed to reveal any sign of meteoric impact. Quietly, the
item slipped from the news as it became apparent that the
experts would be unable to find an explanation.

There are interesting factors about the centre of this enormous
geophysical display of energy. Arthur's Table stands beside the
Bala Fault. Around it are various prehistoric remains, including
a giant hilltop earthwork over the other side of the fault containing a vitrified stone (one that has been subjected to great heat).
On Arthur's Table's own flanks is a superb stone circle known as
Moel Ty Uchaf. This circle, composed of fairly small stones by
megalithic standards, has a groundplan geometry that both
Thom and Critchlow[13] have found to embody some sophisticated geometric expressions.

I learned from Keith Critchlow that two scientists, a few days
after the event, while investigating the mountain found that

Moel ty Uchaf Circle on Arthur's Table mountain near Corwen,
Wales, which is sited adjacent to the Bala fault. (*Author's photo*)

they obtained very high readings on their geiger counter when close to the circle. It was this anecdote which prompted us to include geiger monitoring in the Dragon Project. The circle itself is in very good condition with probably all its stones intact; there are two gaps but these seem to have been original entrances or openings.

Stonehenge is far more famous than Moel Ty Uchaf, if nowadays less enchanting. One of the best attested instances of UFOs being witnessed over the great prehistoric structure occurred in October 1977 when two families camping near the site saw and filmed a display of aerial lights. This experience and what the film shows has been hotly disputed by sceptics and some UFO researchers. The consus of opinion seems to be that the witnesses were fooled by Army flares. Yet on a television investigation it was claimed that there had been no Army exercise that night.

A reader of *The Ley Hunter*, A. Moncrieff Davidson, has written to tell me of an incident at Stonehenge on 20 June, the day *before* the midsummer solstice celebrations when the rising sun appears behind the Heel Stone, a few years after World War Two:

> I learned there would be a partial eclipse at the hour of sunrise . . .
> and decided to try and film it at Stonehenge. My wife and I arrived
> in our car an hour or so before the Heel Stone hour; weather was
> normal for date and hour. We parked the car on a track tangential to
> the NW side of the enclosure and I got my cine-camera ready.
>
> While we waited, quite suddenly there was a clap of thunder and a
> ball of fire hit the middle of the track, about ten yards ahead of the
> car, but left no mark on the road. I was glad I was *in* the car.
>
> At the correct moment the sun came up very clearly over the
> distant horizon and appeared perched on the Heel Stone partially
> eclipsed.

A name that constantly crops up in French UFO reports is that of Draguignan in the far south-east of France, not far from another important UFO haunt around Valensole. It is a UFO 'repeater' site[14] and the name 'Draguignan' apparently relates to 'dragon'—the Chinese symbol for earth forces, and possibly the European symbol as well. Very close to the town is a dolmen known as *Pierre de la Fee*—The Fairy's Stone. A legend associated with it says that a flame gushes out of the ground at the site. This must be viewed as significant in the context of the ideas being discussed here.

In Sweden, a connection has been noted between UFO incidence and megalithic sites in an area some 40km north of Stockholm.[15]

There are doubtless many more anecdotal snippets of this type. The problem is that most prehistoric sites are in remote or inaccessible regions, and no one keeps round-the-clock and year-long vigils at such sites scanning the skies for UFOs. Even at Rollright, our Dragon Project monitors are on site for only a very small percentage of the year, and even they must sleep sometimes (though reports of anomalous nocturnal illumination within the circle is being investigated at the time of this writing). At popular sites such as Stonehenge and Avebury, where there are a lot of people in the daytime, there would need to be a very considerable event for it to be noticed above the business of tourism. It must be recalled, as well, that many henges to not share the main patterns of UFO incidence.

If stone circles and some other megaliths and UFOs are connected, as their siting patterns and anecdotal information suggests, it strongly indicates that the ancients were involved with such phenomena in some way. What this involvement might have been has to be speculation, but in the light of the evidence and discussion contained within these chapters a remarkable scenario can be assembled.

It is first necessary to picture what Neolithic society was like. Not completely the barbaric, savage, woad-painted ideas of the archaeologists (this image might be true of the Iron Age and later stages of the Bronze Age, but not of the Neolithic period); not completely the wistful 'golden age' image of modern New Agers, either, but something in between. Basing his ideas on the researches of Bruce Chatwin, John Michell suggests in his *The Old Stones of Land's End*[16] that the early Neolithic peoples must have been nomadic, like the Australian aboriginals, wandering the Earth in fixed patterns between locations where the spirits dwelt, where the powers existed. A perpetual sacred journey, following the spirit of the land.

As is the case with the Australian aboriginals, the sacred places would have hardly been marked . . . a spring, a stone, a hilltop. A natural shrine near some fissure in the ground. The archaic peoples would have *known* the sites without the need to monumentalize them. Gradually, as we know from the archaeological record, this wandering life came to an end, and settled communities begin to develop.

It was about this time that the 'megalithic revolution' began in Britain. Stones and earth began to distinguish the sacred places, the totemic sites. But in the aeons of wandering the sacred ways of the landscape, the ancients would have developed great wisdom by their inner visions, their communion with Nature and their observation of the sky and the land. All phenomena would have been noted and absorbed into their developing cosmogeny. (We can recall here the aborigines of Lake Manchester and their 'min-min globes' mentioned in Case 29.)

But the pattern changed. The intuitive, tranquil rhythms of consciousness—the lunar, yin, 'right brain' functions—began to be accompanied by more strident orchestrations of the mind as the settled life took hold. The human mind developed the added mental dimensions of intellect, analytical thought—the solar, yang, 'left brain' functions. Both these horses of human brain-function were skilfully harnessed and handled so the carriage of the human mind could be pulled. The activities of these people as recorded in their structures reflect this dual awareness of the world. That is why when an astronomer finds evidence of astro-nomical practices at megalithic sites he is no more right or wrong than the psychic who receives impressions of strange and wonderful powers at them. The mistake occurs when a par-ticular group claim that the sites could *only* have been used for the particular purposes that their findings indicate. Because we are a culture with a fragmented—some people more politely call it 'compartmentalized'—system of knowledge, created by a cultural mind that is excessively dominated by solar or left-brain functions, our inability to comprehend the dual—or rather harmonized—state of consciousness lying behind the megalithic structures has made it difficult for us to interpret them in an integrated way. Yes, there was objective astronomy; yes, there were sepulchral rites. But there was also magic and mysticism, and each of these elements served the others. What is it that makes a site sacred? Wholiness.

The sites with optimum confluences of conditions would have been divined. Studies of the motions of the Sun and Moon would have been made, and their effect on the human mind and the Earth's body would have been noted and matched over the generations. The spectres and strange lights flitting through their environment would have been observed by these great people. The places in the landscape where they could sense the powers coursing most strongly through their beings would be studied. The nature of such places would be recognized by well-tried acts of divination by people with keenly sensitive sense perceptions. The occasional glows and currents of force emanating from certain hilltops would have long previously identified such sites as holy, as places for magical and spiritual gatherings. A place to talk with Nature; a place for the spirit to depart from the body. The emanations from odd stones and outcrops would have been felt at certain times by countless hands down the generations. The emerging solar consciousness would eventually lead to stones being artificially placed at certain locations and in particular configurations to enhance the sensations. These configurations would echo fundamental geometric patterns inherent in Nature; these too would come to be noted, recognized and reproduced. The relationship of certain divining responses with particular kinds of geological conditions and the movement of the Sun and Moon would be observed and remembered. It would be found to be possible to emulate and strengthen subtle energetic conditions found in natural situations. Mankind began the terrible process of 'improving on Nature'.

The ring of stone, the megalithic mounds, were the sacred sites at which space, time and mind were most effectively linked: the early, working temples. Not symbolical—*practical*.

It was at these locations that the great, lost act of ancient knowledge could be performed. Here the ancient wisdom was fashioned into an elemental technology. While present-day magicians can modify external matter, and use the archaic patterns of force, to compare them with the scope and power of the ancient geopsychic wizards is like comparing a candle with the Sun. At these sacred places, or 'hierophanies', the manifestation of unusual powers, or 'krakophonies', took place, to use Eliade's terms.

From their rings of stone the geopsychic wizards or shamans would have been able to ensnare the responsive aerial lights. They would have learnt under what conditions such manifestations would be most likely to appear—generations of meticulous observation would have ensured that—and from where in the landscape they were most likely to emerge. The electromagnetic nets and grids formed by the megalithic settings would have attracted and captured the longer lasting lights, like flies in a spider's web. To eyes that had the memory of generations behind them, it might even have been known what routes certain lights would take when they issued from certain spots: perhaps here we have a clue to the leys, marking the traditional routes of the 'spirits'. The shamanic net of energized megaliths would have ensured the proximity of the lights.

Instead of the incoherent, unfocussed output of the modern human brain, the most intense mental signals could have been generated by the geopsychic practitioner. Even today a practising magician can be awesome in his or her powers of mental projection and PK expertise. The ancient geopsychic wizards would have provided the shamanic channel for forms constellated within the unconscious to come forth and take transient form sustained by the terrestrial emanations glowing in the atmosphere. In this way, the gods *did* appear on Earth. This supreme act of the ancient natural science would allow the societies of the day to have direct, social, conscious contact with what the *Tibetan Book of the Dead* calls the 'knowledge holding deities'. Aspects of what could be experienced as inner vision could be exteriorized in this way—an outward representation of profound mental processes: it was the first sacrament. Mind manifested in matter—the archaic source that fed the Christian belief in transubstantiation; the prehistoric memory preserved in the Grail legend: the lost secret of antiquity—transient, external visions: a sort of psychic cinema. Not for entertainment but for the instruction of conscious awareness. This was surely the period of time that the myths, folk memory and archaic texts refer to, when gods 'walked' the Earth and communicated directly to mankind. Solar heroes, Earth Mothers, demons and giants—all the representations of the forces of physical and mental Nature may actually have taken on tenuous form in the ancient world. It is easy to understand how the vague, inchoate racial memories of this time have come to be misinterpreted in our day and age as references to ancient astronauts.

The gods would have been known and named—in such a way that archetypal influences would have been recognized and tabulated. Certain forces would have specific, traditional forms —geopsychic icons. Like Jung's Philemon they would have communicated things not known to the conscious minds of the awe-filled congregations. It would have been a way for the conscious awareness of a whole culture to have a partial but direct glimpse into the inner secrets of Nature; a sort of social mysticism. It was a geophysical looking-glass for peering deep into the collective human soul.

The very shamanistic acts being practised would have been enhanced by the electromagnetic environment being created within the circle at the time of such interactions. It would have been a precise science, the remnants of which we dismiss as 'magic' today.

This elemental technology would have required a 'mix' of conditions that were elusive. Cosmic, atmospheric, geological and human factors had to be combined. Therefore it is probable that several megalithic 'geopsychic stations' must have been used at the appropriate times in areas where the required conditions were known to sometimes occur. It must have been a remarkable feat to have pulled the whole thing off; the gross effort of such societies must have been directed towards the accomplishment of such a technology—the monument-building displays of prehistory certainly support such an observation. All the mundane aspects of life would have been subordinated to the fantastic engineering and mental effort required. The insights that the visualized aspects of universal wisdom would have communicated to these late Neolithic and Early Bronze Age peoples would have ensured that they lived lives that were materially simple and in close harmony with the planet. Consequently, as archaeology has confirmed, their secular remains are slight compared with the remains of their sacred megalithic engineering.

'Seeing is believing' must have been as true in the past as it is now: atmospherically sustained pictorial representations of the fundamental powers of the mind and of physical Nature must have had an enormous effect on the people of the time. Social stability would have been a predictable outcome, and so it seems to have been.

The complex infrastructure of geophysical knowledge and psychic expertise required to achieve the consummation of the elemental technology would have been difficult to maintain, however. For myself, I feel the knowledge in the British Isles is likely to have been at its peak around the third millenium B.C. in Ireland. The Boyne Valley monuments (Chapter 6), for example, can be seen as a working system of the whole ancient science, as if those who constructed them did so not simply to use the equipment but because they wanted the instruments of their knowledge to last to a future age. Their acquired wisdom would surely have let them realize that the peak they had achieved would, by the very laws of Nature they saw so graphically portrayed, eventually decline. They would have realized that such a knowledge as theirs, sustained by oral traditions, was particularly susceptible to the quirks of Nature and humankind.

At some point 'The Knowledge' became the province of specialists, as the 'left-brain', solar function of consciousness— necessary for the development of the elemental technology— got out of hand and began to develop at the cost of other aspects of the mind. Perhaps groups of practitioners of The Knowledge dispersed and set up institutions in other societies. There seems to have been a major effort in making the physical parts of the system around 1800 to 1600 B.C. Within a few centuries, the physical parts of the elemental technology seem to have been all but lost. The inexplicable vitrified forts of Scotland—sacred hilltops containing stone structures which have been subjected to incredible and widespread heat that recent research has failed to explain—may have been brought about during this declining process.

To watch the lowering of human behaviour and achievement through the later parts of the Bronze Age and the Iron Age is literally like watching a light go out. Certainly, there were wise men, and their colleges doubtlessly kept some of The Knowledge alive, but the whole society was no longer informed by the wisdom and visionary knowledge possessed by the shamans. Society no longer had a direct channel to supernormal knowledge; priests had to be used as intermediaries—priests who had themselves lost the understanding of how to activate the outer mechanisms to present their inner visions. It was word of mouth, ritual display, with costumes emulating the splendour of the geopsychic icons, and symbolism. As left-brain function-ing, the male aspect of consciousness, attained dominance, society became ever more patriarchal and materialistic. Inevitably, the worst images orthodox archaeologists have of prehistoric life came to pass.

Give human beings a similar situation anywhere on Earth, and similar reactions will occur. It is certain that The Knowledge would have been practised elsewhere. Perhaps the secrets of the Art of the Covenant related to the practice of the old elemental science. The Gnostics and Templars and other heretics may have had access to fragments of the archaic information. But everywhere the loss of understanding seems to have occurred; we only have the stone instruments left, empty now, poorly understood and unused.

While fragments of The Knowledge have certainly survived
into the present day, the vital parts—those relating to the linking
of consciousness with the physical world—seem to be completely forgotten. The factors relating to the development of
human psychic abilities are still fairly intact, even if science is
only just getting round to studying them, and if the missing parts
of the old technology, the physical knowledge, could be linked
to these, then the great secret of antiquity could probably be put
into practice again. There are certain hints that some groups are
attempting to do just this—the 'conspiracy' schools of thought
may have some validity. Many would pay a great price to redis-
cover the vital missing pieces of the ancient wisdom, for they
would then have access to supernormal knowledge which could
be used for good or ill.

The ancient people who built the megalithic structures were
clearly involved in something practical as well as sacred, and
that practice gave them a very special, very mysterious relationship with the Earth.

★   ★   ★   ★

There will be those who will be unable to accept such a scenario.
It can only be speculation, of course. Yet it fits what is being
gleaned about those societies and structures of long ago. More
importantly, we have the *fact* that those shapeshifting forms
and beings are still witnessed today. Someone you meet in the
supermarket or pass in the street may have had an involuntary
confrontation with such a spectacle. They will not tell you about
it, because they must bury their experience—there is no place for
it in the world they inhabit. But if these experiences have
actually taken place, and they have, *then it is the rest of society
that is fooling itself*, not the UFO witnesses.

I see in my memory now the Adam Qadmon image that I
witnessed materializing in the Kent skies: anyone who has seen
such a thing, and there are thousands of us, *know* that the
speculations I have given vent to here cannot be lightly dismissed. These phenomena exist, and there has to be a function in
Nature that produces them. The patterns they display match
patterns discernible in megalithic building practices: the connection has to be speculation, but it is not empty speculation.

The two vital elements in the paradigm put forward in these
pages to explain the nature of UFOs are in the first stages of being

investigated today. The psi abilities of human beings are being observed and tested—to a chorus of complaint from left-brain, patriarchal thinkers—and with the new discovery of Brady's quartz-fracture lights we may soon know more about the UFO form itself.

If all this work succeeds, we may find ourselves in the position of knowing the secret of UFOs. Like the ancients, we shall have to decide how best to use it. We flirt increasingly with the spiritual and physical destruction of our race; we need something as revolutionary as this geopsychic epiphany to shock us, to short-circuit the dangerous, mindless games that occupy so many of the resources of our present culture.

Perhaps—just perhaps—Mother Earth holds the last card yet.

Epilogue

I have written these chapters both as a UFO researcher and as a UFO witness. I do not claim to have presented a watertight, totally scientifically convincing argument (nobody has so far—nor have the belief systems ranged against the existence of UFOs), but I have sought to weld certain patterns, evidence and ideas into a paradigm that best accommodates the UFO phenomenon as we know it.

The relationship of UFOs with the Earth is something more than theorizing—the evidence actually points to such a link. The idea of UFOs occasionally responding to mental cues is more speculative—*but it can be tested*. If the article quoted in Chapter 7 about Dr. Brady's work in Colorado is correct, and his work continues, it should be possible to establish whether or not observers can influence the behaviour of laboratory—produced quartz-fracture lights in non-physical ways. The paradigm put forward here predicts that such an influence would occur.

In the meantime, I would have thought that a useful exercise for practical UFO researchers would be to organize long-term skywatches at the ancient sacred sites in their own country-side—particularly megalithic ones. If some of the ideas presented in this work are in any way correct, then the ancient peoples may have already done the groundwork for optimum UFO observation—quite literally. Let us experiment with relying on the wisdom of the ancients—*we* have little to offer, after all. Maps of ancient sites and geological sheets should be essential equipment for all practical ufologists.

To those who allow themselves to believe that there is no core UFO phenomenon, may I refer them back to the challenge put forward in Chapter 1. I am laying myself on the line as much as I know how—anything in an attempt to demonstrate that there really is something to be studied in the UFO enigma.

It is time such study got under way. It is time we obtained the measure of the problem—there has been far too much left-brain bickering. We share the planet with an awesome, wonderful, instructive phenomenon that could change all our lives.

Appendix

The best way for anyone interested in the topics discussed in this book to keep abreast of current developments—and sometimes to be invited to take part in direct field research—is to subscribe to the small magazines and research groups involved. These disseminate information and the latest thinking on the subjects, provide forums for discussion and provide a focus for research. Subscription to them has the happy effect of not only keeping the subscriber in the forefront of what is going on, it also supports the under-funded work in ufological and Earth Mysteries research.

A careful perusal of the chapter references in this book will reveal the addresses of a number of excellent publications. In addition I have quoted or benefited from the following major journals and research groups:

Flying Saucer Review, West Malling, MAIDSTONE, Kent, England (the world's leading UFO journal).

BUFORA Journal, 6 Cairn Avenue, LONDON W5 (organ of one of the foremost UFO research associations).

Magonia, 64 Alric Avenue, NEW MALDEN, Surrey, England (the thinking reader's UFO publication).

Fortean Times, BM-Fortean Times, LONDON WC1N 3XX (the world's leading magazine of strange phenomena, including UFOs and exceptional geophysical events).

The Ley Hunter. P.O. Box 13, WELSHPOOL, Powys, Wales (the leading research journal studying ancient mysteries and associated phenomena; edited by the present author).

The Institute of Geomantic Research, 142 Pheasant Rise, Bar Hill, CAMBRIDGE, England (an excellent research group busily publishing rare geomantic texts and organizing field research projects).

The Dragon Project (the major study of potential unusual energies at ancient sites, closely associated with *The Ley Hunter*, from where details can be obtained. Volunteer monitors are regularly required).

References

Chapter 1:
1. Hendry, A., *The UFO Handbook*, U.S.A. 1979 (Sphere edition 1980).
2. I challenge sceptics to test themselves only against my two 1967 experiences, even though I have seen a few other highly probable UFO events. As these involved lights seen at night there is always the remote possibility that some mundane explanation might be forthcoming; therefore vindication of such accounts would not necessarily be conclusive. Since 1970 I have not been fortunate enough to witness any further UFO occurrences.

Chapter 2:
1. McGregor, A., *The Ghost Book* (Robert Hale, 1955).
2. *ibid.*
3. Hynek, J. A., *The UFO Experience*, 1972 (Corgi edition 1974).
4. *BUFORA Journal*, Vol. 6, No. 5.
5. Devereux, P. & York, A. in *The News* (now *Fortean Times*), Nos. 11 and 12.
6. *Flying Saucer Review* (*FSR*), Vol. 17, No. 3.
7. *Northern UFO News* (NUFON, 8 Whitethroat Walk, Birchwood, Warrington, Cheshire), February 1978.
8. Webb, R. in *FSR*, Vol. 24, No. 4.
9. *BUFORA Journal*, Vol. 7, No. 1.
10. *Lantern* (3 Dunwich Way, Oulton Broad, Lowestoft, Suffolk), No. 21.
11. *FSR: Case Histories*, No. 6.
12. *BUFORA Journal*, Vol. 8, No. 1.
13. *BUFORA Journal*, Vol. 8, No. 1.

14. Hynek, J. A., op. cit.
15. Devereux, P. & Thomson, I., *The Ley Hunter's Companion* (Thames & Hudson, 1979).
16. *BUFORA Journal*, Vol. 7, No. 2.
17. Hynek, J. A., op. cit.
18. Malthaner, H. in *FSR*, Vol. 18, No. 4.
19. Hynek, J. A., op. cit.
20. *NUFORA Journal*, Vol. 7, No. 2.
21. *BUFORA Journal*, Vol. 7, No. 2.
22. *FSR*, Vol. 17, No. 1.
23. Hynek, J. A., op. cit.
24. *Journal of Transient Phenomena* (Newchapel Observatory, Newchapel, Stoke-on-Trent, Staffs.), Vol. 1, No. 2.
25. *FSR: Case Histories*, No. 5.
26. *FSR: Case Histories*, No. 4.
27. *FSR*, Vol. 22, No. 5.
28. Harris, L. in *FSR*, Vol. 22, No. 5.
29. Devereux, P. in *The Ley Hunter* (*TLH*), No. 75.
30. Devereux, P. *et al* in *Southern Report*, Southern Television, February 1977.
31. Personal investigation.
32. McGregor, A., op. cit.
33. Pattison, C. in *Paranormal & Psychic Australian* (P.O. Box 19, Spit Junction, 2088, NSW), Vol. 3, No. 6.
34. *ibid.*
35. *BUFORA Journal*, Vol. 9, No. 2.
36. Jenkins, S., *The Undiscovered Country* (Spearman, 1976).
37. Evans Wentz, W. Y., *The Fairy Faith In Celtic Countries*, 1911 (Colin Smythe edition 1977).
38. Winthrop, J., *A Journal of Transactions of Massachussetts and Other New England Colonies 1630-1644*, 1790.
39. McClure, K. & S., *Stars, and Rumours of Stars*, privately printed, 1980 (from 14 Northfold Road, Knighton, Leicester).
40. Vallee, J., *Passport To Magonia*, 1970 (Tandem edition 1975).
41. Bord, J. & C., *Alien Animals* (Elek/Granada, 1980).
42. Winthrop, J., op. cit.
43. Bord, J. & C., op. cit.
44. *ibid.*
45. Styles, S., *The Mountains of North Wales* (Gollancz, 1973).
46. *NUFORA Journal*, Vol. 7, No. 2.

47. *NUFORA Journal*, Vol. 8, No. 1.
48. *BUFORA Journal*, Vol. 7, No. 1.

Chapter 3:
1. Constable, T., *The Cosmic Pulse Of Life*, 1976 (Spearman edition 1977).
2. I have been involved with attempting to capture certain effects in the atmosphere around megaliths using infra red film. See Chapter 6.
3. Keel, J. in *FSR*, Vol. 17, No. 3.
4. Keel, J., *Our Haunted Planet*, 1971 (Futura edition 1975).
5. Keel, J., *Operation Trojan Horse*, 1970 (Abacus edition 1973).
6. Vallee, J., *Passport to Magonia*, 1970 (Tandem edition 1975).
7. Vallee, J., *Messengers Of Deception* (And/or Press, 1979).
8. Campbell, S. in *Journal of Transient Aerial Phenomenon*, Vol. 1, No. 3.
9. Persinger, M. & Lafrenière, G., *Space-Time Transients And Unusual Events* (Nelson-Hall, 1977).
10. The minerals that make up the rock masses are prone to distortion and dislocation during and after their formation. McCartney was, in fact, engaged in such research a number of years ago. (McCartney, P.C., *The Mossbauer Analysis of Tin Ores and their Non-Stoiciometry*, unpublished dissertation, University of London, 1974).

    Distortion of minerals can produce a dipole (charge separation) in them—the piezo-electric effect—which may lead, in turn, to the ionization effect of the surrounding air. It is suggested that this may be the basis of a mechanism to explain the production of UFOs. It is quite conceivable that energy interchanges in such processes may lead to the manifestation of light energy, which could produce the UFO phenomena.

    Distortion and dislocation of minerals will be accentuated in and around areas of high tectonic stress, such as highly faulted and intruded zones. Earthquake activity, particularly that of low intensity, seems to provide a suitable environment for the location of current 'hot spots' where the likelihood of UFO production would be highly favoured.
11. Michigan Anomaly Research Bureau, P.O. Box 1479, Grand Rapids, Michigan 49501.

12. Jung, C. G., *Flying Saucers—A Modern Myth Of Things Seen In The Sky*, 1959 (RKP edition 1977).
13. Randles, J. & Warrington, P., *UFOs—A British Viewpoint* (Robert Hale, 1979).
14. Magee, J. in *FSR*, Vol. 24, No. 3.
15. Randles, J. in *Lincolnshire Dragon* (16 Packhorse Lane, Swineshead, Boston, Lincs.), No. 4.
16. See for example Jenny Randles, again, and Hilary Evans in *Common Ground* (14 Northfold Road, Knighton, Leicester), No. 1.

Chapter 4:
1. Playfair, G. L. and Hill, S., *The Cycles Of Heaven* (Souvenir Press, 1978).
2. Gribbin, J., *The Climatic Threat* (Fontana, 1978).
3. Playfair, G. L. and Hill, S., op. cit.
4. Gribbin, J., op. cit.
5. Gauquelin, M., *Cosmic Influences*, 1973 (Futura edition 1976).
6. Playfair, G. L. and Hill, S., op. cit.
7. *ibid.*
8. Lieber, A., *The Lunar Effect*, 1978 (Corgi edition 1979).
9. Puharich, A., *Beyond Telepathy*, 1962 (Picador edition 1975).
10. Devereux, P. & York, A. in *The News* (*Fortean Times*), Nos. 11 and 12.
11. Corliss, W. R., *The Unexplained*, Bantam, 1976.
12. Devereux, P. and York, A., op. cit.
13. Corliss, W. R., op. cit.
14. Markson, R. & Nelson, R. in *Weather*, Vol. 25, p. 350, 1971.
15. Anon. in *Scientific American*, Vol. 106, p. 464, 1972.
16. Charman, N. in *New Scientist*, 26 February 1976.
17. Stenhoff, M. in *BUFORA Journal*, Vol. 7, No. 3.
18. *BUFORA Journal*, Vol. 7, No. 3.
19. *BUFORA Journal*, Vol. 7, No. 3.
20. Anon. in *Comptes Rendus*, No. 35.
21. *Monthly Weather Review*, No. 15, 1887.
22. *Nature*, Vol. 103, p. 284, 1919.
23. *Fortean Times*, No. 31.
24. Stenhoff, M. giving lecture in London under auspices of BUFORA, March 1979.
25. Ashby, D. & Whitehead, C. in *Nature*, Vol. 230, p. 180, 1971.

26. Huntington, E. in *Monthly Weather Review*, No. 28, 1900.
27. The very best place to confirm this is in the *Handbook of Unusual Natural Phenomenon*, a goldmine of papers and reports collected by William Corliss, from which some of the accounts in this chapter were gleaned. Available from The Sourcebook Project, Glen Arm, MD 21057, U.S.A.

Chapter 5:
1. Muir-Wood, Robert, *On the Rocks: A Geology of Britain* (BBC Publications, 1978).
2. Calder, Nigel, *Restless Earth* (Omega edition, 1975).
3. Hallam, A., 'Continental Drift and the Fossil Record', *Scientific American*, November 1972. Reprinted in *Readings From* Scientific American: *Planet Earth* (W. H. Freeman, 1974).
4. Dewey, John F., 'Plate Tectonics', *Scientific American*, May 1972. Reprinted in *Readings From* Scientific American: *Planet Earth*.
5. Gribbins, John, *This Shaking Earth* (Sidgwick and Jackson, 1978).
6. Muir-Wood, Robert, op. cit.
7. Science Foundation Course Team, *Earthquake Waves and the Earth's Interior: The Earth as a Magnet* (Open University Science Foundation course, 1979).
8. Gribbins, John, op. cit.
9. Gribbins, John, and Plagemann, Stephen, *The Jupiter Effect* (Fontana, 1977).
10. Calder, Nigel, op. cit.
11. Middlemiss, F. A., *British Stratigraphy* (Introducing Geology, 2, Allen and Unwin, 1974).
12. *ibid.*
13. *ibid.*
14. *ibid.*
15. *ibid.*
16. John, Brian S., *The Geology of Pembrokeshire* (Pembrokeshire Handbooks).
17. Middlemiss, F. A., op. cit.
18. *ibid.*
19. Haining, P., *The Great English Earthquake* (Robert Hale, 1976).
20. Rona, Peter A., 'Plate Tectonics and Mineral Resources', *Scientific American*, July 1973. Reprinted in *Readings From* Scientific American: *Planet Earth*.

21. Open University Course Team, *The Earth's Physical Resources, 3: Mineral Deposits* (Open University Second Level Science Course, 1974).
22. *ibid.*
23. Applied Geochemistry Research Group, Imperial College of Science and Technology, *The Wolfson Geochemical Atlas of England and Wales* (Clarendon Press, 1978).
24. Elsasser, Walter M., 'The Earth as a Dynamo', *Scientific American*, May 1958. Reprinted in *Readings From* Scientific American: *Planet Earth*.
25. Open University Science Foundation Team, *The Earth as a Magnet*, op. cit.
26. Elsasser, Walter M., op. cit.
27. Open University Course Team, *Mineral Deposits*, op. cit.
28. *ibid.*

Chapter 6:
1. Burl, A., *Prehistoric Avebury* (Yale, 1979).
2. MacKie, E., *Science and Society in Prehistoric Britain* (Elek, 1977).
3. Hawkins, G., *Stonehenge Decoded* (Souvenir Press, 1965).
4. Hadingham, E., *Circles And Standing Stones*, 1975 (Abacus edition, 1978).
5. Bird, C., *Divining* (Macdonald & Janes, 1980).
6. Hitching, F., *Pendulum* (Fontana, 1977).
7. Underwood, G., *The Pattern Of The Past*, 1969 (Abacus edition, 1972).
8. *Dowsing and Archaeology* ed. Tom Graves (Turnstone Press, 1980).
9. Graves, T., *Dowsing* (Turnstone Press, 1976).
10. An example of this sort of work can be found in *TLH* No. 90, in which an account is given of Miss Geraldine Cummins psychic study of two Irish sites.
11. A comprehensive account of folklore associated with pre-historic sites is provided by Janet and Colin Bord's *The Secret Country* (Elek, 1976).
12. Thom, A., *Megalithic Sites In Britain* (OUP, 1967).
13. Brennan, M., *The Boyne Valley Vision* (Dolmen Press, 1980).
14. Brennan, M. in *TLH*, No. 90.
15. Pennick, N., *The Subterranean Kingdom* (Turnstone Press, 1981).

16. Atkinson, R., *TLH*, No. 90.

17. Devereux, P. and Thomson, I., *The Ley Hunter's Companion* (Thames & Hudson, 1979).

18. The only well-researched ley I know of which displays a repeated correlation with UFO activity is the one which runs south from Stonehenge, through Old Sarum, Salisbury Cathedral, Clearbury Ring and Frankenbury Camp. Every TLH site on this line has a history of unusual aerial phenomena.

19. Devereux, P. in *TLH*, No. 88.

20. This material is available from the Institute of Geomantic Research (see Appendix).

21. Morrison, Tony, *Pathways To The Gods* (Michael Russell, 1978).

22. Pennick, N. in *TLH*, No. 90.

23. Michell, J., *The Old Stones Of Land's End*, 1974 (Pentacle Books edition, 1979).

24. Forrest, R. in *TLH*, No. 87.

25. Hitching, F., *Earth Magic* (Cassell, 1976).

26. We had a further anecdote along these lines. When archaeological researcher John Barnatt was surveying the Derbyshire henge of Arbor Low a man visiting the site claimed that the skylarks were attracted to the site and others on the moor because of the ultrasound such places gave off!

27. Robins, G. V. in *TLH*, No. 87.

28. Bentall, R. in *New Scientist*, 22 April 1976.

29. Steel, J. in *TLH*, No. 89.

30. Lethbridge, T. C., *The Legend Of The Sons Of God*, 1972 (Sidgwick and Jackson edition, 1973).

31. Williamson, T. in *New Scientist*, 8 February 1979.

32. Michell, J., *The Flying Saucer Vision* (Sigdwick and Jackson, 1967).

33. Critchlow, K., *Time Stands Still* (Gordon Fraser, 1979).

34. Michell, J., *The View Over Atlantis*, 1969 (Abacus edition, 1973).

35. MacKie, E., op. cit.

36. Méreaux-Tanguy, P. in *Atlantis* (30 Rue de la Marseillaise, F94300, Vincennes), No. 307.

Chapter 7:
1. Devereux, P. and York, A. in *The News* (*Fortean Times*), Nos. 11 and 12.
2. Devereux, P. and York, A. in *TLH*, Nos. 66, 67, 68.
3. Devereux, P. in the Foreword to Anthony Roberts' *Sowers of Thunder* (Rider, 1978).
4. Graves, R., *The White Goddess* (Faber, 1961).
5. Michell, J., *The View Over Atlantis* (Garnstone Press, 1969).
6. BUFORA, 6 Cairn Avenue, London W5.
7. McClure, K. and S., *Stars, And Rumours Of Stars* (privately printed, 1980: from 14 Northfold Road, Knighton, Leicestershire).
8. Pugh, R. J. and Holiday, F. W., *The Dyfed Enigma* (Faber & Faber, 1979).
9. *Journal of Transient Aerial Phenomena*, Vol. 1, No. 1.
10. Vallee, J. and J., *Challenge To Science*, 1966 (Spearman edition, 1967).
11. Goddard, J., *Handbook of Leys and Orthoteny* (privately printed, 1966).
12. Brander, J. in *New Scientist*, 21 February 1980.
13. Lagarde, F. in *FSR*, Vol. 14, No. 4.
14. Quoted by David Fideler in *Fortean Times*, No. 31.
15. Fideler, D. in *Fortean Times*, No. 32.
16. Pye, M. in *The Sunday Times*, 29 March 1981.
17. Evans, H. in *Common Ground*, No. 1.
18. *Fortean Times*, No. 10.
19. Eaton, H. in *Royal Meteorological Society, Quarterly Journal*, Vol. 13, p. 305, 1887.
20. Bonney, A. in *Royal Meteorological Society, Quarterly Journal*, Vol. 13, p. 306, 1887.
21. Matts, E. in *Weather*, Vol. 19, p. 228, 1964.
22. Matthews, J. in *Weather*, Vol. 19, p. 291, 1964.
23. Creighton, G. in *FSR*, Vol. 14, No. 6.
24. Supplied by Barry Gooding to me personally, with other Warminster data.
25. Supplied to me directly and written in the hand of John Rowston.
26. *BUFORA Journal*, Vol. 6, No. 5.
27. Randles, J. and Warrington, P., *UFOs—A British Viewpoint* (Robert Hale, 1979).
28. Lagarde, F., op. cit.

29. Charman, N. in *New Scientist*, 26 February 1976.
30. Fideler, D. in *Fortean Times*, No. 32.
31. *Central Somerset Gazette*, 22 November 1979.

Chapter 8:
1. Heering, J. in *Editecs* (P.O. Box 190, 40100 Bologna, Italy), Vol. 11, No. 1.
2. See for example—again—Corliss' *Handbook of Unusual Natural Phenomena.*
3. Quoted by Andrija Puharich in a lecture at the University of Toronto, 13 October 1976.
4. Noted by Jan Heering in *FSR*, Vol. 24, No. 5.
5. Lovelock, J. E., *Gaia: A New Look At Life On Earth* (OUP, 1979).
6. Huxley, A., *The Doors Of Perception & Heaven And Hell,* 1954 (Penguin edition, 1959).
7. Jung, C. G., *Memories, Dreams, Reflections,* 1961 (Fontana edition, 1967).
8.

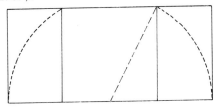

9. Earp, F. in *Northern Earth Mysteries* (15 Convent Court, Park Grove, Hull, England), No. 11.
10. Devereux, P. & Thomson, I., *The Ley Hunter's Companion* (Thames and Hudson, 1979); a recent report handed to me states that a group of people on a pilgrimage up the Tor on midsummers day in 1981 witnessed a glowing orange form being emitted from the ruined tower on the hill's summit. The atmospheric phenomenon 'earthed' itself close to Chalice Wall at the foot of the Tor. One witness stated that she believed that 'what we saw was the magnetic field . . .'. Much was made of the dragon-like forms of the discharge phenomenon.
11. Porter, W. in *Fortean Times*, No. 5.
12. *Tanat Chronicle*(Plough Shop, Llanrhaeadr-ym-Mochnant, Powys, Wales), Autumn, 1980.
13. Critchlow, K., *Time Stands Still* (Gordon Fraser, 1979).
14. *FSR: Case Histories*, No. 14.

15. Reported in private correspondence to John Steele—a Dragon Project co-ordinator—by Lennart Lidfors in 1979.
16. Michell, J., *The Old Stones Of Land's End* (1974).

Index